# Charitable Real Property Tax Exemptions in New York State

# Charitable Real Property Tax Exemptions in New York State

## Menace or Measure of Social Progress?

*by Peter Swords*

Association of the Bar of the City of New York
New York 1981

Distributed by
COLUMBIA UNIVERSITY PRESS

Printed in the United States of America

Library of Congress Catalog Card Number: 81–67553
ISBN: 0–231–05402–5

# Contents

THE ASSOCIATION OF THE BAR
OF THE CITY OF NEW YORK
42 WEST 44TH STREET
NEW YORK 10036

COMMITTEE ON PHILANTHROPIC ORGANIZATIONS

CARROLL L. WAINWRIGHT, JR.
CHAIRMAN
ONE CHASE MANHATTAN PLAZA
NEW YORK 10005
(212) 530-5332

CAROLYN C. CLARK
SECRETARY
ONE CHASE MANHATTAN PLAZA
NEW YORK 10005
(212) 530-5334

During 1979 it became apparent to the members of the Committee on Philanthropic Organizations of The Association of the Bar of the City of New York that widespread misconception existed concerning the rationale for and the economic effect of the exemption from real property taxes granted under New York law to charitable organizations. This misconception extended to legislators and other public officials, many of whom were facing serious fiscal problems in their units of local government and were searching for sources of additional revenue. The public policy issue involved in the real property tax exemption was so important and so interrelated with the policy of granting other tax privileges to charitable organizations that the Committee concluded it should sponsor an independent, scholarly examination of the historic, philosophic, economic and legal considerations involved in the real property tax exemption.

The Committee consulted with Professor Harvey Goldschmid and Associate Dean Peter deL. Swords of the Columbia University School of Law. It was agreed that Dean Swords would undertake an in-depth study and, with advice and assistance from Professor Goldschmid, would prepare a report of his findings. Funding for this project was obtained through generous grants from The New York Community Trust, the Edward John Noble Foundation, the Robert Sterling Clark Foundation and The New York Times Company Foundation.

The following report is the result of this undertaking initiated more than two years ago. The Committee believes that it is the most thorough study ever exclusively directed to the exemption from real property taxes granted to charities under New York's Constitution and laws. We believe the report will be a useful tool for legislators and other policymakers in addressing this important issue. We further believe that it will be of use to lawyers and others faced with legal questions involving the real property tax exemption.

*COMMITTEE ON PHILANTHROPIC ORGANIZATIONS*

CARROLL L. WAINWRIGHT, JR. Chairman

*Class of 1981*

HELENE L. KAPLAN
EILEEN C. SCHWAB
ROBERT J. TASK
PHILIP T. TEMPLE
PETER M. WARD
SIDNEY S. WHELAN, JR.

*Class of 1982*

CAROLYN C. CLARK
DAVID L. DEITZ
HOWARD R. DRESSNER
DANIEL L. KURTZ
JO-UNA SPADAFORA
SYDNEY A. WOODD-CAHUSAC

*Class of 1983*

JORGE L. BATISTA
JOHN B. KOEGEL
MICHAEL G. MACDONALD
JOHN G. SIMON
STEPHEN L. SOLOMON

April 3, 1981

# Acknowledgments

I have been greatly helped by many people in completing this study and my thanks go to them all. To begin with, I am grateful to a battery of talented Columbia Law students: William A. Escobar, Raymond O. Gietz, David Retter, Mark Schnabl, Richard L. Schwartz and Windell C.M. Singley. Elizabeth Dvorkin, a Lecturer at Columbia Law School at the time, ably assisted me with Chapter 5. Three bright lights, then at the Hunter High School, helped with the many computations made in Section B of Chapter 2: Lynn Hudson, Nancy Lewin and especially Andrea Schawaroch. In the closing stage of the study, Leslie Morgan provided me with invaluable statistical assistance. I am also indebted to Mark Rollins, a graduate student in philosophy at Columbia, who clarified my views on some of the study's underlying policy issues.

Much thanks is owed to the staff of the Columbia Law School Library and especially to Sam Cohen, Barbara Rubin Kessler and Philip Oxley. I am, of course, dearly indebted to the staff of Columbia Law School's Secretariat who made the production of the manuscript possible and particularly to its Director, Virginia Woods.

Throughout I have been enormously helped by the advice and encouragement of the members of the Committee on Philanthropic Organizations and especially by its Chairman, Carroll L. Wainwright, Jr. A word of special thanks goes to Ronald Schramm, a graduate student in economics at Columbia, who helped me immeasurably with many of the public finance issues involved in the study and did much of the work on the Note at the end of Chapter 1 and Section D of Chapter 2 on the Service Charge Law.

Finally, no words can express my gratitude to my dear friend and colleague Professor Harvey J. Goldschmid of the Faculty of Columbia Law School. From beginning to end, he has provided me with invaluable insight and encouragement and has helped me enormously with the manuscript. His support has been inestimable.

PETER DEL. SWORDS

*New York, New York*
*April, 1981*

# Charitable Real Property Tax Exemptions in New York State

# Introduction

This study examines the real property tax exemption accorded to nonprofit charitable[1] organizations in New York State. Conclusive findings indicate that the charitable exemption does not significantly interfere with the financing of local governments, that any erosion of the property tax base has not come about through the devotion of property to charitable purposes, and that available evidence strongly suggests that the charitable exemption will not pose problems in the future. Why the charitable exemption is good social policy and why it would be unfair to subject property used for charitable purposes to the tax will also be demonstrated.

The study is organized as follows: Chapter 1 is a simple primer on the New York State real property tax system, an understanding of which is necessary for considering the exemption questions. Chapter 2 describes and explains the New York real property tax exemption system with particular focus upon charitable exemptions. Chapter 3 surveys prior New York studies that have evaluated the charitable property tax exemption. Chapter 4 reports on an extensive analysis made of the amount

1. As explained below, the term "charitable" is used in an embrasive sense throughout the Introduction and in much that follows.

of exempt property by type in New York. Chapter 5 provides an analysis of the New York decisional law interpreting the purposes for which property can be granted a charitable exemption, and Chapter 6 examines the theoretical justifications for the charitable real property tax exemption.

Concern over the problem of real property tax exemptions—the exemption for nonprofit charitable organizations is only a small part of this larger category—has been chronic in New York for most of this century. Rapid and recurring increases in the costs of local government, which receives a significant part of its funding from the real property tax, have intensified this concern. The fear, of course, is that the growth in the amount of exempt property causes a serious erosion of the tax base.

Chapter 3 reviews the many authoritative studies on the problem of real property tax exemptions that have been done in New York since the turn of the century. An ebb and flow of concern over tax base erosion runs throughout these studies. In 1970, the tide of concern was running particularly high. In that year, the Joint Legislative Committee to Study and Investigate Real Property Tax Exemptions published a report, detailed below, predicting that by 1985 one-half of the value of all real property in New York State would be exempt.[2] The following year Alfred Balk published his book *The Free List* with the revealing subtitle *Property Without Taxes.*[3] This extremely readable book sounded a national alarm about "how sievelike the United States property tax exemption system has become."[4] Balk suggested that one-third of the value of all property goes untaxed and that the proportion was still rising.[5] Earlier the influential Advisory Commission on Intergovernmental Relations, after noting that "the expression of concern over the decreasing generalness of the general property tax is well jus-

2. See notes 20–21 and accompanying text infra.
3. A. Balk, The Free List (1971).
4. Id. at 6.
5. Id. at ch. 2.

tified by the erosion of the property tax base that has occurred over the past half century or more and continues to occur,"[6] exclaimed,

> The seemingly endless procession of narrowing the property tax base has progressed so far, and in such diverse directions, as to necessitate some forthright determination not only on where it should stop, but how much of it should be repealed. Step by step, exemptions place heavier burdens on those still required to pay, or reduce the responsibility of local government by inducing them to depend increasingly on fiscal aid.[7]

In 1977 the state legislature established a Temporary State Commission on the Real Property Tax[8] "to undertake a comprehensive review of the real property tax, including but not limited to, assessment administration, exemptions and equity of application."[9] Part of the impetus for the establishment of the commission was the finding that "the proliferation of tax exemptions for a multiplicity of purposes, the often imprecise statutory basis for such exemptions, and their unforeseen use and abuse, have eroded the real property tax base."[10] It is the purpose of this study to determine whether the concern over property tax exemptions as it relates to the charitable exemption is justified and in this connection to examine critically whether the real property tax exemptions accorded to property used by nonprofit organizations for charitable purposes promotes or retards the general public welfare of the State of New York.

A review of the voluminous amount of material that has been produced on the subject of real property tax exemption shows a recurring failure to distinguish between exemptions granted

6. U.S. Advisory Commission on Intergovernmental Relations, The Role of the States in Strengthening the Property Tax, Vol. 1, 76 (1963).
7. Id. at 77–78.
8. 1977 N.Y. Laws, ch. 889.
9. Id.
10. Id.

to publicly held property and exemptions granted to privately held property. Furthermore, seldom are distinctions made between different types of exemptions granted to privately held property. Hence conclusions are frequently made about one type of exempt property on the basis of a finding made about all exempt property.

In the course of this study many types of exemptions will be considered, but the central purpose is to inquire into the status, impact and justification of the charitable exemption. By "charitable exemption" reference is made to the real property tax exemptions granted by section 421 of the Real Property Tax Law[11] to property owned by organizations established and conducted for a number of stated charitable purposes which property is used for such purposes. Several of these purposes are also exempted by the New York State Constitution.[12] One of the purposes enumerated in section 421 and listed in the Constitution is the purpose "charitable"; others include such purposes as "religious," "educational," "hospital," "moral or mental improvement of men, women or children" and "scientific." "Religious" and "educational" are given constitutional protection in addition to "charitable" and the rest of the enumerated purposes are not. For purposes of this study all of these purposes are from time to time included under the term "charitable." This is done not only for ease of reference but because it is believed that properly analyzed all of the specifically enumerated purposes, including the "religious" and "educational" purposes, are properly included under the broader concept "charitable," as all promote purposes beneficial to the community.

When the value of property charitably exempt is compared to the value of the vast amount of property exempt under other provisions, the relative significance of the charitable exemp-

11. N.Y. Real Prop. Tax § 421 (McKinney 1972).
12. See N.Y. Const. art. XVI, § 1.

tions is sharply diminished. As will be shown in Chapter 4, most exempt property is held by one unit of government or another. Indeed, it is usually the local municipality in which charitably exempt property is located that holds most of the jurisdiction's exempt property. Other private exemptions include exemptions given to promote business, agriculture and housing. Exemptions are given to veterans and to senior citizens.

Most opinion regarding property tax exemptions is critical. Such exemptions are seen as attempts to curry political favor and as threats to the integrity of the tax base. This study will examine the strength of these criticisms, which, as already mentioned, often make no distinction between the various kinds of exemptions. It is not uncommon for charitable exemptions specifically to be tarred by a brush that should be painting a much wider area.[13]

To determine what fraction of the value of all property is charitably exempt, one has to consider each municipality individually. Looking at the aggregate values of all municipalities as could be done, for example, by adding the exempt values of all New York assessing units and dividing that total by the sum of the value of all property, leads to the false conclusion that some percent of the value of all property in New York State is exempt. This is incorrect because the 991 Upstate municipalities and New York City assess property within their jurisdictions at very different percents of actual full market value.[14] This is

13. In this connection it may be noted that Alfred Balk in his book The Free List (see note 3 supra) does distinguish between the various types of exemptions.

14. Chapter 4 contains this study's findings on the impact of property tax exemptions in terms of the amount of assessed value made up by various types of exempt property. A division is made between New York City and Upstate municipalities because the sources of data are different. On the basis of aggregate figures—which, it should be recognized, are infested with the differential assessment problem just mentioned—as of 1978, 54% of all assessed property in New York State is in New York City and 46% is in Upstate municipalities, and 66% of the assessed value of all exempt property in New York State is in New York City and 34% is in Upstate municipalities.

called the differential assessment problem. The solution is to consider each municipality individually[15] and make findings as to average value of all municipalities based on these figures.[16]

In regard to what portion of a municipality is exempt from property taxation, it might be noted that recently one township, Hardenburg, has given rise to much agitation. Over the years a considerable portion of property in Hardenburg had become exempt. In response, in late 1976 the town assessor granted exemptions to many of the homes in this township whose owners had become "ministers" in the Universal Life Church with the result that nearly all of Hardenburg's property was off its tax rolls. The State Board of Equalization and Assessment ruled that these latter exemptions were invalid and ordered that the properties be placed back on the tax rolls. At the time of this writing the matter is still in litigation.[17] While it is certain that Hardenburg has experienced an exemption problem, Hardenburg is only one municipality in nearly 1,000 and its unique circumstances hardly justify any general conclusions about property tax exemptions in New York.

It is found in Chapter 4 that for the last year (1978) for which data are available, the average percent of the percents that the assessed value of private exempt property made of the assessed

15. Even by this method the data are not entirely firm because within individual municipalities different parcels of property will be assessed at different percents of actual full market value.

16. For example, if the percents that the value of exempt property made up of all property at three separate municipalities were 20, 10 and 3, then the average of these three would be 11%, but if the municipality with 20% of its value exempt had four or five times as much value as the other two municipalities, the average derived by adding all values would be quite different. This cannot be done because of the differential assessment problem.

17. See League of Women Voters of New York State, Toward an Evaluation of the Property Tax System in New York State, 65 (1979). This situation was referred to in section 3 of the 1977 legislation establishing the Temporary Commission on Real Property Tax, where it noted that "some taxpayers, seeking relief from what they believe to be unfair burdens, have dramatized the erosion of the tax base through exemption by attempting to gain exemptions under the letter but not the spirit of the law." 1977 N.Y. Laws, ch. 889.

value of all of the 991 Upstate municipalities was 3.7%. For these purposes the category private exempt property includes property exempt under provisions other than the charitable exemption sections. Consequently the figure for charitable exemptions would be lower but not much lower as charitable exemptions probably make up the largest part of private exemptions. Moreover, the indications are that this percent is decreasing. In 1973 it stood at 4.04%. Only thirty-one Upstate municipalities had private exempt property in excess of 15% in 1978. For the last year (1979) for which New York City data are available, the value that charitably exempt property made up of all property was 5.1%, down from 5.3% in 1970, although up somewhat from earlier years. In contrast, the average of the percents that the assessed value of all other exempt property[18] made up of all value for the 991 Upstate municipalities in 1978 was about 17% and for New York City the comparable figure in 1979 was about 36%. The conclusion is very clear: for most municipalities the value of charitable exemptions constitutes only a small part of the value of all property.

Nonetheless, the most significant legislative response to concern over property tax exemptions was an enactment in 1971 aimed solely at restricting charitable exemptions. Section 421 was amended to give municipalities an option to remove the exemption from a number of charitable purposes which had theretofore been mandatorily exempt.[19] Section 1 of this enactment, prefaced "Legislative findings and intent," clearly indicates that concern over tax base erosion motivated the legislation. It makes reference to studies that show the amount of the assessed value of property in New York that is exempt from real property taxes. The figures used are the same as those published the year before in a report by the Joint Legislative Committee

18. "All other exempt projects" include public wholly exempt and partially (both public and private) exempt property.

19. 1971 N.Y. Laws, ch. 414.

to Study and Investigate Real Property Tax Exemptions.[20] (The committee was chaired by Assemblyman Daniel Becker and the report will be referred to as the Becker Committee Report.) Thus, it may fairly be concluded that the 1971 legislation, which operated to restrict charitable exemptions, was largely in response to the Becker Committee Report.

An alarm was sounded by the Becker Committee in its conclusion that if the relative growth rates of exempt and taxable property continued at the same rate as they had been growing, by 1985, 50% of all the assessed value in New York State would be exempt.[21] This prophecy will be proven false. Chapter 4 shows that on average only about 20% of assessed value of Upstate municipalities is exempt, and the amount appears to be decreasing. The amount of exempt property in New York City has risen to a high of 41.5% of all value, but New York City contains only about half of all the assessed value in the state.[22]

As shown in some detail in Chapter 4, the bulk of this growth of exempt property in New York City has been in exemptions granted to government-owned property, particularly public authorities and government-owned and assisted housing and noncharitable private exemptions. Indeed, charitable exemptions, which constituted about 23% of the value of all exempt property in the city in 1910, by 1979 came to constitute only about

20. See Final Report of the Joint Legislative Committee to Study and Investigate Real Property Tax Exemptions, N.Y. Leg. Doc. No. 15 (1970) [hereinafter cited as the Becker Committee Report].

21. See Becker Committee Report, supra note 20, at 5 and 35–36. As shown in Chapter 4 it appears that the Becker Committee Report made its alarmist finding in part on the basis of erroneous arithmetic, i.e., on the basis of the figures used it would take a considerably longer time before one-half of all New York property became exempt. (Note that so long as exempt property grows at a faster rate than taxable property at some point 50% and more of all property would become exempt.) Chapter 4 also critically examines the methods and the appropriateness of the data used by the Becker Committee Report.

22. Above it is said that New York City contains 54% of all assessed value in the state. Since New York City assesses its property at a higher percent of full market value than Upstate municipalities, it is likely that a true figure would be lower than 54%. See note 92 and accompanying text, Chapter 4 infra.

12% of such value. As suggested above, noncharitable exemptions are also a much larger factor in Upstate municipalities than charitable exemptions (although not nearly so large a factor as in New York City).

In sum, the Becker Committee Report correctly detected a growth in the value of exempt property but failed to make clear that the source of this growth was the increase in government-owned property, and particularly the growth of such property in New York City. It was hardly a statewide phenomenon, and charitable exemptions, both in New York City and in Upstate municipalities, were not a significant factor. And yet the principle response to the Becker Committee Report was legislation designed to limit exemptions accorded to charitable property.[23]

Furthermore, two significant Court of Appeals cases, which strictly applied this new law so as to narrow the scope of charitable exemptions, expressly cited the legislative findings of the 1971 enactment as justification of their holdings.[24] Thus severe limits on charitable exemptions from property taxation resulted in response to a perceived problem having virtually nothing to do with charitable exemptions.

On the basis of the data summarized above, it is a major finding of this study that the value of charitably exempt property in a large preponderance of New York State municipalities is relatively small. If it were assumed that the amount of (the value of) charitably exempt property relative to the amount of (the value of) other property is an accurate index of the extent of fiscal hardship that charitable exemptions cause to local governments or to property owners who are subject to the tax, it

23. As noted in Chapter 2, section D, during the same session that this legislation was passed there was also enacted a law to impose a service charge on certain exempt property both governmentally and privately held. 1971 N.Y. Laws, ch. 417. See N.Y. Real Prop. Tax §§ 102, 400, 420 and 498 (McKinney 1972). At the time of this writing this legislation has not been implemented.

24. See Association of the Bar of New York v. Lewisohn, 34 N.Y.2d 143, 155, 313 N.E.2d 30, 35, 356 N.Y.S.2d 555, 563 (1974) and American Bible Society v. Lewisohn, 40 N.Y.2d 78, 86, 351 N.E.2d 697, 701, 386 N.Y.S.2d 49, 53–54 (1976).

would have to be concluded that for the overwhelming majority of New York municipalities charitable exemptions do not significantly contribute to such hardships.

It is far from certain, however, that such an assumption should be made, i.e., it is far from certain that charitable exemptions accorded to real property, even assuming they were significant in scope, would contribute to the fiscal hardship of local governments or to property owners who are subject to the tax.

The conventional wisdom embraced by this assumption seems to rest upon a view that at some earlier time before the advent of exemptions all property within a jurisdiction was taxable. When exemptions were granted and property that had previously paid the tax no longer did, property remaining taxable was made to bear a larger tax burden, i.e., a smaller amount of property had to produce the same amount of taxes. In a word, the tax base was eroded. Such a view assumes that in the natural course of things all property within a jurisdiction would pay taxes.

This postulate, however, is open to serious question. Property taxes are in fact paid by people, not by real estate itself. As people use property productively they gain the capacity to pay taxes. People who own homes and who relate to property in other ways also have such capacity. But, for example, if property is not used or not used productively, no capacity to pay the tax will be generated. In these circumstances, the initial view that all property within a jurisdiction ought naturally to be taxed becomes clouded. Tax bases are not given a priori; they must be chosen, and the grounds upon which the choice is made necessarily involve social policy value judgments. The clear suggestion is that only certain kinds of property will be chosen to be taxed.[25] If it is decided that certain other kinds of property ought not to be taxed then it cannot be said that the

25. The use of property in a manner that society has decided is properly subject to tax is referred to throughout this Introduction as a "taxable use."

tax base has been eroded by granting such property exemptions because the property is not part of the tax base to begin with.

There are good reasons why a society might conclude that charitable uses should not be subject to the property tax. Implicit in this assertion is that concommitant claim that certain other uses are appropriately subject to tax. These other uses are what will be referred to as taxable uses in the following analysis. An important predicate to justifying this view is the finding made in Chapter 1 that most of the uses to which property taxes are put are not for the benefit of property. A division is made of such uses between people-related expenditures and property-related expenditures. On very conservative estimate (i.e., where there is any doubt expenditures are allocated to property-related expenditures), it is found that 75% of property tax revenues are spent on people-related uses and 20% are spent on property-related uses.[26] This finding supports a conclusion that for the most part the property tax is a general revenue-raising tax similar, for instance, to the income and sales taxes. The central issue then is what uses of property ought to be subject to a property tax used for general revenue-raising purposes and what uses ought to be exempted.

After pointing out that property taxes are not paid by real estate but rather by people by virtue of their relationship to property, Chapter 6 concludes that there are two natural classes of people who by virtue of their relationship to property held for charitable purposes[27] might be expected to pay the tax: the recipients of their services and those who contribute to their support. In most cases recipients either cannot or will not pay a charge sufficient to recover the before-tax costs of these

26. The remaining 5% is spent on revenue used to fund noncurrent expenditures (e.g., capital outlays, etc.).

27. For the discussion that follows it is useful to keep in mind that the term "charitable purposes" is broadly conceived and includes both purposes designed to relieve the distress of the helpless as well as purposes designed to promote the moral and cultural development of man (e.g., the arts).

services. Consequently, if a tax were imposed upon charitable organizations and defrayed by its inclusion in a charge made to the recipients of their services the likely result would be a decrease in the level of consumption and therefore provision of these services. There are, of course, sound reasons in social policy, however, why it would be contrary to the general welfare to let charitable services decline in this manner. It is, for example, a benefit to society for private universities not to have income and wealth alone determine who their students are. If tuition were raised to meet a tax charge it is likely that some poor but talented students could not attend those institutions or would be forced to go to school out of state. This would be harmful to higher education.

Furthermore, in many cases the extension of their services to as many recipients as possible is a principal purpose underlying the existence of charitable organizations. It has been decided that it is beneficial to the community to have such services provided. It is of benefit to those who directly partake of their services, to those who might partake of their services (e.g., those who might get sick and use a hospital or those who might develop a taste for art and use a museum) and to all of those who feel enriched because they are living in a society in which such organizations exist. To encourage the sufficient provision of these services it has correlatively been decided that the recipients of these services be charged less than their costs or nothing at all. It would work against these decisions to impose what might be characterized as a secondary charge in the form of a tax burden.

In sum, there are good reasons for not expecting the tax to fall upon the recipients of charitable services: both practical reasons—they could not or would not pay—and for reasons grounded in social policy—the likely result in increasing the charge to them would be a reduction in the level of charitable services and attendant social dislocation.

The alternative, then, is that contributors to charitable organizations bear the burden of tax. It may be that they could pay for its defrayal and it may even be that they would pay, but the question is whether they ought to pay. If it is concluded that there are good reasons why they should not pay, the further question that arises is why should others who bear a different relationship to property be expected to pay? In considering these questions a sharp distinction is made between those who receive direct benefits from their relationship to property and those who do not but rather provide direct benefits to others. It will be shown that it is appropriate to subject the first group to general revenue tax and to exempt the second.

In the first group are included those who own homes. They directly benefit from such ownership. A similar conclusion applies to those who rent, assuming that the tax is shifted to them. Furthermore, owners of commercial property directly benefit from their ownership, or, if the tax is shifted to the consumers of their goods and services, these consumers directly benefit from their consumption. In these and similar ways those in the first group directly benefit from their relationship to property.

Contributors to charitable organizations comprise the second group. They do not generally directly benefit[28] from their contributions but rather provide direct benefits to others. Someone must pay the tax to finance general government expenditures. Chapter 6 concludes that in defining the tax base it is entirely justifiable as a matter of tax policy to resolve that that burden of financing government revenue should fall upon those in the first group who are themselves directly benefited from their

28. Chapter 6 argues in some detail that while indirect or intangible benefits might inure to those who contribute to charitable organizations—for instance the social esteem derived or the satisfaction of "doing good"—these are of a radically different nature than the kind of benefits received by those in the first group and that this distinction provides a solid basis for subjecting the first group to tax and exempting the second. In some instances, it may be the case that contributors receive some direct benefits from their contributions (e.g., the contributor to a school whose child attends the school), but even in such instances, it is usually the predominant effect of the contribution to benefit others and the distinction holds.

relationship to property in the ways described above and not upon those who contribute to charitable organizations since the principal purpose and effect of making the contribution is to benefit others.[29]

Consistent with the general position that the charitable sector should not be expected to share in the support of government through the payment of a general revenue raising tax, it might, however, be argued reasonably that if the effect of the charitable exemption is to preempt property that would otherwise be put to uses that all would agree would make the property properly subject to tax, then the charitable exemption should not be sustained. It is far from axiomatic, however, that if exempt property held by charitable organizations were made available it would be picked up and applied to taxpaying uses and further that it would be assessed at the same value that it had in the hands of its previous charitable owners. It would appear that the conventional wisdom alluded to above rests upon the additional assumption that the demand for property for taxpaying uses is in excess of its supply, and in the words of Dean Netzer, "Any tax exemption shuts out taxable uses in reality as well as in theory."[30] Might it not rather be the case that the availability of property is such that taxpaying uses acquire all such property as it needs, and that property owned by charitable organizations does not usually "preempt sites that would otherwise be occupied by"[31] such uses. Is it not likely, except in a few rare cases, that if a taxpaying use had a strong

29. Chapter 6 points out that as well as providing direct benefits to others (e.g., to the recipients of a charitable service such as patients in a hospital or museum attendees), many of these charitable organizations are in the nature of a public good since many members of society will derive satisfaction (or "utility" in the terminology of an economist) from the mere presence of such organizations in their community even though they do not directly benefit from them. They will "free-ride" on the support provided by contributors and so are beneficiaries of such support.

30. Netzer, Property Tax Exemptions and Their Effects: A Dissenting View, Proc. 65th Am. Conf. Tax., Nat'l Tax. A. 268, 281 (1973).

31. Id.

demand for exempt property owned by a charitable organization it would be able to acquire such property or at least find an adequate unimproved substitute? In summary, it is at least arguable that in most circumstances existing taxpaying uses acquire all the property needed, and consequently that the charitable exemption system does not operate to diminish, by any significant margin, the level of taxpaying uses. To the extent that this is so, it follows that charitable property tax exemptions do not cause a fiscal hardship to local governments or to property owners who are subject to the tax.[32] From this perspective it is fair to say that the problem of tax base erosion stems not from the availability of charitable exemptions but from the lack of demand for property for taxpaying uses. A shrinking general economy would erode the tax base but not, in any important way, an ascendant charitable sector.

This analysis suggests that the property tax exemption accorded to charitable uses costs society relatively little if anything. On the other hand, it is widely recognized that in several significant ways, charitable organizations benefit society in an economic sense. Because many of these organizations provide goods and services that would otherwise be provided by the government, e.g., private schools and hospitals, their existence actually reduces the cost of government and its need for tax revenues. Furthermore, these organizations provide employment and otherwise enter into the commerce of the community by purchasing locally sold goods and services and the like. Consequently, it is likely that many of these activities may enter into the government's tax base and thus produce a higher level of tax revenues than would be the case if the charitable organization did not exist. Finally, many of these organizations may

32. Of course to the extent that additional government services are required to service property held by charitable organizations, their presence might cause some additional expenditures, but since, as will be shown below, most of the revenue raised by the property tax goes to support government services that do not benefit property, this qualification is a minor one.

attract visitors from outside the jurisdiction, which will generate income for such ancillary services as hotels, restaurants and commercial parking garages.[33] Some of this income may also enter into the tax base.

Indeed, if these two analyses as to the costs and benefits of charitable property tax exemptions are combined, it could be concluded that the net economic effect of charitable organizations upon a community is positive. This follows from the probability that charitable exemptions do not shut out taxable uses and that the presence of charitable organizations may well operate to increase local governments' tax base and consequently cause a higher level of revenue than would be the case without these organizations.

In spite of the fact that there are sound and sufficient reasons in social policy why charitable organizations should not be subject to the tax, nonetheless, if the exemption were removed, it is likely that additional tax revenues would be collected from some charitable organizations. The tax base would be expanded somewhat with a consequent decrease in the tax burden that property used for taxable use had before the exemption's removal. Some contributors might increase their contributions, although it is probable that many would not and that the net result of the exemption's removal would likely be a reduction in the level of services provided by charitable organizations. To the extent, however, that some contributors continued to contribute at the same level as they had before the exemption's removal, charitable service would be reduced but government revenues would be increased. Some contributors might cease contributing altogether and spend such funds as would otherwise have been contributed to charitable organizations in a manner that might lead such funds into the tax base. In this case charitable services would also be reduced and government

33. This is particularly true of cultural organizations in large cities such as New York City. See D. Netzer, The Subsidized Muse 24–25 (1978).

revenues increased. In both cases, as mentioned, the burden on taxpaying uses might be lessened. In this context, it may be asked whether a particular society can afford charitable organizations.

Thus, even recognizing that charitable uses do not preempt taxable uses it might nevertheless be decided that charitable uses ought to be taxed so as to increase the level of revenue for government support and perhaps to lower the tax burden on taxable uses, which had come to be perceived as being too high. In crude terms such a judgment might be articulated in the following terms: "It is all right if you want to spend your money on or devote your resources to charitable purposes, but if you do, don't expect to be relieved from supporting government. We need all activities and endeavors in our tax base and cannot afford to leave any out even though they operate to promote the general welfare and advance no private interests." Such a judgment would hardly be the sign of a flourishing civilization. Considerations similar to these may have been behind the questions asked by Mark Graves in a letter included in the 1927 Report of the Special Joint Committee on Taxation and Retrenchment: "Instead of exemptions being the measurement of a taxation menace, may they not be a measurement of social progress? May they not be the measurement of benefits which society is able to and should afford?"[34]

Our society has benefited enormously from its voluntary sector of charitable organizations. As mentioned, many of the services provided by charitable organizations are similar to those provided by the government. Further, many may not usually be provided by our governmental system but are similar to those supported by governments in other countries, e.g., state-supported religions and opera companies in Europe. Our soci-

34. Preliminary Report by the Special Joint Committee on Taxation and Retrenchment, Tax Exemption in State of New York, N.Y. Leg. Doc. No. 80, 144 (1927).

ety is greatly enriched by the advantages of pluralism that flow from having a voluntary sector of charitable organizations operating parallel to our governmental system, a sector able to discover new needs and experiment in providing ways of meeting them in a manner that simply is not possible for government agencies. In discussing the policy behind the tax exemptions generally, John Gardner has eloquently pointed out:

> It would be difficult to exaggerate the importance of this policy in preserving and fostering the pluralism so characteristic of our society. The fact that our system encourages such diversity of initiative in the vitally important areas of education, science, religion and philanthropy has contributed to the richness and variety of our national life.[35]

It is in this sense that the exemption may be justified for those who view the exemption as a tax expenditure. This approach characterizes exemptions as indirect government subsidies given to exempt organizations in order to encourage their provision of charitable services. Exemptions are said to be functionally equivalent to direct subsidies since they entail tax revenues foregone by the government. Instead of providing the subsidy through the exemption mechanism, a tax could be levied on the property of an exempt organization and a direct grant in an equal amount returned to it. There is a major difference, however, between providing subsidies by a system of exemptions and doing it by direct grants. Under the exemption system it is those interested in providing charitable services who decide whether or not the subsidy should be given (e.g., by establishing a museum), whereas under the system of direct grants it is government agencies that decide. It follows, therefore, that the evident advantages of pluralism resulting from a voluntary sector of charitable organizations are more effectively promoted by the exemption system.

A private sector, operating parallel to the government in a

35. J. Gardner, No Easy Victories 140 (1968).

joint effort to advance the public good, is likely to produce a more imaginative and flexible response to society's needs than would be the case if this responsibility were left to the government alone. An important result of the considerable freedom in which private initiatives are allowed to operate under the charitable exemption system is their ability to discover new needs and to experiment with diverse ways of meeting these new needs. This productive attribute of the charitable exemption system argues strongly for a broad interpretation of the term "charitable." If the term is construed too narrowly, it is likely that efforts to address new community needs arising as an inevitable result of a dynamically evolving society might not be classified as charitable and consequently would be excluded to the detriment of the general welfare from the advantages accruing from a system of private initiative.

The law of charity[36] has long recognized the need to keep the definition of charity flexible. Lord MacNaughton, in *Commissioners for Special Purposes of Income Tax v. Pemsel,*[37] offered what has come to be regarded as the classic definition of "charity":

> Charity in its legal sense comprises four principal divisions: trusts for the relief of poverty; trusts for the advancement of education; trusts for the advancement of religion; and trusts for other purposes beneficial to the community, not falling under any of the preceding heads.[38]

This definition is closely paralleled by the Restatement of Trusts (Second). Its section 368 (What Purposes Are Charitable) provides:

> Charitable purposes include (a) the relief of poverty; (b) the advancement of education; (c) the advancement of religion; (d) the promotion of health; (e) governmental or municipal purposes; (f) other purposes the accomplishment of which is beneficial to the community.[39]

36. Reference is made here to the law of charitable trusts.
37. (1891) A.C. 531.
38. Id. at 583.
39. Restatement (Second) of Trusts § 368 (1959).

It will be noted that both formulations contain the embrasive concept of purposes that are beneficial to the community;[40] this plainly allows for great flexibility in determining whether a particular activity is charitable. It is significant in this connection that the regulatory scheme that applies to organizations exempt from federal income taxes as charitable organizations expressly defines the word "charitable" "in its generally accepted legal sense,"[41] by which is meant the law of charitable trusts.

What constitutes a charitable exemption for purposes of New York property tax exemption has been unclear from the inception of the statutory scheme in the late nineteenth century. At that time, some sixteen separate purposes were enumerated as being exempt and no attempt was made to define those purposes.[42] Some of these purposes would seem naturally to be included within others, e.g., "bible" within "religious" or "scientific" within "educational." Indeed, as suggested, they might all be included under the term "charitable" if that purpose is construed broadly.

As shown in Chapter 5, little clarity was brought to this issue by early judicial decisions. The matter became further confused by a 1938 amendment to the New York State Constitution and a 1971 amendment to that section of the Real Property Tax Law that provides the charitable exemption. In 1938 the Constitution was amended to provide, in effect, that exemptions from

40. Indeed, it appears that the various purposes listed in the above definitions before the catchall "beneficial to the community," e.g., relief of poverty or advancement of religion, are species of the genus "beneficial to the community."

41. See Treas. Reg. § 1.501(c)(3)-1(d)(2)(1959).

42. These purposes were: moral and mental improvement of men and women, religious, charitable, missionary, hospital, educational, patriotic, historical, cemetery, bible, tract, infirmary, scientific, literary, library and for the enforcement of law relating to children or animals. In the late Twenties the following two purposes were added: "bar association" and "playground." See Chapter 2, Section B.

property taxes for property used for religious, educational or charitable purposes could not be repealed and all others could.[43] In 1971 the Real Property Tax Law was amended as noted above to provide that certain purposes, including the constitutionally protected purposes, must be exempt, while others could be made exempt or not at the choice of each local municipality.[44] As also noted above, this legislation appears to have been made in direct response to the Becker Committee Report, which had wrongly attributed tax base erosion to charitable exemptions. This gave rise to a number of cases coming from jurisdictions, particularly New York City, which had made the election to remove the exemption from nonmandatory purposes, in which the taxpayer argued that a particular activity constituted a purpose that was constitutionally protected. For a period it appears that as a result of the 1971 legislation the Court of Appeals rejected "public benefit" from the test of what qualifies for exemption—i.e., it rejected the concept that is at the very heart of the traditional definition of charitable purpose. This rejection was expressly attributed to the Becker Committee Report.[45] A fairly narrow definition to the term "educational" may also have been prescribed.

More recently, however, the Court of Appeals seems to have moved back into the mainstream of what is thought to be a charitable purpose in finding that purposes "which are necessary to the public good"[46] are charitable, educational and for the moral improvement of men, women or children. Thus it would appear that the Court of Appeals now accords a broad flexibility to the nature of purposes which qualify for exemp-

43. N.Y. Const. art XVI § 1.
44. See note 19 and accompanying text supra.
45. Association of the Bar of New York v. Lewisohn, 34 N.Y.2d 143, 155, 313 N.E.2d 30, 35, 356 N.Y.S.2d 555, 563 (1974).
46. Mohonk Trust v. Board of Assessors of Gardnier, 47 N.Y.2d 476, 484, 392 N.E. 2d 876, 880, 418 N.Y.S.2d 763, 767 (1979).

tion, i.e., to purposes which have here been included under the broad term "charitable." This is a highly desirable development since it allows for a system of private initiative in defining the nature of public good and in determining ways to provide that good.

# 1

# A Primer on Real Property Taxes in New York State

A general familiarity of the property tax in New York is necessary for understanding the rest of this study.[1] To begin, the property tax today applies only to real property[2]—generally, land and improvements.[3] Revenues raised by the real property tax are used exclusively by local jurisdictions—counties, cities, towns, villages, school districts, fire, water and special districts[4] —which generally levy and collect the taxes.[5] There are 991

1. For a general description of the tax, see Final Report of the Temporary State Commission on State and Local Finances, Vol. 2, The Real Property Tax (1975) [hereinafter cited as the Feeney Commission]. See also, League of Women Voters, Toward an Evaluation of the Property Tax System in New York State (1979) for a general review of the real property tax, including an interesting examination of the effect of the property tax on education, housing, land and economic development. This report contains a useful bibliography on the property tax.

2. Effective January 1, 1939 New York by constitutional amendment removed from taxation all personal property. N.Y. Const. art. XVI, § 3. This had previously been done by legislative enactment. 1933 N.Y. Laws, ch. 470. See N.Y. Real Prop. Tax § 300 (McKinney 1972).

3. N.Y. Real Prop. Tax § 102(12) (McKinney 1972) defines "real property."

4. A special district is a town or county improvement district established to improve services, for example, health or sanitation, provided to the community. See N.Y. Real Prop. Tax § 102(16) (McKinney 1972).

5. The New York State Constitution provides that all of these jurisdictions may be authorized by the legislature to impose the real property tax. N.Y. Const. art. VIII, § 1. However, not all of these municipalities make assessments. Property is primarily assessed by cities and towns (and in some cases by villages)

taxing municipalities in addition to New York City. In 1928 the state stopped collecting property tax revenues for its purposes.[6]

The property tax is a very significant source of revenues for most local jurisdictions.[7] The table below sets out by source the amounts of revenue collected in 1978 by all units of local government (including New York City).

| | |
|---|---|
| *Revenues* | |
| Real Property Taxes | $8,586,494,000 |
| Non-Property Taxes | 3,819,130,000 |
| Assessments | 48,762,000 |
| State Aid | 6,744,288,000 |
| Federal Aid | 5,598,821,000 |
| Other Revenues | 2,758,441,000 |
| Total Revenues | $27,555,934,000 |
| *Borrowings* | |
| Bonds | $931,275,000 |
| Notes | 753,860,000 |
| Total Borrowings | $1,685,135,000 |
| Total Revenues and Borrowings | $29,271,067,000 |

Source: New York State Comptroller, Special Report on Municipal Affairs, table 1-A, N.Y. Leg. Doc. 92 (1979) (for fiscal year ending 1978).

It will be seen that revenues from the real property tax constitute the single largest source of financing for local government. At one time property taxes were the major means of financing local government services. There has been a tremendous

defined as "assessing units." N.Y. Real Prop. Tax § 102(1) (McKinney 1972). In general, the assessment of one locality may be used by others as, for example, when a village or school district will rely upon the assessment by a town of property subject to their tax that is within the town's assessing boundaries. Two counties, Nassau and Tompkins, are the assessing units for all of the municipalities contained within their borders. The nature and meaning of "assessment" is discussed below.

6. See Report of Temporary State Commission on the Constitutional Convention, Local Finance 22 (1967).

7. See Feeney Commission, supra note 1, at 6.

growth in intergovernmental grants to local municipalities over the past sixty to seventy years, and as a result property taxes have come to defray a smaller part of municipalities' operating budgets. The 1979 Report of the Temporary State Commission on the Real Property Tax notes that real property tax revenues, which supplied 46% of all local revenues in 1946, made up only 30% of all local revenues in 1975.[8] Property tax revenues, however, remain, as the figures above suggest, an important continuing source of funding for local governments. The certain availability of this revenue source as compared, for instance, to the vagaries of intergovernment grants contributes to its significance. For many jurisdictions the property tax is the only available tax source. Only large cities have had success with the sales and income taxes.

The Temporary State Commission on the Real Property Tax "found that New York's real property tax burdens are . . . among the highest" of a 12-state sample chosen to make interstate comparisons.[9] The states were comparable industrial states.[10]

It is of obvious importance for this study to develop information on the purposes for which funds raised by the real property tax are used. This is done in a note at the end of this chapter, the results of which are now summarized. Two general categories of uses are established: property tax funds used for property-related expenditures and property tax funds used for people-(nonproperty) related expenditures. Typical property-related

8. Report of the New York State Temporary State Commission on the Real Property Tax 10 (1979) [hereinafter cited as the Gerber Commission]: "These trends occurred in virtually all local governments and school districts. What accounts for the declining relative importance of property tax collections? Simply, local government expenditures rose more rapidly than did property tax collections. Only substantial increases in federal and state aid to localities made it possible for local government programs and services to continue to be funded at present levels." Id.

9. Id. at 13. They were California, Connecticut, Florida, Illinois, Massachusetts, Michigan, New Jersey, New York, North Carolina, Ohio, Pennsylvania and Texas. Steven Gold also suggests New York has one of the nation's highest property tax burdens. S. Gold Property Tax Relief, ch. 2 (1979).

10. Id.

uses include sanitation, highway and public safety. Typical people-related uses include education, social services, health, culture and recreation. This distinction is of importance since the justification of the property tax exemption for charitable, etc., purposes is clearly related to the uses to which property tax revenues are applied. To the extent these revenues are used for people-related services, the exemption's justification is strengthened as these services do not benefit charitable organizations per se. This point is developed in the Introduction.

Based on an extremely "conservative" allocation of expenditures between the two uses (i.e., where there is any doubt an expenditure is allocated to property-related expenditures), it is found that about 70% of all revenues raised by the property tax are used to fund people-related services, about 25% of such revenues are used to fund property-related services, and about 5% of such revenues are used to fund noncurrent expenditures (e.g., capital outlays, etc.). These estimates are "conservative" for a number of reasons. First, some of the expenditures allocated to property-related expenditures may be more properly allocated to people-related expenditures. For example, within the catchall expenditure category "All Other" are included expenditures for bus lines, airports, cemeteries and markets. Second, the expenditure category "General Government," which on the "conservative" basis is allocated entirely to property-related expenditures, may be more properly allocated in part to property-related expenditures and in part to people-related expenditures, since presumably "General Government" expenditures, expenditures for the mayor's office, for example, are used to fund management services that are provided to both uses. Finally, and most importantly, all of the expenditures allocated entirely to property-related expenditures most likely fund services that in part benefit people in their individual capacities as well as property per se. For example, "Public Safety" (police, correction, etc.) expenditures clearly fund services that protect people in their individual capacities as well as property. To take account of these considerations, allocations are made on less "conservative" assumptions—first by assuming that 25% of property-related expenditures are more properly allocated to people-related expenditures, and second by assuming that 50% of property-related expenditures are more properly allocated to people-related expenditures. On the first assumption it is found that about 75% of all revenues raised by the property tax are used to fund people-related services, 20% property-related services and 5% nonrecurrent expenditures. On the second assumption it is found that about 80% of all revenues raised by the property tax are used for people-related services, 15% for property-related services and 5% for nonrecurrent expenditures. It is believed that the figures based on the first assumption, viz., 75% for people-related services, 20% for property-related services and 5% for nonrecurrent services, more closely reflect the actual allocation of real property tax revenues.[11] A final point of importance for this study is that the data suggest that the trend is toward greater amounts of property tax revenues being used for people-related services and smaller amounts for property-related services.

The real property tax in New York is an ad valorem (according to value) tax, i.e., the tax is levied on the value of real property and is computed as a percent of that value. The value for these purposes is called the "assessed value." The assessed value is determined for all property each year by the local assessor of each assessing unit and entered onto the tax rolls of that unit. For those parcels of property that are subject to tax, the tax rate is applied against the property's assessed value (a simple multiplication process) to determine their tax liability. For most jurisdictions the tax rate is expressed as a dollar

11. For the reasons suggested above this first assumption is also a conservative one, i.e., people-related expenditures are probably understated even under this first assumption.

amount per $1,000 of assessed valuation.[12] For example, if the tax rate is $87.50 and a particular parcel is assessed at $100,000, its annual real property tax liability would be $8,750.[13] The same rate is applied to all taxable property within the municipality regardless of type of property, that is different types or classes of property, e.g., commercial or residential, are not taxed at different rates.

The tax rate is derived in rough outline as follows. First, the municipality determines its annual budget. Next, it anticipates the amount of nonproperty tax revenues—e.g., intergovernmental grants, sales tax revenues, fine revenues, receipts from the sale of goods and services, etc.—it will have available to meet that budget. This amount is subtracted from the annual budget, and the remaining amount is raised by real property taxes. The rate is fixed by reducing a fraction whose numerator is the remaining amount to be raised and whose denominator is the total assessed value of taxable property in the jurisdiction. For example, if a municipality's budget is $750,000 and it projects nonproperty tax revenues of $500,000, it would have to raise $250,000 in property taxes. If the municipality had a total assessed valuation of taxable property of $1,000,000, its tax rate would be $25,[14] i.e., $25 for each $1,000 of assessed value of taxable property. In this sense the real property tax is a "tax of last resort," i.e., a source of financing from which the balance of municipal costs is defrayed after all other sources are estimated.[15]

There are some jurisdictions where it may not be strictly

12. Sometimes the tax rate is referred to as the mill rate. In New York City it is expressed as a dollar amount per $100.

13. Expressed in percentage terms, the tax rate would be 8.75% (.0875), or as a mill rate, 87.5 mills. Many parcels are subject to several taxes, each for a different local jurisdiction in which they are situated. For example, a parcel with an assessed valuation of $100,000 may have levied against it a county rate of $9.06, a town rate of $46.50 and a school district rate of $32.60. Its annual tax bill would then be the sum of $906 + $4,650 + $3,260, or $8,816.

14. $250,000/$1,000,000.

15. Feeney Commission, supra note 1, at 16.

accurate to call the property tax a "tax of last resort." Article VIII, section 10 of the New York State Constitution limits the amount of money that can be raised by tax on real property for any fiscal year to 2%[16] of the average full valuation of taxable real estate on the last completed assessment roll and the four preceding years' rolls.[17] Full valuation for each year is reached by applying to the assessed valuation of each such year the equalization rate[18] for that year as determined by the State Board of Equalization and Assessment. There is no such limit on the amount that can be raised for the payment of interest on and the redemption of the principal of indebtedness. In a jurisdiction such as New York City, where the practice generally has been to raise the fullest amount possible from the real property tax, the rate appears to be fixed in such a manner that property is taxed up to the 2½% limit. In practical terms it appears that in these jurisdictions the tax rate that would return an amount (unrestricted by the Constitution) necessary to repay debt, interest and principal is added to the tax rate that would produce an amount equal to the 2½% limit.

Municipalities differ widely in their per capita amounts of the assessed value of taxable property. These differences are related in part to the fact that commercial and industrial properties (which tend to have relatively high assessed values) are distributed unevenly throughout the state. In any event, there are "rich" and "poor" municipalities and municipalities between the extremes. Differences also exist in the demand for property tax revenues to finance local services. Some municipalities have high social services budgets and large student populations, resulting in a strong demand for property tax revenues. Others have relatively low levels of demand for the provision of public

16. The percent limit is lower for some municipalities and goes as high as 2½% for New York City.

17. N.Y. Const. art. VIII, § 10.

18. For an explanation of equalization rates see text accompanying note 31 infra.

services and consequently relatively small needs for property tax revenues. For these reasons the real property tax burden differs among the many taxing units.[19]

There is probably no thornier set of problems in the field of real property taxation than those which arise out of assessing (or setting a monetary value to) the worth of real property. The law commands that property shall be assessed at full value.[20] The statute does not define the term "full value" but courts have said that it is the price at which property would change hands under ordinary circumstances between a buyer who is willing but not compelled to buy and a seller who is willing but not compelled to sell.[21] Full value, then, is market value.[22] (Below it is indicated that in many cases property is assessed at only a fraction of market value, notwithstanding that the ordinary meaning of "full value" would seem to suggest that this is wrong. This fact constitutes one of the sharpest thorns in the nettle of New York property taxation.)[23] Evaluating the worth of property involves a subjective judgment on the part of a local assessor. Three generally accepted methods of appraisal are used to help make this judgment as objective as possible: the market, income and cost methods.[24] The market method com-

19. The difficult issues regarding school financing and more particularly inter-municipality differences in educational resources arise in large part from these differences.

20. N.Y. Real Prop. Tax § 306 (McKinney 1972).

21. People ex rel. Parklin Operating Corp. v. Miller, 287 N.Y. 126, 38 N.E. 2d 465 (1941).

22. Full value as so defined cannot apply to instances involving specialized property, as, for example, might be the case with a public utility or church, for which there is no market. Other concepts of value are used in these instances. What constitutes "value" whether called "full value," "market value" or whatever is, of course, an enormous subject fraught with conceptual ambiguities and dependent on varying factual contexts. It is beyond the scope of this simple introduction to real property taxes. See J. Bonbright, The Valuation of Property (1937).

23. Indeed, as suggested below, one aspect behind the current concern over exemptions can be traced to this fact.

24. Pepsi-Cola Co. v. Tax Commission of the City of New York, 19 A.D. 2d 56, 240 N.Y.S. 2d 770 (1st Dept. 1963). Only a very brief description of these

pares the property in question to similar parcels that have recently been sold. The income method capitalizes the income generated by the property, and the cost method determines the cost of replacing the structure being appraised and takes into account depreciation for loss of value over time.[25] In actual practice, all three methods may be used when information is available.

For many years in New York real property has been assessed at only a fraction of full market value.[26] For example, a home with an actual full market value of $100,000 might be assessed at only 30% of that value and would accordingly be entered on the tax rolls at $30,000. Differences in the fraction of actual full market value at which property is taxed occur within an assessing unit between properties of the same type (called "intraclass inequity"[27]) and between different types or classes of property (called "interclass inequity"[28]) as, for example, when homes might be assessed at 30% of full market value and commercial properties at 80%. In addition, differences exist between various assessing units in the fraction of full market value at which

methods will be given as the subject is not central to this study. For a more complete explanation, see Feeney Commission, supra note 1, at 20.

25. The value of land determined by this approach must be estimated separately, using either the market or the income method.

26. The Court of Appeals, in Hellerstein v. Assessor of Islip, 37 N.Y.2d 1, 332 N.E.2d 279, 371 N.Y.S.2d 388 (1975), a decision invalidating fractional assessments under the statutory provision requiring assessments to be made at full value, noted that the custom of fractional assessments appears to be as old as the statute, one of the oldest in the state. Id. at 4, 332 N.E.2d at 281, 371 N.Y.S. 2d at 390. Hellerstein includes a fairly comprehensive discussion of the history of fractional assessment in New York.

27. "Inequality of assessment within classes of property (intraclass inequities) is greater than among classes in most municipalities. Homeowners on the same block often pay widely disparate portions of the local tax burden, while residing in homes of similar value. Often it depends only on when the individual purchased the property." Gerber Commission, supra note 8, at 23.

28. "In many municipalities, different classes of real property are, on average, assessed at different percentages of full value, which creates inequities among classes (interclass inequities). In most municipalities, owners of commercial property pay considerably more than homeowners." Gerber Commission, supra note 8, at 22.

property is taxed.[29] This practice of differential assessment is not peculiar to New York, being common in many other jurisdictions.[30]

Equalization rates are established by the State Board of Equalization and Assessment to equalize these differences between assessing units.[31] To establish these rates the board regularly surveys properties on a sample basis within each assessing unit to determine yearly the average fraction of full value at which property is assessed in each unit. This is important, for instance, where a school district comprises two or more towns and relies upon the towns' assessments for its tax purposes. If differences exist among the towns in the average percentage of full value at which properties are assessed, to apportion taxes for school district purposes among these towns in proportion to total assessed values in each town would be manifestly unfair. Equalization rates are used to make necessary adjustments.

To give a sense of the wide range of equalization rates, the 1978 rates of two representative counties are set out below.[32]

It is not known with certainty why these differences exist. Assessors quite understandably are loathe to admit to or explain these differences. Differences between assessing units might be related to the fact that taxing units faced with the need of changing the level of their tax revenues (almost invariably upward) prefer to adjust assessed value rather than tax rates—a method that is less visible and therefore less likely to engender opposition. Since assessing units differ widely in changes in the levels of their operating budgets, if adjustments are effected

29. The Feeney Commission notes that "The assessor and the town board usually have a recognized level of assessment at which the town wishes to maintain property. In theory, this is perfectly proper since equal treatment of all properties will spread the tax burden equally. In practice, variations creep in to produce substantial distortions in the established level." Feeney Commission, supra note 1, at 20. Such distortions were salient for the Court of Appeals in Hellerstein v. Assessor of Islip, 37 N.Y.2d 1, 332 N.E.2d 279, 371 N.Y.S.2d 388 (1975) discussed below.

30. See S. Gold, Property Tax Relief, ch. 1 (1979).

31. N.Y. Real Prop. Tax § 202 (McKinney 1972).

32. State Tax Rep. N.Y. (CCH) ¶ 20-360.

| COUNTY OF SUFFOLK[32] | CITIES AND TOWNS | VIL-LAGES |
|---|---|---|
| BABYLON | 9.65 | |
| VG. OF AMITYVILLE | | 28.69 |
| VG. OF BABYLON | | 20.37 |
| VG. OF LINDENHURST | | 12.81 |
| BROOKHAVEN | 7.64 | |
| VG. OF BELLE TERRE | | 9.77 |
| VG. OF BELLPORT | | 91.54 |
| VG. OF OLD FIELD | | 8.55 |
| VG. OF PATCHOGUE | | 21.71 |
| VG. OF POQUOTT | | 119.20 |
| VG. OF SHOREHAM | | 11.85 |
| VG. OF PORT JEFFERSON | | 10.58 |
| VG. OF | | 7.14 |
| VG. OF | 7.10 | |
| VG. OF EAST HAMPTON | | 8.99 |
| VG. OF SAG HARBOR | | 12.59 |
| HUNTINGTON | 8.15 | |
| VG. OF ASHAROKEN | | 34.55 |
| VG. OF HUNTINGTON BAY | | 8.14 |
| VG. OF LLOYD HARBOR | | 8.10 |
| VG. OF NORTHPORT | | 13.22 |
| ISLIP | 105.17 | |
| VG. OF BRIGHTWATERS | | 12.93 |
| VG. OF OCEAN BEACH | | 9.01 |
| VG. OF SALTAIRE | | 15.80 |
| RIVERHEAD | 9.62 | |
| SHELTER ISLAND | 16.69 | |
| VG. OF DERING HARBOR | | 16.63 |
| SMITHTOWN | 10.60 | |
| VG. OF HEAD OF THE HARBOR | | 8.16 |
| VG. OF NISSEQUOGUE | | 8.49 |
| VG. OF VG. OF THE BRANCH | | 13.05 |
| SOUTHAMPTON | 8.87 | |
| VG. OF NORTH HAVEN | | 6.60 |
| VG. OF QUOGUE | | 7.62 |
| VG. OF SOUTHAMPTON | | 13.72 |
| VG. OF WESTHAMPTON BEACH | | 12.87 |
| VG. OF SAG HARBOR | | 12.54 |
| SOUTHOLD | 11.70 | |
| VG. OF GREENPONT | | 12.72 |

| COUNTY OF SULLIVAN | CITIES AND TOWNS | VIL-LAGES |
|---|---|---|
| BETHEL | 10.81 | |
| CALLICOON | 11.32 | |
| VG. OF JEFFERSONVILLE | | 24.40 |
| COCHECTON | 10.56 | |
| DELAWARE | 11.54 | |
| FALLSBURGH | 23.66 | |
| VG. OF WOODRIDGE | | 112.06 |
| FORESTBURG | 72.22 | |
| FREMONT | 1.95 | |
| HIGHLAND | 1.27 | |
| LIBERTY | 18.71 | |
| VG. OF LIBERTY | | 83.97 |
| LUMBERLAND | 2.87 | |
| MAMAKATING | 9.87 | |
| VG. OF BLOOMINGBURGH | | 16.04 |
| VG. OF HURTSBORO | | 39.82 |
| NEVERSINK | 19.47 | |
| ROCKLAND | 20.23 | |
| THOMPSON | 18.24 | |
| VG. OF MONTICELLO | | 71.88 |
| TUSTEM | 2.43 | |

through changing the fraction of actual value at which property is assessed, different ratios of assessed value will develop. Interclass differences may occur as a result of an unannounced policy to tax commercial and industrial property at a higher effective rate than residential property, perhaps on the belief that the first two types of property can more easily defray the tax by passing it onto their consumers.[33] Since the nominal tax rate for all types of property must be the same, a way of effecting this

33. The Feeney Commission suggests that public utilities usually bear the highest assessment ratios of any type of property because of their monopoly ability to shift the tax to consumers and notes that "the transfer of costs by pricing imposes a burden on consumers of goods and services outside the service area. This 'exporting' of taxes is seen as beneficial to the local taxpayer." Feeney Commission, supra note 1, at 22.

policy is to assess different classes of property at different fractions of actual full market value. Finally, intraclass differences may exist simply because a local assessor is unable or unwilling to revalue property in his unit each year and does so only when property is sold.[34]

Among property of the same class, differences in levels of assessment are commonly expressed by a statistical measure called the coefficient of dispersion; very simply put, the coefficient of dispersion is the difference, on average, in percents of variation from what parcels would be assessed at if a uniform fraction of full market value were used and the fractions at

34. The Feeney Commission, after noting that the State Board of Equalization and Assessment had recently conducted some studies on New York assessors, stated that, "Those studies certainly tend to confirm the general experience that the typical assessor is a part-time elected official with a substantial burden in the form of parcels to assess. There is no reason to believe that his compensation has improved beyond adjustments for increases in the cost of living since 1957. There is also only slight reason to believe that the degree of 'professionalization' has changed markedly. It remains likely that the average assessor is still a local resident, employed full-time in some other vocation, who has little or no specific training in the appraisal of real estate and who applies a maximum of 200 to 300 hours per year to his job." Feeney Commission, supra note 1, at 18. The Feeney Commission discusses this phenomenon, which is sometimes called "price-level stagnation" (or the "welcome stranger"—newcomers are "welcome" because the assessed value of the old-timers' tax burden is shifted to them). Feeney Commission, supra note 1, at 20-22. The Gerber Commission quotes a wit to the following effect:

> To find a value good and true,
> Here are three things for you to do:
> Consider your replacement cost
> Determine value that is lost,
> Analyze your sales to see
> What market value really should be,
> Now if these suggestions are not clear
> Copy the figures you used last year.

Gerber Commission, supra note 8, at 24.

The Court in Hellerstein v. Assessor of Islip, 37 N.Y.2d 1, 332 N.E.2d 279, 371 N.Y.S.2d 388 (1975) notes, among others, the following reason for partial valuation: taxpayers are not likely to associate higher valuations with higher taxes or will be less contentious about high valuations if they do not exceed their view of true value. Id. at 11. See R. Kuttner, Revolt of the Haves, ch. 7, The Crooked Assessor Revisited (1980) for a brief and critical discussion of the history and present practice of property tax assessments.

which they are actually assessed.[35] The lower the percentage, the more uniform the assessments. The State Board of Equalization and Assessment has said: "A perfect coefficient of dispersion would be zero and is unobtainable; an acceptable one would be 10%, according to experts in the field."[36] Based on data supplied by the State Board, the Gerber Commission noted that in 1974 only thirteen of 991 assessing units met this standard with respect to residential property and that more than two-thirds of these units had coefficients in excess of 20% and about one-third in excess of 30%.[37]

As mentioned, not only does nonuniformity of assessment exist between property of the same class, but commonly there exists nonuniformity in the average ratios applied to different classes of property within the same assessing unit. The table set out below, taken from the Gerber Commission, based on 1974 data, shows this phenomenon.

A manifest unfairness results when two properties of identical actual value are taxed at the same rate and are assessed at different fractions of actual value. Property that is assessed at

35. For a simple example, assume three parcels, A, B and C, with actual market values of $50,000, $40,000 and $20,000, which are assessed respectively at $20,000, $6,000 and $10,000. The average ratio of assessment for these three parcels would be .35. The actual ratios of the three parcels are respectively .40, .15 and .50, which average out to .35. If they were all assessed at the average ratio, their respective assessed values would be $17,500, $14,000 and $7,000 ($50,000 × .35 = $17,500, etc.). Thus, parcel A is assessed about 14% too high; B, 57% too low; and C, about 43% too high. Averaging these differences produces a coefficient of dispersion of 38%. This example was taken from Appendix A—"The Coefficient of Dispersion"—from the Gerber Commission. Gerber Commission, supra note 8, at 73.

36. New York State Board of Equalization and Assessment, Improving Real Property Tax Administration: A Primer for Local Officials 3–4 (1979), quoted by Feeney Commission. Feeney Commission, supra note 1, at 44.

37. Gerber Commission, supra note 8, at 25. Where the coefficient of dispersion is 30%, this means that in an assessing unit with an average assessment ratio of 50%, two homes with equal actual market values of $60,000 might be assessed respectively at $39,000 (30% higher than would be the case if the average ratio were used) and $21,000 (30% lower than would be the case if the average ratio were used).

38. Gerber Commission, supra note 8, at 30.

**1974 MEAN ASSESSMENT RATIOS FOR MAJOR PROPERTY CLASSES, CITIES AND TOWNS IN NEW YORK STATE WITH POPULATION GREATER THAN 50,000[38]**

| Cities | Residential | Apartment | Commercial | Industrial | Vacant |
|---|---|---|---|---|---|
| Albany | 26% | 34% | 55% | — | — |
| Binghamton | 26 | 31 | 44 | — | — |
| Buffalo | 42 | 60 | 66 | — | — |
| Mount Vernon | 25 | 42 | 42 | — | — |
| New Rochelle | 35 | — | 58 | — | — |
| Niagara Falls | 50 | 57 | 59 | — | — |
| Rochester | 28 | 44 | 39 | 42 | — |
| Rome | 50 | — | 57 | — | — |
| Schenectady | 25 | 29 | 47 | — | — |
| Syracuse | 34 | 45 | 40 | — | 17 |
| Troy | 75 | 91 | 92 | — | — |
| Utica | 39 | 46 | 43 | — | — |
| White Plains | 26 | — | 45 | — | — |
| Yonkers | 26 | 43 | 48 | — | — |
| *New York City* | | | | | |
| Bronx | 42 | 86 | 82 | 72 | — |
| Brooklyn | 34 | 60 | 71 | 73 | — |
| Manhattan | 52 | 74 | 71 | 64 | — |
| Queens | 26 | 48 | 58 | 52 | — |
| Richmond | 28 | 42 | 46 | — | — |
| *Towns* | | | | | |
| Amherst | 23 | — | 31 | — | — |
| Babylon | 10 | — | 12 | — | — |
| Brookhaven | 9 | — | 14 | — | 7 |
| Cheektowaga | 12 | — | 15 | — | — |
| Clarkstown | 98 | — | 111 | — | — |
| Colonie | 13 | — | 19 | — | — |
| Greece | 17 | — | — | — | — |
| Greenburgh | 31 | 51 | 44 | — | 18 |
| Hempstead | 15 | 26 | 26 | — | 10 |
| Huntington | 9 | — | 12 | — | 6 |
| Irondequoit | 17 | — | — | — | — |
| Islip | 12 | — | 16 | — | 15 |
| North Hempstead | 14 | 23 | 23 | 19 | 13 |
| Orangetown | 17 | — | 23 | — | 13 |
| Oyster Bay | 15 | — | 21 | — | 11 |
| Ramapo | 97 | 102 | 109 | — | 97 |
| Smithtown | 12 | — | — | — | 6 |

**1974 MEAN ASSESSMENT RATIOS FOR MAJOR PROPERTY CLASSES, CITIES AND TOWNS IN NEW YORK STATE WITH POPULATION GREATER THAN 50,000[38]**

| Cities | Residential | Apartment | Commercial | Industrial | Vacant |
|---|---|---|---|---|---|
| Tonawanda | 16 | — | 24 | — | — |
| Union | 16 | — | 22 | — | — |

Note: Where no sample mean ratio is reported for a class, either the class was not sampled or the sample was judged too small (i.e., fewer than 10) to permit a reasonable estimate.
Source: 1974 Market Value Survey by New York State Division of Equalization and Assessment.

the higher fraction will pay a larger amount in taxes than property assessed at a lower fraction of actual value. Basic principles of tax equity require that equals be treated equally. The patterns described above suggest that considerable inequity exists in the implementation of the New York property tax system. Indeed, the Gerber Commission found that the tax is "apportioned on a random basis."[39] Manifest inequity in assessment practices has prompted criticism of the administration of the assessment process.[40] To remove this inequity all property would have to be assessed at the same fraction of actual value. It will be recognized, however, that if this were done a large shifting of the tax burden among properties would result.[41] At the class level, for example, to the extent that commercial or industrial property was assessed at a higher fraction of full value and residential property at a lower fraction, there would be a shift in tax burden from the former classes of property to

39. Gerber Commission, supra note 8, at 22.

40. See, e.g., H. Aaron, Who Pays the Property Tax? 12–17 (1975).

41. In Hellerstein v. Assessor of Islip, 37 N.Y.2d 1, 332 N.E.2d 279, 371 N.Y.S.2d 388 (1975) the court noted that Bonbright observed that uniform underassessment would not work and that its great vice " 'is that the percentage of undervaluation is rarely a matter of common knowledge so that it is extremely difficult to ascertain whether there is uniformity in the proportion or whether, through incompetence, favoritism, or corruption of the assessors, some portion of the taxpaying body are bearing the others' burdens as between individuals or local groups.' " Id. at 13, 332 N.E.2d at 286, 371 N.Y.S.2d at 398.

residential property. Within classes of the same type of property, where the coefficient of dispersion is high, there would be significant shifting among individual parcels of like property.[42]

The inequity that results from fractional assessment was clearly of great concern to the Court of Appeals when in the 1975 *Hellerstein*[43] case it mandated that all property in the town of Islip be assessed at full value (in the sense of full actual market value) and in effect prohibited the long practice of fractional assessments. As of this writing, the full impact of *Hellerstein* has not been felt as the state legislature has on a number of occasions postponed its implementation.[44]

A sufficient review of the general operation of the New York real property tax system has been made to support some possible further explanations for the current interest in the question of exemptions. When and if *Hellerstein* is fully implemented

42. If all the property in an assessing unit were brought up to full value, the tax rate would go down (assuming no increase in the amount of revenues to be raised), but the overall tax burden would remain the same. There would be, however, a shifting of the tax burden among individual pieces of property because they were assessed at different fractions of actual full value before all property was brought to full value. In the example given at note 35, if the tax rate were $25 per $1,000, the home assessed at $39,000 would pay $975 in taxes and the home assessed at $21,000 would pay $525. If both properties were revalued to their actual value of $60,000 and the tax rate were halved to $12.50 per $1,000, they would both pay a tax of $750. The first home's tax liability would be lowered and the second home's tax liability raised by $225.

43. Hellerstein v. Assessor of Islip, 37 N.Y.2d 1, 332 N.E.2d 279, 371 N.Y.S. 2d 388 (1975).

44. See 1977 N.Y. Laws, ch. 888; 1978 N.Y. Laws, ch. 163; 1980 N.Y. Laws, ch. 880. Hellerstein, while involving only the Town of Islip, has statewide application. At the time of this writing there is considerable legislative interest in enactments designed to introduce in effect a classification system among classes of property. Mark Willis has noted, "The switch to 'full value' assessment since 1975 has been slow. To date, only a small part of the state's real estate has been brought into compliance. In addition to the high cost of revising the property tax rolls, communities are reluctant to make a major tax change when it is possible the state legislature will amend the law." Willis, "Reforming New York City's Property Tax: Issues and Options," 1 Fed. Res. Bank N.Y.Q. Rev. 14 (1980).

and all property is revalued, a great deal of tax shifting will inevitably occur.[45] One way of minimizing the extent of such shifting would be somehow to expand the tax base, and, at least theoretically, one neat way of expanding the tax base would be to subject to tax property heretofore exempt, i.e., limit or eliminate property tax exemptions. To the extent the tax base is expanded, *ceteris paribus,* the tax liability of property in the base before the expansion will be reduced. Thus, a property whose tax burden would increase when revalued, having previously been valued at a lower fraction of actual full value than the average of other property, might have its enlarged burden somewhat minimized as a result of the expanded tax base.[46]

A similar problem has also arisen with tax refund claims based on inequality. When a taxpayer alleges inequality, he must show

45. Mark Willis described the potential shift in New York City resulting from implementing the Hellerstein mandate there as follows:

> Current property tax practices in New York City contrast sharply with these requirements of state law. Properties in the city are assessed at differing percentages of market value. These assessment variations, in turn, produce wide differences in effective tax rates, particularly between residential and nonresidential properties. For example, the property taxes paid by owners of single-family houses in the city are only about half of what they would be if the property tax were levied on the basis of market values. At the other extreme, owners of office buildings tend to pay a relatively large share of taxes—over 60 percent more than they would if the tax burden were distributed according to actual property values. These and other disparities in effective tax rates mean that a switch to a uniform tax system would result in a major reallocation of the tax load among the different property groups. The size of these tax shifts underscores the potential for economic disruptions from the court's mandating of full market value assessment.
>
> Not only do effective tax rates in New York City differ by property type, but they also differ by borough. For example, single-family houses in Manhattan are assessed on average at a much higher percentage of market value than houses in other boroughs. In fact, Manhattan appears to be the most heavily taxed borough overall. Consequently, a switch to a uniform tax system would reduce the share of taxes paid by owners of Manhattan properties by some 30 percent. At the opposite end of the scale, Staten Island property owners would face a two-thirds increase since they now pay only a fraction of their proportional share.

Id. at 14–15.

46. This theoretical point weakens when it is recognized that it assumes either that an organization whose tax exemption is removed would be able to pay the tax, or, if not, be able at least to find a successor that would be willing and able to pay the tax and in whose hands the property would be used so as to be assessed at a value at least equal to what the property was assessed at when it was exempt.

that his property was assessed at a higher percent of full value than other property in the assessing unit. To do this the taxpayer must prove the ratio of assessed value to full value used in the assessing district in which the property is situated. In the past this could only be done by a complicated and very expensive process pursuant to which both parties to the proceeding selected a number of parcels to be appraised and produced witnesses to attest to the appraisal. The costs of these inequality proceedings effectively eliminated all but a few wealthy taxpayers from bringing these suits. To meet this problem a series of amendments were made to the Real Property Tax Law that ultimately, as interpreted by the courts, allowed taxpayers to use the State Board's equalization rate to prove the ratio of assessed value to full value used in the taxing district.[47] As noted, the equalization rate is produced each year by the State Board of Equalization and Assessment and is the average percentage of full value at which all property in a particular district is assessed.[48]

In those districts where commercial property has been assessed at a higher fraction of full value than residential property, these changes provide an attractive opportunity for inequality proceedings. "This has given rise to fears that the payment of refunds to the owners of commercial property will result in a significant shift of tax burden to residential homeowners and cause a serious erosion in the tax bases of assessing units."[49] As in the case of a move to full valuation, it might be

47. Guth Realty Inc. v. Gingold, 41 A.D.2d 479, 344 N.Y.S.2d 270 (4th Dept. 1973), aff'd, 34 N.Y.2d 440, 315 N.E.2d 441, 358 N.Y.S.2d 367 (1974); 860 Executive Towers, Inc. v. Board of Assessors of the County of Nassau, 84 Misc. 2d 525, 377 N.Y.S.2d 863 (Sup. Ct. 1975), aff'd, 53 A.D. 2d 463, 385 N.Y.S.2d 604 (2d Dept. 1976), aff'd sub nom., Pierre Pellaton Apartments v. Board of Assessors of Nassau, 43 N.Y.2d 769, 372 N.E.2d 801, 401 N.Y.S.2d 1013 (1977).

48. See text at note 31 supra.

49. Slewett & Farber v. Board of Assessors of Nassau, 97 Misc. 2d 637, 642, 412 N.Y.S. 2d 292, 296 (Sup. Ct. 1978). Elsewhere the Court noted that as a result of these changes: "Municipalities were soon beseiged with a startling wave of protests and proceedings based on inequality. It has been estimated

thought that the distress that would result from the shift in the burden of taxes ensuing the resolution of numerous inequality proceedings in taxpayers' favor could be relieved through an expansion of the tax base brought about by a restriction of exemptions.

## Note on the Governmental Services and Functions Financed With Funds Raised by the Real Property Tax

An important question related to an examination of property tax exemptions is how the revenues from the property tax are distributed. If the revenues or benefits are distributed, for the most part, among property owners in a manner somewhat proportionate to their level of property ownership, then the tax can be considered a charge for property-related services. It would be efficient and equitable to tax all property owners in such a

---

that statewide refunds in these proceedings may reach one billion dollars and this figure may admittedly be on the low side. In the City of New York alone one estimate places the cost of rebates between 1.7 and 2.7 billion dollars." Id. at 64, 412 N.Y.S. 2d at 296 (citations omitted). Since 1978 Nassau County has paid out more than $46 million in commercial property tax refunds, has lost $30 million from commercial assessment rolls, and faces 35,000 refund claims from businesses seeking tax relief based on the 1975 State Supreme Court decision, known as the 860 Executive Towers decision. In response to this threat in mid-1979 the legislature amended the law in effect to retroactively validate all classified assessments and to impose upon taxpayers bringing inequality proceedings the obligation of pleading inequality in comparison to properties of the same type rather than to all properties. 1978 N.Y. Laws, ch. 478. This statute was declared unconstitutional. Slewett & Farber v. Board of Assessors, supra.

In 1979 the legislature amended the statute again to eliminate the use of the state equalization rate in inequality proceedings except for those involving residential property. 1979 N.Y. Laws, ch. 126. A lower court decision involving an inequality claim brought with respect to commercial property located in New York City upheld the validity of the 1979 law and declared a City Administrative Code provision that required that in inequality proceedings comparisons be made to "other real property of like character" to be controlling. Colt Industries Inc. v. the Tax Commission of the City of New York, 183 N.Y.L.J., June 4, 1980 at 10, col. 2 (Sup. Ct. June 3, 1980). (1980). At the time of this writing the whole area is in flux and it is impossible to tell what the ultimate resolution of these problems will be. The above, somewhat topical analysis has only been offered to provide background to help explain why the question of tax exemption has been raised again.

case, as property owners are paying the tax and receiving the benefits on a quid pro quo basis. On the other hand, if there is no direct relationship between payment of the tax and benefits from it, there must be some other justification for the tax than the benefit principle, perhaps an ability-to-pay criterion.

This brief note analyzes the distribution of benefits from the property tax for localities within New York State. By examining the distribution of benefits among the owners of property and the community at large, it will be shown that the property tax is used in such a way as to benefit the community at large.

Property taxes, excluding those raised by school and fire districts, are seldom earmarked for any specific expenditure function. The approach taken here is to assume that revenues from the property tax, other than those specifically earmarked for school and fire districts, go into a general fund and then are distributed proportionately among the various expenditures of a taxing unit. First, however, all nonproperty tax revenues earmarked for specific expenditure categories are eliminated from these specific categories.[50] While a large portion of the property tax may not be collected for any specific expenditure purpose, by this method its de facto use can, nevertheless, be determined.

Data used in this note are taken for the most part from the annually published *Special Reports on Municipal Affairs by the State Comptroller* of New York State.[51] Expenditure categories as set forth in the *Special Reports* comprise the following functions: General Government, Public Safety, Health, Sanitation, Highways, Social Service Programs and Administration, Culture and Recreation, Education, All Other, Interest, Capital Outlay and Debt Service. These expenditure categories have been aggregated into three main areas: 1) Property-Related

50. Revenues whose use can be explicitly identified account for a little over 50% of all revenues.

51. New York State Comptroller, Special Report on Municipal Affairs, N.Y. Leg. Doc. No. 92 (1979) (for local fiscal year ending in 1978), and N.Y. Leg. Doc. No. 97 (1971) (for local fiscal year ending in 1970).

expenditures, 2) People-Related expenditures and 3) Noncurrent expenditures. Because determining the placement of individual expenditure categories is somewhat arbitrary, the most conservative approach possible has been taken, placing only Education, Social Services, Health and Culture and Recreation under the People-Related expenditures category. Capital Outlay and Debt Services have been placed in the area Noncurrent expenditures, and all other functional categories have been placed in Property-Related expenditures. (Below a less conservative approach is used.) Obviously, it could be argued that expenditures such as those for Public Safety or Sanitation partially benefit the community exclusive of property ownership as well, but determining where the line should be drawn for such a division becomes rather difficult.[52]

Table 1 presents for the years 1960, 1965, 1970, 1975 and 1978 a breakdown of the property tax's use as distributed between Property-Related, People-Related and Noncurrent expenditures in all New York State taxing units. Even with the very conservative approach used here, it is clear that People-Related expenditures take up the lion's share of the property tax revenue. Data for the most recent year available, 1978, show that 68% of all the property tax in all taxing units goes toward People-Related expenditures.

It can be seen that a definite trend exists in each of the three summaries toward greater reliance on the property tax for sup-

52. The conservative nature of this estimate becomes even more apparent when it is understood that the functional categories All Other and General Government are included in the analysis as Property-Related expenditures. All Other is defined in the case of cities as expenditures related to the operation of a city-owned bus line, airport, cemetery, dock, market, off-street parking, community beautification, publicity such as advertising of natural resources and benefits of the city, authorized agencies, employer's share for fringe benefits payments and economic opportunity. General Government represents expenditures for City officers, board of contract and supply or purchasing agent, law department, civil service commission, city engineer, elections, city court and municipal buildings and offices. Without question, some of these expenditures fall more appropriately under the People-Related expenditures category.

**Table 1**
**Expenditure Distribution by Function of Property Tax Revenues of New York State Taxing Units. Years: 1960, '65, '70, '75 and '78[1]**

| Year | Property-Related Expenditures<br>General Government<br>Public Safety<br>Sanitation<br>Highways<br>Interest<br>All Other | People-Related Expenditures<br>Education<br>Social Services<br>Health<br>Culture and Recreation | Noncurrent Expenditures<br>Capital Outlay<br>Debt Service-Principal |
|---|---|---|---|
| | *New York City* ($1,000s) | | |
| 1978 | $ 804,494 | $2,189,423 | $235,800 |
| % | 25 | 68 | 7 |
| 1975 | 658,197 | 1,833,394 | 414,570 |
| % | 23 | 63 | 14 |
| 1970 | 539,366 | 1,255,589 | 115,791 |
| % | 28 | 60 | 6 |
| 1965 | 449,380 | 878,601 | 22,042 |
| % | 33 | 65 | 2 |
| 1960 | 377,556 | 562,529 | 89,600 |
| % | 37 | 55 | 9 |
| | *Upstate Taxing Units* ($1,000s) | | |
| 1978 | $1,346,449 | $3,677,167 | $294,730 |
| % | 25 | 69 | 6 |
| 1975 | 955,167 | 2,945,674 | 242,933 |
| % | 23 | 71 | 6 |
| 1970 | 597,930 | 1,851,270 | 91,989 |
| % | 24 | 73 | 3 |
| 1965 | 448,879 | 1,009,012 | 98,663 |
| % | 29 | 65 | 6 |
| 1960 | 676,477 | 1,276,604 | 175,253 |
| % | 32 | 60 | 8 |
| | *All Taxing Units* ($1,000s) | | |
| 1978 | $2,234,210 | $5,854,599 | $590,434 |
| % | 26 | 68 | 7 |

**Table 1**
**Expenditure Distribution by Function of Property Tax Revenues of New York State Taxing Units. Years: 1960, '65, '70, '75 and '78[1]**

| Year | Property-Related Expenditures<br>General Government<br>Public Safety<br>Sanitation<br>Highways<br>Interest<br>All Other | People-Related Expenditures<br>Education<br>Social Services<br>Health<br>Culture and Recreation | Noncurrent Expenditures<br>Capital Outlay<br>Debt Service-Principal |
|---|---|---|---|
| 1975 | 1,475,587 | 4,905,075 | 669,273 |
| % | 21 | 70 | 9 |
| 1970 | 1,134,232 | 3,103,697 | 214,006 |
| % | 25 | 70 | 5 |
| 1965 | 903,584 | 1,897,551 | 106,907 |
| % | 31 | 65 | 4 |
| 1960 | 676,477 | 1,276,604 | 175,253 |
| % | 32 | 60 | 8 |

Source: For a summary of the method used to compile Table 1, see the Appendix immediately following this note. For the data upon which this table is based see Bureau of the Census, U.S. Department of Commerce, 1977 Census of Governments, vol. 4, no. 5 (1979) (Governmental Finances, Compendium of Government Finances); New York State Comptroller, Special Report on Municipal Affairs, N.Y. Leg. Doc. No. 92 (1979) (for local fiscal years ending in 1978), and N.Y. Leg. Doc. No. 97 (1971) (for local fiscal years ending in 1970); Budget Services Unit, New York State Statistical Yearbook 1979-80 (1979); Department of Finance, New York City, Annual Report of the Comptroller, pts. 2, 2A (1961 to 1979 inclusive) (Operating Accounts—Summary 1, Expense Budget—Statement 4) (Data for fiscal years 1960–61 through 1978).

1. 1978 is the most recent year for which data are available.

port of People-Related expenditures. This is most evident in the case of New York City, where People-Related expenditures increase as a share of property taxes from 55% in 1960 to 68% in 1978. This is not surprising as expenditures for Education and Social Services became of increasing importance to localities in the late 1960s and the 1970s.

For the years considered, Education accounts for around 50% of the property tax expenditures of all taxing units. Although Social Services account for around 20% of current expenditures of all taxing units, 60% of these expenditures, on average, are provided for by either the state or federal government, thus lessening the support needed from the property tax. People-Related expenditures increased most rapidly between 1965 and 1970. At the same time, intergovernmental aid also increased rapidly but more so for Property-Related expenditures. The result of this imbalance was a greater reliance on the tax for People-Related expenditures. Table 1 confirms this.

Without question, the New York State property tax is used for People-Related expenditures to a far greater extent than for Property-Related expenditures and, therefore, is not an exclusive charge for property-related services.[53] Furthermore, it has been shown that because of the increased importance of People-Related expenditures within taxing units and the relatively declining contribution of governmental aid for such expenditures, a natural outcome is a greater role for the property tax in providing for People-Related expenditures.

Table 1, above, presents a conservative estimate of the distribution of property tax revenues for People-Related expenditures by assuming that all General Government, Public Safety, Sanitation, Highways, Interest and All Other expenditures are Property-Related expenditures. In Tables A-1 and A-2 this assumption is relaxed by first assuming 25% and then 50% of these expenditures are People-Related.

## Appendix

This appendix provides a detailed description of the method and source used in determining the data used in Table 1.

The general approach used in deriving Table 1 is to examine expenditures of localities and segregate from these expenditures those which came from nonproperty tax sources, and were earmarked for specific funtional categories and which

53. For a similar conclusion, see D. Netzer, Economics of the Property Tax 59–60 (1966).

**Table A-1**
**Expenditure Distribution by Function of Property Tax Revenues of New York State Taxing Units. Years: 1960, '65, '70, '75 and '78 (Assumes 25% of Table 1 Property-Related Expenditures are People Related.)**

| Year | Property-Related Expenditures | People-Related Expenditures | Noncurrent Expenditures |
|---|---|---|---|
| | | *All Taxing Units* ($1,000s) | |
| 1978 | $1,675,658 | $6,413,152 | $590,434 |
| % | 19 | 74 | 7 |
| 1975 | 1,106,690 | 5,273,972 | 699,273 |
| % | 16 | 75 | 9 |
| 1970 | 850,674 | 3,387,255 | 214,006 |
| % | 19 | 76 | 5 |
| 1965 | 677,688 | 2,123,447 | 106,907 |
| % | 23 | 73 | 4 |
| 1960 | 507,358 | 1,445,723 | 175,253 |
| % | 23 | 68 | 8 |

Source: See note to Table 1.

**Table A-2**
**Expenditure Distribution by Function of Property Tax Revenues of New York State Taxing Units. Years: 1960, '65, '70, '75 and '78. (Assumes 50% of Table 1 Property-Related expenditures are People Related.)**

***All Taxing Units***
**($1,000s)**

| Year | Property-Related Expenditures | People-Related Expenditures | Noncurrent Expenditures |
|---|---|---|---|
| 1978 | $1,117,105 | $6,971,704 | $590,434 |
| % | 13 | 80 | 7 |
| 1975 | 737,794 | 5,642,865 | 669,273 |
| % | 10 | 80 | 9 |
| 1970 | 567,116 | 3,670,813 | 214,006 |
| % | 13 | 83 | 5 |
| 1965 | 451,792 | 2,349,343 | 106,907 |
| % | 16 | 81 | 4 |
| 1960 | 338,239 | 1,614,843 | 175,253 |
| % | 16 | 76 | 8 |

Source: See note to Table 1.

accordingly did not come from the locality's property tax. This was accomplished by the removal of such revenue sources as intergovernmental aid and borrowing.

Intergovernmental aid to all taxing units was eliminated on the basis of functional breakdowns of state aid to all localities, and federal aid to New York City. This omits explicit federal aid to Upstate localities, considered acceptable because a large portion of federal aid is channeled through state agencies. Furthermore, data for the most recent year available, 1978, show about 60% of federal aid to all localities went to New York City. Assuming a large fraction of the remaining 40% of the federal aid to other localities was in the form of general revenue sharing, it appears that the omission of these data does not seriously affect the results in Table 1. Nevertheless, to the extent that this omission does have an effect on the results in Table 1, it would most likely exaggerate the importance of property tax support for People-Related expenditures because more federal aid to Upstate localities was probably earmarked for People-Related expenditures. Upstate intergovernmental aid was determined as the difference between aid to all taxing units and New York City for all relevant years.

After the removal from total expenditures of earmarked non-property tax revenues as well as those expenditures not related to the property tax, such as expenditures for publicly operated utilities, one arrives at a new functional distribution of expenditures by localities supported by general revenues alone, of which the property tax is a significant portion (about 34% in 1978). It is assumed that the distribution of expenditures of these general revenues represents the distribution of expenditures of property tax.

There is now examined in detail a typical year in Table 1.

Table 1-A of the State Comptroller's *Special Report on Municipal Affairs* for 1978[54] indicates that total expenditures (excluding Noncurrent expenditures) of all New York State taxing

54. New York State Comptroller, Special Report on Municipal Affairs, N.Y. Leg. Doc. No. 92 (1979) (for local fiscal year ending in 1978).

units was $21,572,651,000 for 1975. Table 1-M of the same report provides the following functional breakdown of all current expenditures.

**Table B-1**
**All Units Current Expenditures—1975**
**($1,000s)**

| Function | Amount |
|---|---|
| General Purpose | |
| General Government | $1,225,862 |
| Public Safety | 1,943,629 |
| Health | 1,407,395 |
| Sanitation | 448,888 |
| Highways | 530,517 |
| Social Service Programs and Administration | 4,967,206 |
| Culture and Recreation | 365,297 |
| Education | 7,540,270 |
| All Other | 1,790,924 |
| Utilities and Special Districts | 326,248 |
| Interest on Debt | 1,026,415 |
| Total Current Expenditures | $21,572,651 |

Source: New York State Comptroller, Special Report on Municipal Affairs, table 1-A, N.Y. Leg. Doc. No. 92 (1979) (for local fiscal year ending in 1978).

There is now removed some of the nonproperty tax revenues earmarked for specific expenditure categories. Table I-42 of the New York State Statistical Yearbook[55] provides the required information. Table I-42, for example, shows that total state aid to localities in 1975 was $5,762,131,000, and of this total $1,-214,689,000 financed Social Services. This intergovernmental aid to Social Services is subtracted from the total Social Services current expenditures of $4,967,206,000 shown in Table B-1. By matching categories between Tables B-1 and I-42, all earmarked state funds to localities are eliminated.

As stated earlier, no functional breakdown of federal aid to all

55. Budget Services Unit, New York State Division of the Budget, New York State Statistical Yearbook-1979, 80, table I-42 (1979).

localities is available, but there is one for New York City. "Part 2—Operating Accounts—Summary 1," of the *New York City Annual Report of the Comptroller,*[56] 1974–75 provides a functional breakdown of federal aid to New York City. By matching categories between this table and Table B-1, earmarked federal funds to New York City are eliminated. Continuing with this example, there is eliminated $1,568,896,000 from Social Services in Table B-1. Part 2 of the *Annual Report of the Comptroller* also provides us with state aid data to New York City. This permits one to determine state aid to Upstate localities by subtracting New York City aid information from aid information for all localities.

The example traced above began with Social Service expenditures of $4,967,206,000. After identifying and subtracting state and federal aid for Social Services, only $2,167,921,000, or 44%, of the initial amount remained. This amount is aggregated with other People-Related expenditures to determine the percentage of general revenues going toward People-Related expenditures. This, in turn, reflects the percentage of the property tax used for these expenditures. The above procedure is the same for all years and services identified in Table 1.

Use of Tables 1-P for New York City and 1-Mn for Upstate localities from the *Special Report* in addition to the tables already mentioned permits one to duplicate the above procedure for New York City and Upstate localities.

Tables 1-G through 1-K of the *Special Report* permit one to examine in detail the sources and uses of educational revenues within state localities. For example, Table 1-G presents the following financial information concerning all school districts in New York State for 1975:

The availability of the above data obviates the need for an approximation of property tax support for this expenditure cat-

56. Department of Finance, New York City, Annual Report of the Comptroller, pt. 2 (1975) (Operating Accounts-Summary 1) (Data for fiscal year 1974–75).

**Table B-2**
**Sources and Uses of Funds of all New York State School Districts (Excluding Higher Education)—1975.**
**($1,000s)**

| | |
|---|---|
| *Revenues* | |
| Real Property Taxes | $3,617,474 |
| Nonproperty Taxes | 42,696 |
| State Aid | 2,948,307 |
| Federal Aid | 515,452 |
| Other Revenues | 377,724 |
| Total Revenues: | $7,501,653 |
| *Borrowings* | |
| Bonds | $374,422 |
| Notes | 133,160 |
| Total Borrowings: | $507,582 |
| Total Revenue and Borrowings: | $8,009,235 |
| *Expenditures* | |
| Current Expenditures | $6,952,885 |
| Capital Outlay | 453,439 |
| Debt Service | |
| Principal | 443,268 |
| Interest | 237,784 |
| Total Expenditures: | $8,087,376[1] |

Source: New York State Comptroller, Special Report on Municipal Affairs, table 1-G, N.Y. Leg. Doc. No. 92 (1979) (for local fiscal year ending in 1978).

1. This figure does not equal the amount under Education in Table B-1 for 1975 because Table B-1 represents only current expenditures and not capital expenditures and includes current expenditures for higher education.

egory as was made for the other categories. Rather, one can work directly with the above information, segregating it from the rest of the analysis on both the sources and uses sides.[57]

Finally, Municipal Assistance Corporation revenues generated in 1978 came from state aid and the New York City sales

57. Table 1-L of the Special Report permits the same procedure to be followed for Fire Districts which are also units supported by the property tax. Their presence, however, is far less significant than the presence of School Districts with respect to the results of this study.

tax. All utility revenues are assumed generated by sources other than the property tax. All borrowing for all categories is assumed to be used for capital expenditure or to service the principal on debt.

Table B-3 presents the estimated distribution of general revenue support and, in turn, property tax support for current and capital expenditures categories in 1975 for all localities. This approximation, of course, represents the outcome of the techniques and data sources described above.

**Table B-3**
**Distribution of General Revenues and Property Tax Revenues in 1975 for All Units by Expenditure Function[1]**
**($1,000)**

| Function | General Revenue Support | Percent | Property Tax Support[2] |
|---|---|---|---|
| General Government and Other[3] | $1,529,342 | 14 | $446,181 |
| Public Safety | 1,863,297 | 17 | 541,792 |
| Health | 959,585 | 9 | 286,831 |
| Sanitation | 448,888 | 4 | 127,481 |
| Highways | 330,100 | 3 | 95,610 |
| Social Services and Administration | 2,167,921 | 20 | 637,403 |
| Culture and Recreation | 365,297 | 3 | 95,610 |
| Interest | 777,687 | 7 | 223,091 |
| Capital Outlay and Debt Service | 2,240,169 | 21 | 669,272 |
| Total | $10,685,286 | 100% | $3,187,013 |

1. Education is not included here as that can be obtained without approximation from Table B-2.
2. The percentages are applied to a base of $3,187,013 in property taxes which represents non-Education-related property tax revenues.
3. General Government and Other have been aggregated due to the nature of available earmarked revenue data.

Now that property tax support of the expenditure functions identified in Table B-3 has been approximated, these can generate a final expenditure distribution of property tax revenues utilizing data on Education from Table B-2. Table B-4 presents the combination of estimated data from Table B-3 and actual Education data from Table B-2.

**Table B-4**
**Final Distribution of Property Tax Revenues by Expenditure Function in 1975 for All Units[1]**
**($1,000s)**

| Function | Property Tax Support | Percent |
|---|---|---|
| General Government and Other | $446,181 | 6% |
| Public Safety | 541,792 | 8 |
| Health | 286,831 | 4 |
| Sanitation | 127,481 | 2 |
| Highways | 95,610 | 1 |
| Social Services and Administration | 637,403 | 9 |
| Culture and Recreation | 95,610 | 1 |
| Education[2] | 3,809,538 | 55 |
| Interest | 223,091 | 3 |
| Capital Outlay and Debt Service | 669,272 | 10 |
| Total | $6,932,809 | 100% |

1. Aggregates may differ slightly in Table 1 due to rounding.
2. Includes Higher Education and therefore disagrees slightly with Table B-2.

Table B-4 provides the base from which one can estimate Property-Related, People-Related and Noncurrent expenditures for 1975 in Table 1.

# 2

# The Structure and History of Charitable Real Property Tax Exemptions

## Section A—An Explanation of the New York State Property Tax Exemption System

This section briefly summarizes the law in New York in relation to real property tax exemptions. The next section gives a short history of the development of the "charitable"[1] exemption. Section C suggests a way by which property tax exemptions should be analyzed, and section D discusses the Service Charge Law.

Constitutional provisions on property tax exemptions are brief. They permit the repeal of exemptions except for religious, educational and charitable exemptions, exempt personal property from tax, and prohibit the passing of any private law granting exemptions. Article XVI, section 1 of the New York State Constitution[2] provides in part that: "Exemptions from taxation may be altered or repealed except those exempting real or personal property used exclusively for religious, educational or charitable purposes as defined by law and owned by any corporation or association organized or conducted exclusively for one or more of such purposes and not operating for

1. "Charitable" is used here in the broad sense to cover religious, educational and numerous other like private purposes that are of a charitable nature.
2. N.Y. Const. art. XVI, § 1.

profit." Section 3 exempts intangible personal property from the property tax[3] and section 17 provides, in part, that: "The legislature shall not pass a private or local bill in any of the following cases . . . granting to any person, association, firm, or corporation, an exemption from taxation on real or personal property."[4]

The law on real property tax exemptions is contained for the most part in Article 4 of the New York Real Property Tax Law (RPTL).[5] Title 1 of Article 4 covers public property and Title 2 covers private property. Very briefly, under Title 1 (RPTL §§ 400–418) property of the following public bodies is exempt: the United States (RPTL § 401), the State of New York (RPTL § 404), municipal corporations, i.e., local government units such as counties, cities, towns, and villages (RPTL § 406), school districts (RPTL § 408), special districts (RPTL § 410), public authorities (RPTL § 412), industrial development agencies (RPTL § 412-a), public housing, including publicly assisted housing and limited-profit nursing homes (RPTL § 414), the United Nations (RPTL § 416) and foreign governments (RPTL § 418).[6]

Exemptions for private property are provided under Title 2 (RPTL §§ 420–489). These private real property tax exemptions may be categorized as falling into five general classes.[7] First are exemptions designed to spur economic development and revi-

3. N.Y. Const. art. XVI, § 3.

4. N.Y. Const. art XVI, § 17.

5. N.Y. Real Prop. Tax (McKinney 1972). Certain other laws exempt real property such as provisions in the Public Authorities Law exempting the property of various public authorities and some exemptions are granted under local laws pursuant to provisions in the Private Housing Finance Law.

6. As will be shown in Chapter 4, the great bulk of exempt property is public property, particularly property belonging to municipal corporations. No attempt is made herein to describe or explicate how these public property exemptions have been construed or applied or the many limitations and special qualifications that relate to them.

7. The following classification scheme is not given or even suggested in the statute and is made here only to facilitate treatment of the material. Sometimes a distinction is made between wholly and partially exempt property. Where this distinction appears relevant it will be noted.

talization. Second are exemptions designed to encourage residential construction and rehabilitation. Third are exemptions provided to certain classes of individuals, viz., veterans and the elderly. Fourth are a number of miscellaneous exemptions that do not fit into any of the above classes or in any other single descriptive class. And fifth are exemptions provided to charitable, religious, educational and similar organizations, which are the chief subject of this study. There follows a brief description of these five classes of exemptions. Except for the treatment of the fifth category—charitable exemptions—the descriptions are extremely limited, offer only a general idea of the nature of these exemptions and in no way suggest the very detailed and complex nature of some of the provisions.

*Economic Development Exemptions*

RPTL § 485b allows municipalities to provide a partial exemption to real property constructed, altered, installed or improved after July 1, 1976 for purposes of commercial, business or industrial activity. For the first year an exemption of 50% of the increase in assessed value due to construction, etc., is allowed; thereafter the amount is reduced by 5% each year until the tenth and last year when a final exemption of 5% is allowed. The municipality may reduce at its option the per centum of exemption. If the property is not used for eligible purposes the exemption ceases. A similar exemption is granted in New York City (RPTL §§ 489-aaa et seq.) for the construction and reconstruction of industrial structures and the reconstruction of specially needed commercial structures, the former allows an exemption beginning at 95% to be reduced by 5% a year over eighteen ensuing years.

RPTL § 485(3) allows municipalities to grant partial exemptions to eligible business facilities (as defined in the Commerce Law) certified by the New York State job incentive board to the extent authorized by local law for any increase in the assessed value of the property attributable to expenditures for capital improvements consisting of the construction, reconstruction, erection or improvement of depreciable property.

*Veterans and Elderly Exemptions*

RPTL § 458 provides that real property owned by veterans, their spouses or unmarried surviving spouses, dependent fathers, mothers or children under the age of twenty-one and purchased with proceeds made available to such veterans by virtue of their service (e.g., veterans' pensions) is exempt to the extent that such moneys are applied to their purchase up to an assessed value of $5,000. Similarly, real property bought with proceeds collected by popular subscription and owned by disabled veterans (or their close relatives) of World Wars I or II or the Korean or Vietnam War is entitled to an exemption up to $5,000.[8]

RPTL § 467 provides that municipalities can exempt the residence of persons sixty-five or older up to 50% of assessed valuation. No exemption is allowed if the property owner's income exceeds $3,000 or such other sum not less than $3,000 or more than $8,000 as provided by local law. If a child is living in the residence and attends public school the property shall not be exempt from taxation for school purposes.[9]

8. Interestingly, subdivision 5 of this section provides in part that "if the ratio between the exemption granted under this section and the total assessed value of the real property for which such exemption has been granted increases or decreases due only to a change in the manner of assessing real property by a court-ordered full value assessment in the tax district in which the property is located, the amount of the exemption heretofore or hereafter granted shall be increased or decreased in such subsequent year in the same proportion as the total assessed value has been increased or decreased." N.Y. Real Prop. Tax § 458(5)(a)(McKinney 1972).

9. N.Y. Real Prop. Tax § 467-b (McKinney 1972) allows municipalities to give a tax abatement for the forebearance of taking advantage of allowable rent increases under the regulated rent provisions occupied by senior citizens. N.Y. Real Prop. Tax § 467-c allows New York City to exempt certain housing from a tax equal to rent increases that might have been imposed on persons sixty-two or older but which increases were foreborne.

In addition exemptions are granted for industrial waste facilities (RPTL § 477), air pollution control facilities (RPTL § 481), solar and wind energy systems (RPTL § 487), structures and buildings essential to the operation of agricultural and horticultural lands (RPTL § 483), certain real property used in the manufacture of steel (RPTL § 485-a) and partial exemption to land used for timber production (RPTL 480-a).

*Housing Development Exemptions*

RPTL § 489 allows municipalities to exempt from taxation any increase in the assessed value of rehabilitated structures through upgrading, eliminating health and fire hazards, effecting improvements to conserve energy or improving outside walls for historic or landmark purposes. (This exemption is referred to as the J-51 program in New York City.) Very generally, RPTL § 421-a provides a property tax exemption on the increase in assessed valuation from the new construction (or in some cases rehabilitation) of multiunit dwellings. The exemption declines over a ten-year period so that the property will pay full taxes in the eleventh year after completion. RPTL § 484 exempts real property owned by urban development corporations. Finally, RPTL § 422 exempts from taxation real property owned by a not-for-profit corporation and used to provide housing for the handicapped or aged persons of low income (and for numerous other purposes, including housing for faculty members, students, employees, nurses, interns, resident physicians, researchers and other personnel and their immediate families in attendance or employed at colleges, universities, hospitals etc.) or to provide facilities to offer health care to sick or disabled persons of low income.

*Miscellaneous Exemptions*

There follows a brief listing of some of the miscellaneous real property tax exemptions provided by the law.

RPTL § 450 exempts property owned by an agricultural society and permanently used for a meeting hall or exhibition grounds.

RPTL § 452 exempts real property owned by veterans' organizations.

RPTL § 454 exempts real property in any Indian reservation owned by the Indian nation, tribe or band occupying them.

RPTL § 474 exempts real property owned by dental societies. (Not allowed in New York City.)

RPTL §§ 456 and 476a provide certain exemptions for railroad purposes.

RPTL § 478 exempts off-street parking facilities providing underground shelters.

RPTL § 479 exempts fallout shelters.

RPTL § 480 exempts tracts of forest land.

RPTL § 488 exempts real property owned by a retirement system.

RPTL § 482 provides a partial exemption at the option of the municipality for farmland taken by the state for enforcing a quarantine.

RPTL § 486 exempts real property owned by medical and dental expense indemnity and hospital corporations.

*Charitable Exemptions*

Section 421 of the Real Property Tax Law,[10] entitled "Nonprofit organizations," is the major statutory provision covering exemptions of real property for charitable purposes[11] and is the

10. N.Y. Real Prop. Tax § 421 (McKinney 1972).
11. "Charitable" is used here in its broadest sense. See note 1 supra.

provision with which this study is chiefly concerned.[12] There are a number of other sections in Title 2 (Private Property) of Article 4 (Exemptions) covering purposes that might be considered charitable, but for the most part these provisions are very narrowly drawn and appear to apply to only one or a very few existing organizations. They are briefly discussed below.

Subdivision 1 of section 421 is the principal provision of this section. Those provisions of subdivision 1 contained in paragraphs (a), (b) and (d) and of particular importance to this study follow with some brief comments.[13]

Paragraph (a) of subdivision 1 provides:

> (a) Real property owned by a corporation or association organized or conducted exclusively for religious, charitable, hospital, educational, moral or mental improvement of men, women or children or cemetery purposes, or for two or more such purposes, and used exclusively for carrying out thereupon one or more of such purposes either by the owning corporation or association or by another such corporation or association as hereinafter provided shall be exempt from taxation as provided in this section.

Paragraph (b) provides in part:

> (b) Real property owned by a corporation or association which is not organized or conducted exclusively for religious, charitable, hospital, educational, moral or mental improvement of men, women or children or cemetery purposes, or for two or more such purposes, but which is organized or conducted exclusively for bible, tract, benevolent, missionary, infirmary, public playground, scientific, literary, bar association, medical society, library, patriotic or historical purposes, for the enforcement of laws relating to children or animals, or for two or

12. The section on nonprofit organizations was renumbered from section 420 to section 421 by 1971 N.Y. Laws, ch. 417. As this law, providing for a service charge (see section D infra) has at the time of this writing not been implemented, the nonprofit organizations' section is technically still section 420, but it is numbered as section 421 in the consolidated laws and widely referred to as such. It shall be referred to as section 421 in this study.

13. They are referred to in the next section as the "central section 421 provisions."

> more such purposes, and used exclusively for carrying out thereupon one or more of such purposes either by the owning corporation or association, or by another such corporation or association as hereinafter provided, shall be exempt from taxation; provided, however, that such property shall be taxable by any municipal corporation within which it is located if the board of such municipal corporation, after public hearing, adopts a local law, ordinance, or resolution so providing.

Thus, all municipalities must exempt real property, which otherwise qualifies, that is owned by organizations established for purposes enumerated in paragraph (a) and used for such purposes and may or may not at its option exempt real property, which otherwise qualifies, that is owned by organizations established for purposes enumerated in paragraph (b) and used for such purposes.[14] It may be noted that in addition to the purposes required to be exempt by Article XVI, section 1,[15] viz., religious, educational and charitable purposes, paragraph (a) enumerates hospital, moral or mental improvement of men, women or children and cemetery purposes. Chapter 5 provides an analysis of what some of these purposes, particularly those listed in paragraph (a), have been construed to mean and so no definitions of these terms will be given here.

Paragraph (c) permits municipalities to select for taxation only some of the paragraph (b) purposes and leave others exempt. Paragraph (d) provides:

> (d) Real property such as specified in paragraphs (a) and (b) of this subdivision shall not be exempt if any officer, member or employee of the owning corporation or association shall receive or may be lawfully entitled to receive any pecuniary profit from the operations thereof, except reasonable compensation for services in effecting one or more of such purposes, or as proper beneficiaries of its strictly charitable purposes; or if the organization thereof for any such avowed purposes

14. The impact of this difference is discussed in Chapter 5.
15. See note 2 supra.

be a guise or pretense for directly or indirectly making any other pecuniary profit for such corporation or association or for any of its member[16] or employees; or if it be not in good faith organized or conducted exclusively for one or more of such purposes.

Simply put, for real property to qualify for an exemption under section 421 it must satisfy three requirements: it must 1) be owned by a corporation or association (including trusts)[17] i) organized or conducted ii) exclusively for one or more of the stated purposes, and 2) be used exclusively by such organization to conduct thereupon one or more such purposes. Finally, 3) no one associated with the organization can derive any profit (in a monetary sense) from its activity.

The first part (i) of the first requirement provides the organization seeking exemption *be organized or conducted* exclusively for one or more enumerated purposes. Up until 1971 the statute required only that the organization be organized for an exempt purpose.[18] In pre-1971 cases close attention was paid to an organization's organizing documents, e.g., its certificate of incorporation or trust instrument, to determine whether it was organized for an exempt purpose. See *In re DePeyster's Estate* [19] An organization whose establishing papers permitted it to engage in nonexempt purposes would presumably not be entitled to exemption. In 1971 the law was changed to provide that the organization must be organized *or conducted* for an exempt purpose.[20] Recently, the Court of Appeals[21] in taking account

16. As in original. It probably should read "members."
17. Mohonk Trust v. Board of Assessors of Gardnier, 47 N.Y.2d 476, 482–483, 392 N.E.2d 876, 879, 418 N.Y.S.2d 763, 776 (1979).
18. 1958 N.Y. Laws, ch. 959.
19. 210 N.Y. 216, 104 N.E. 714 (1919). For some this focus may have survived the 1971 changes. See Shrine of Our Lady of Martyrs of Auriesville v. Board of Assessors of Glen, 40 A.D.2d 75, 337 N.Y.S.2d 786 (3d Dept. 1972), aff'd, 33 N.Y.2d 713, 304 N.E.2d 563, 349 N.Y.S.2d 993 (1973) and 5 Op. Counsel SBEA No. 103 (1976).
20. 1971 N.Y. Laws, ch. 414.
21. Mohonk Trust v. Board of Assessors of Gardnier, 47 N.Y.2d476, 393 N.E.2d 876, 418 N.Y.S.2d 763 (1979). This case is discussed in considerable detail in Chapter 6.

of the 1971 changes noted that before such change it was irrelevant to consider whether an organization formed under a broad charter permitting it to engage in both exempt and nonexempt activities in fact conducted only exempt activities. After pointing out that the test was now "organized or conducted,"[22] it concluded: "Hence, the determination of an organization's primary purpose may turn upon the extent to which it pursues the various purposes for which it was created, and is not necessarily dependent solely upon the language of the document pursuant to which the organization operates."[23]

The second part (ii) of the first requirement provides that the organization be organized or conducted *exclusively* for exempt purposes.[24] In *Association of the Bar of New York v. Lewisohn,* [25] the Court of Appeals noted that the term: " 'exclusive,' as used in the context of these exemption statutes, has been held to connote 'principal' or 'primary.' Hence, purposes and uses merely auxiliary or incidental to the main exempt purpose and use will not defeat the exemption."[26]

Both the first and second requirements provide respectively that the organization be devoted to one of several enumerated purposes, e.g., religious, educational or charitable, and that the property be used for one or more of such purposes. As noted this aspect of section 421 is discussed at some length in Chapter 5.

The second requirement is that the property sought to be

22. Id. at 484, 392 N.E.2d 880, 418 N.Y.S.2d 767.

23. Id. It is unclear as to how the Court would rule if an organization's founding documents permitted it to engage solely in nonexempt activities although it in fact only pursued clearly exempt purposes. It does seem likely, however, that if an organization's founding documents expressly limited it to exempt purposes and it in fact engaged in substantial amount of nonexempt activity (so much at least that it could not be said that its primary purpose was an exempt purpose) that it would not be entitled to exemption.

24. As will be pointed out below the meaning of "exclusively" for this first requirement of the tri-part formulation is the same for the second requirement.

25. 34 N.Y.2d 143, 313 N.E.2d 30, 356 N.Y.2d 555 (1974).

26. Id. at 153, 313 N.E.2d 35, 356 N.Y.S.2d 561 (citations omitted).

exempt be used exclusively for an exempt purpose. As noted "exclusively" here also means "principal" or "primary." A considerable amount of litigation has developed around this requirement. Typically, the owning organization is clearly organized and conducted for exempt purposes, but a particular use of a part of its property is called into question. As will be pointed out below, if a part of property otherwise exempt is used for nonexempt purposes it shall not be exempt.[27] For example, the question of whether or not an exemption ought to be accorded to housing owned by hospitals or colleges or to a farm owned by a religious organization has been raised.[28]

The third requirement, the nonprofit requirement, has presented few interpretive difficulties; generally speaking commercial activity can be engaged in only if it is merely incidental and supportive of the primary exempt purpose.[29]

To have property declared exempt under section 421, the first step is to make such a request to the local assessor of the assessing unit in which the property is located. If this attempt is unsuccessful there are various administrative and judicial

27. See text accompanying note 32 infra.

28. In In re Syracuse University, 124 Misc. 788, 209 N.Y.S. 329 (Sup. Ct. 1925), aff'd, 214 A.D. 375, 212 N.Y.S. 253 (4th Dept. 1925) dormitories, infirmaries, a farm and the chancellor's residence of a university were held to be exempt under the educational purposes category. Apartments used for residential purposes for hospital personnel were held to be exempt under the hospital purposes category. St. Lukes Hospital v. Boyland, 12 N.Y.2d 135, 187 N.E.2d 769, 237 N.Y.S.2d 308 (1962). A farm owned by the Jehovah's Witnesses used primarily to produce food for members of the order was held to be exempt under the religious purposes category. Watchtower Bible and Tract Society v. Haring, 8 N.Y.2d 350, 170 N.E.2d 677, 207 N.Y.S.2d 673 (1960). Over 90% of the produce was used for these purposes. The rationale of these decisions is that the use of the property was promotive of and a natural incidence of the primary exempt purposes of the organizations.

29. Shrine of Our Lady of Martyrs of Auriesville v. Board of Assessors of Glen, 54 Misc.2d 145, 281 N.Y.S.2d 544 (Sup. Ct. 1967), modified, 40 A.D.2d 75, 337 N.Y.S.2d 786 (3d Dept. 1972), aff'd, 33 N.Y.2d 713, 304 N.E.2d 563, 349 N.Y.S.2d 993 (1973).

remedies that may be pursued to correct an assessor's erroneous judgment.[30]

There are several other consequential provisions in section 421, a brief summary of which follows.[31] Subdivision 2 covers cases where property owned by an organization organized or conducted for exempt purposes uses part of such property for exempt purposes and part for nonexempt purposes. Only that part used for exempt purposes is exempt and that part used for nonexempt purposes is subject to taxation, express reference in this latter connection being made to property leased for other than exempt purposes. However, where an exempt organization leases part or all of its property to another organization that is organized and operated for exempt purposes and such other organization uses the leased property for exempt purposes, the leased part will be exempt but only "so long as any moneys paid for such use do not exceed the amount of the carrying, maintenance and depreciation charges of the property or portion thereof, as the case may be."[32] Subdivision 3 covers the case where nonrevenue-producing land otherwise exempt is not in actual use because "of the absence of suitable buildings or improvements thereon."[33] If the construction of such improvements "is in progress or in good faith contemplated" or if such land is held upon the condition that title shall revert if "any building not intended and suitable for"[34] exempt purposes is built thereupon, it shall be exempt. (Subdivision 4 provides that property

30. This subject is beyond the scope of this study. See H. Lee and W. Forester, Review and Reduction of Real Property Assessments in New York, ch. 10, § 10.09 (1978).

31. Because these provisions are not of direct relevance to this study and because they are somewhat prolix, they are summarized for convenience. Reference should be made to the statute for a complete presentation of their content.

32. N.Y. Real Prop. Tax § 421(2) (McKinney 1972). Similar exceptions are made for organizations and property exempt under other sections of the Real Property Tax Law. As they are not directly related to this study a description of these provisions is omitted.

33. N.Y. Real Prop. Tax § 421(3) (McKinney 1972).

34. Id.

otherwise exempt shall not lose its exemption because "it is used as a polling place upon days of registration and election"[35] and subdivisions 5–7 apply to special situations not of relevance to this study). Subdivision 8 provides that properties exempt from taxation under section 421 shall also be exempt from special ad valorem levies[36] and special assessments[37] to the extent provided for in section 490.[38] This is important as the definition of taxation under section 102(20) expressly excludes special ad valorem levies and special assessments.[39] Section 490[40] provides in effect that all property exempt under section 421 shall be exempt from special ad valorem levies and special assessments except for property subject to service charges under section 420.[41]

As noted a number of other sections under Title 2 (Private Property) of Article 4 (Exemptions) provide exemptions to property used for what might be considered "charitable" purposes, giving that term a broad intendment. A number of these provisions are contrary to the Constitution's prohibition of special bills for specific organizations.[42] There follows a brief survey of these provisions.[43]

35. N.Y. Real Prop. Tax § 421(4).

36. "Special ad valorem levy" means a charge imposed upon benefited real property in the same manner and at the same time as taxes for municipal purposes to defray the cost, including operation and maintenance, of a special district improvement or service, but not including any charge imposed by or on behalf of a city or village. N.Y. Real Prop. § 102(14) (McKinney 1972).

37. "Special assessment" means a charge imposed upon benefited real property in proportion to the benefit received by such property to defray the cost, including operation and maintenance, of a special district improvement or service or of a special improvement or service, but does not include a special ad valorem levy. N.Y. Real Prop. § 102(15) (McKinney 1972).

38. N.Y. Real Prop. Tax § 421(8) (McKinney 1972).

39. N.Y. Real Prop. Tax § 102(20) (McKinney 1972).

40. N.Y. Real Prop. Tax § 490 (McKinney 1972).

41. As noted section 420 at the time of this writing has not been implemented. See note 87 infra. For a description of the service charge, see section D, infra.

42. See note 4 supra.

43. Only a very brief description of these sections will be offered in order to

Under what might be called the religious category, RPTL § 430 exempts real property owned by a corporation for the purposes of establishing an interdenominational center; RPTL § 436 exempts real property held in trust by a clergyman for the benefit of the members of his church. RPTL § 460 exempts real property owned by a minister of any denomination engaged in work assigned to him by the denomination and RPTL § 462 exempts property owned by a religious corporation when actually used by the officiating clergymen thereof for residential purposes.

Under what might be referred to as the charitable category,[44] RPTL § 428 provides an exemption to real property owned by a fraternal organization where the entire net income of the property is used to support asylums, homes or schools for the relief of its members; RPTL § 440 exempts property of any infant home corporation used for the care of children; RPTL §§ 464, 466 and 468 exempt property owned by various volunteer firemen and fire control and salvage organizations; RPTL 486 exempts real property owned by certain medical corporations; RPTL § 472 exempts real property used as a college of pharmacy; RPTL § 442 exempts real property owned by soldiers' monument corporations; RPTL § 444 exempts real property owned by a historical society acquired for the purpose of the preservation and erection of monuments; RPTL §§ 446 and 448 exempt lands used for cemetery purposes and RPTL § 438 exempts certain real property used for hospital, playground and library purposes.

Finally, several exemptions are provided under what might be called the educational category. RPTL § 424 exempts certain real property in New York City acquired by a corporation orga-

---

provide a general idea of their nature. No discussion of a technical sort or of some of the detailed provisions of these sections will be given.

44. "Charitable" used here in a somewhat narrower sense than its broadest intendment so as to exclude the religious and educational categories.

nized exclusively as an institute of arts and sciences for the encouragement of the study of and the advancement of knowledge in the arts and sciences. RPTL § 425 exempts real property in New York City used for instruction of women and girls in trades. RPTL § 426 exempts real property owned by a corporation organized to sustain, encourage and promote musical art and to educate the general public in good music provided that such real property is maintained for the production of opera. RPTL § 427 exempts real property acquired under certain conditions by a corporation organized to sustain, encourage and promote musical and performing arts including opera, concerts, ballet, drama and other forms of artistic expression. RPTL § 432 exempts real property owned by a corporation created by an act of the U.S. Congress on a nonprofit basis and organized and used for the purposes of stimulating public interest in drama as an art through the operation of a school. RPTL § 434 allows certain municipalities to exempt real property used as academies of music.

## Section B—The History of Section 421

This section briefly outlines the historical development of the "central section 421 provisions" that are the focus of this study: those provisions exempting property owned by an organization organized or conducted for certain purposes and used for such purposes, viz., paragraphs (a) and (b) of subdivision 1, and those provisions, broadly speaking, requiring that the activities in furtherance of such purposes not be conducted for profit, viz., paragraph (d) of subdivision 1.[45] Certain constitutional amendments are also discussed.

In 1893 the legislature passed a law[46] (set out in part below) that is the progenitor of the central section 421 provisions. Before its enactment most exemptions from real property taxa-

45. See note 13 supra.
46. 1893 N.Y. Laws, ch. 498.

tion were provided by special laws applying to specific individual organizations or by charters establishing particular organizations.[47] Early general tax laws of the state did provide for exemption but their coverage was not comprehensive. For example, an 1801 law provided:

That no houses or lands belonging to the United States or to people of this state, nor any church or place of public worship, nor any personal property belonging to any minister or priest not exceeding in value of one thousand five hundred dollars, nor any college or incorporated academy, nor any schoolhouse, courthouse, goal, alms house, or property belonging to any incorporated library, shall be taxed by any law of this state.[48]

The Revised Statutes of 1828 provided in part that:

Section 1. All land and all personal estate within this state, whether owned by individual or by corporations, shall be liable to taxation, subject to the exemptions herein after specified.

Section 4. The following property shall be exempt from taxation:

3. Every building erected for the use of a college, incorporated academy, or other seminary of learning; every building for public worship; every school-house, courthouse and jail; and the several lots whereon such buildings are situated, and the furniture belonging to each of them.

4. Every poor house, alms-house, house of industry, and every house belonging to a company incorporated for the reformation of offenders, and the real and personal property belonging to or connected with the same . . . .

5. The real and personal property of every public library . . . .

8. The personal property of every minister of the gospel . . . .[49]

47. "The legislature has in numerous instances exempted the real and personal property of particular corporations of this chapter [referring to religious, literary and charitable corporations] from taxation. But this has been done under special laws designating the particular corporation intended to be benefited." Catlin v. Trustees of Trinity College, 113 N.Y.133, 141, 20 N.E.864, 867 (1889).

48. 1801 N.Y. Laws, ch. 178, section 24.

49. Revised Statutes of the State of New York, ch. XIII (1829).

The New York Court of Appeals in a 1901 case noted that the exemptions of the Revised Statutes of 1828 "were not broad enough to embrace the many charitable societies, great and small, which have since multiplied and developed with the growth of the state, and hence exemption was sought in many individual cases by special acts."[50]

Between 1828 and 1896 there was no revision of the tax laws.[51] In 1889 the legislature created the Commissioners of Statutory Revision,[52] charged to "report to the legislature a bill for the consolidation and revision of the general statutes of the state 'relating to the collection and assessment of taxes and the exemption of property from taxation throughout the state.' "[53] A later case said this about the conditions that existed in 1889:

> The subject of taxation has been a great embarrassment to legislative bodies throughout the history of the world. Special interests clash with general interests and seek relief, wholly or in part, from the public burden which is essential to the protection of property and the preservation of order. Claims for exemption multiply, and when the Legislature yields to the pressure of special interests, the precedent breeds a multitude of special statutes and brings confusion into the law. Such was the situation that confronted the Legislature of 1889, which set out to meet the difficulty by an act authorizing the appointment of commissioners to revise and consolidate the statutes relating to different subjects and, among them, to the assessment and collection of taxes and exemption of property from taxation throughout the state.[54]

The commissioners' work resulted in the Tax Law of 1896,[55] but before that enactment the legislature passed in 1893 the exemption law referred to above entitled, "An Act in relation to the exemption of the real property of religious, charitable and ed-

50. In re Huntington's Estate, 168 N.Y. 399, 407, 61 N.E. 643, 645 (1901).
51. Id. at 405, 61 N.E. at 645.
52. 1889 N.Y. Laws, ch. 289.
53. In re Huntington's Estate, 168 N.Y. 399, 405, 61 N.E. 643, 645 (1901).
54. Pratt Institute v. City of New York, 183 N.Y. 151, 155, 75 N.E. 1119, 1120 (1905).
55. 1896 N.Y. Laws, ch. 908.

ucational corporations and associations from taxation," which was repeated verbatim, with exceptions noted below, in subdivision 7[57] section 4 (Exemption From Taxation) of the Tax Law of 1896[58] and much of whose language can be found today in the central section 421 provisions. Chapter 498 reads in part as follows:

> Section 1. The real property of a corporation or association organized exclusively for the moral and mental improvement of men and women or for religious, charitable, missionary, hospital, educational, patriotic, historical or cemetery purposes, or for two or more of such purposes, and used exclusively for carrying out thereupon one or more of such purposes shall be exempt from taxation. But no such corporation or association shall be entitled to any such exemption, if any officer, member or employe thereof shall receive or may be lawfully entitled to receive any pecuniary profit from the operations thereof, except reasonable compensation for services in affecting one or more of such purposes, or as proper beneficiaries of its strictly charitable purposes; or if the organization thereof, for any of such avowed purposes, be a guise or pretense for directly or indirectly making any other pecuniary profit for such corporation or association or for any of its members or employes, or if it be not in good faith organized or conducted exclusively for one or more of such purposes.[59]

The only changes made to the central section 421 provisions in the 1896 enactment of subdivision 7 were certain additions to the enumerated purposes: bible, tract, infirmary, scientific, literary, library and for the enforcement of laws relating to children or animals.

The codification of 1896 was held by the Court of Appeals to be so comprehensive that it operated to repeal all the prior special exemption laws (except where a transfer of property to corporations claiming exemption was made on the promise of state exemption.)[60]

57. The provision was renumbered as subdivision 6 in the 1950s.
58. 1896 N.Y. Laws, ch. 908.
59. 1893 N.Y. Laws, ch. 498.
60. Pratt Institute v. City of New York, 183 N.Y. 151, 75 N.E. 1119 (1905).

Complementing this development and said to be influenced by the work of the commissioners[61] was the amendment to the New York State Constitution in 1901 that provided that "the Legislature shall not pass a private or local bill granting to any person, association, firm or corporation an exemption from taxation on real or personal property" (Constitution, Article III, section 18).

There were only three changes to the central section 421 provisions as set forth originally in subdivision 7 of section 4 of the Tax Law between the time of its enactment and 1958, when it was incorporated into the Real Property Tax Law,[62] a general recodification of the Tax Law, as section 420 (now numbered section 421).[63] In 1927 "bar association" was added to the enumerated purposes[64] and in 1929 "playground" was added.[65] Finally in 1971 subdivision 1 was bifurcated into paragraphs (a) and (b)—the mandatory and optional exemption provisions described above.[66] That this was done because of concern that exemptions were eroding the tax base is clear from the legislative findings that were made part of the law enacting these provisions in section 1:

> The legislature finds that competent studies indicate that real property in this state, having an assessed valuation in excess of twenty-two billion dollars, is exempt from and free from the payment of real property taxes; that this sum constitutes approximately thirty per centum of the total assessed valuation of real property in this state. That of this sum over sixteen billion dollars is in the city of New York and constitutes approximately one-third of the total assessed valuation of real property in such city. The legislature further finds, that the contin-

61. See J. Saxe, Charitable Exemption From Taxation in New York State on Real and Personal Property 18 (1933).
62. 1958 N.Y. Laws, ch. 959.
63. See note 12 supra.
64. 1927 N.Y. Laws, ch. 565.
65. 1929 N.Y. Laws, ch. 382.
66. 1971 N.Y. Laws, ch. 414. See text accompanying note 14 supra.

uous removal from the tax rolls of taxable real property, is a particular hardship on the local governments of this state, who are increasingly burdened by additional taxes, whenever such tax exemptions reduce the tax base, as a means of raising revenue for the conduct of government."

The "competent studies" referred to include the Report of the Joint Legislature Committee to Study and Investigate Real Property Tax Exemptions discussed in the Introduction and in some detail below in Chapter 3.

## Section C—How the Costs and Benefits of Property Tax Exemptions Should Be Analyzed

On the subject of real property tax exemptions it is important to be clear about how one determines the true cost and benefits of such an exemption. Dean Netzer has suggested a useful method.[67] To determine the cost of a real property tax exemption he suggests the first step would be to multiply the tax rate times the assessed value of the property. Many would stop here. This product, however, in turn must be multiplied by "the probability that, were there no tax exemption, either the existing use and value could be sustained or the land and buildings would be used for another purpose with an equally high market value."[68] On this latter point Netzer wonders whether the demand for land for clearly taxable uses is limitless so "that any tax exemption shuts out taxable uses, in reality as well as in theory."[69] Discussing the issue in connection with central cities, where the demand for land is presumably the strongest, he observes:

67. Netzer, Property Tax Exemptions and Their Effects: A Dissenting View, Proc. 65th Am. Conf. Tax., Nat'l Tax. A. 268 (1973).
68. Id. at 280.
69. Id. at 281.

In view of the changing distribution of economic activity in metropolitan areas, that is the trend or degree of decentralization of economic activity, I doubt the queue of precluded taxable users is a very long one. I suspect that, were we to have full taxation of tax exempt organizations and a dramatic reduction in their consumption of land and their occupation of land, in many central cities, there would be no takers for that land.[70]

As a final step in determining the cost of an exemption, to the nominal tax the exempt organization or its replacement would pay (discounted, perhaps, by reason of the fact that the property, for one reason or another, would not sustain a tax at that level) there would be added the incremental costs of governmental services "actually provided to the tax-exempt user of the property and financed from local general revenue (i.e., not from user charges or external grants dependent on the volume of service provided)."[71]

Having established the cost of the exemption, the benefits can be calculated by a similar three-step approach. First, "the social worth of the services provided by use of tax-exempt property"[72] is determined. This value in turn must be multiplied by "the percentage reduction in the volume of services provided [by the organization if it] had to pay property taxes, or the probability that the services would be discontinued entirely."[73] To this product there would have to be added "the incremental costs, if any, of the additional public services that would have to be provided if the tax-exempt user of the site were supplanted by the likely taxpaying users (e.g., replacement of a church by private housing occupied by families with schoolage children)."[74]

70. Id.
71. Id. at 280.
72. Id.
73. Id. This part of the method has a further alternative: "or the percentage increase in charges levied against users for services that, although subsidized, are partly fee-supported (e.g., the post office)." Id.
74. Id. at 200.

This method determines the immediate costs and benefits of the exemption. There are less direct factors to consider. Exempt property, as for example a museum, hospital or university, in addition to providing jobs, can attract persons from outside the municipality who would be likely to make a variety of purchases that might generally stimulate the municipality's economy and produce additional tax revenues. In this respect, it is highly likely that the concentration of exempt corporations in New York City, acts as a strong magnet in drawing spending visitors to the city.[75] As will be noted in Chapter 3 a number of studies that have been done on the real property tax exemption in New York have recognized the strong positive economic affect that many exempt organizations make to their communities.[76]

## Section D—The Service Charge Law

Chapter 1 indicates that for the most part the real property tax is a levy and collection for general municipal purposes as distinguished from a tax to raise "earmarked" money specifically to benefit real property. This characteristic of the real property tax has been concordant with the exemption from taxation of property used to benefit the community at large since such a levy would reduce the level of public benefit provided by organizations owning exempt property by taking funds for taxes that would be used to finance the provision of government services that also promote to public interest.[77] If, however, a charge were made for benefits that accrued specifically to real

75. D. Netzer, The Subsidized Muse 24–25 (1978).

76. See text accompanying notes 23–24, 51, and 77–78, Chapter 3 infra. Methods have been developed to determine these more indirect costs and benefits. See J. Caffrey and H. Issacs, Estimating the Impact of a College or University on the Local Economy (1971). It is believed, however, that this kind of effort does not produce convincing results since the data used are so imprecise and difficult to obtain and many of the assumptions are somewhat speculative.

77. This statement is a simplification of a rationale for the exemption discussed in greater detail below in Chapter 6.

property this justification of the exemption does not apply. Such charges are called benefit taxes.[78] In 1971 the New York State Legislature enacted a law to impose service charges on certain real property, which shall be referred to as the Service Charge Law.[79] This law subjects certain types of publicly and privately owned wholly exempt property to taxation for police protection, fire protection, sanitation, water supply and street and highway construction, maintenance and lighting. Only publicly held property used exclusively for charitable, hospital, educational or cemetery purposes[80] and privately held property owned by an organization organized or conducted exclusively for religious, charitable, hospital, educational or cemetery purposes and [81] used for such purposes are exempted from the service charge.[82] The law was a "response to the problem of wholly exempt real property,"[83] i.e., the problem of tax base

78. R. & P. Musgrave, Public Finance in Theory and Practice 195–198 (1973) [hereafter cited as Musgrave].

79. 1971 N.Y. Laws, ch. 417. This law is entitled "AN ACT to amend the real property tax law, in relation to the imposition of service charges on certain property." The Law amends section 102 of the Real Property Tax Law by adding a new subdivision, numbered 13-a, which defines the term "service charge," and by amending subdivision 20 to include the term "service charge" within the definition of "tax" or "taxation." See N.Y. Prop. Tax §§ 102(13-a) and (20)(McKinney 1972). It adds two new sections to the Real Property Tax Law numbered 400 and 420, which respectively subject certain wholly exempt public property and private property to the service charge. See N.Y. Prop. Tax §§ 400 and 420 (McKinney 1972). It adds a subdivision, numbered 2, to section 490 of the Real Property Tax Law, which subjects property subject to the service charge to special advalorem levies and special assessments for "service charge purposes," i.e., police protection etc. See N.Y. Real Prop. Tax § 490(2) (McKinney 1972). Finally it adds a new section to the Real Property Tax Law, numbered 498, which indicates how the service charge shall be computed. See N.Y. Real Prop. Tax § 498 (McKinney 1972).

80. N.Y. Real Prop. Tax § 400 (McKinney 1972).

81. N.Y. Real Prop. Tax § 420 (McKinney 1972).

82. These purposes include the constitutionally protected purposes, viz., religious, educational and charitable purposes (See N.Y. Const. art XVI, §1), which had to be done since as noted the service charge is defined as a tax. See note 79 supra.

83. Final Report of the Temporary State Commission on State and Local Finances, Vol. 2, The Real Property Tax 128 (1975) [hereinafter cited as the Feeney Commission Report].

erosion due to exemptions, and the notion must have been that since the tax was a type of benefit tax it was appropriate to subject exempt property to its provisions.[84] The Service Charge Law was enacted at the same legislative session that enacted the law[85] bifurcating section 421(1) of the Real Property Tax Law, also done with specific reference to the problem of tax base erosion.[86] Since its enactment the implementation of the Service Charge Law has been regularly postponed.[87]

The final section of the Service Charge Law presents the means for determining a service charge for the subject publicly and privately owned properties. The formula is set forth in section 498 of the Real Property Tax Law as follows:

§ 498. *Service charges.*—(a) Any service charge to which any real property may be subject as provided in section four hundred or section four hundred twenty of this chapter shall be imposed at a rate which shall be a percentage of the rate tax imposed upon real property for which no exemption is allowed. Such percentage shall be computed as provided in subdivision (c) of this section.

(b) For purposes of this section the term "chargeable services and improvements" means services, and improvements necessary or convenient in providing such services, for the following purposes: police protection; fire protection; street and highway construction, maintenance and lighting; sanitation; and water supply. All improvements specified in clause (a) of subdivision one of section four hundred ninety of this chapter shall be deemed chargeable improvements.

(c) The percentage to be applied to the rate of tax imposed on real property for which no exemption is allowed, in order to determine the rate of any service charge, shall be computed as follows:

(1) From (A) the total amount included in the municipal budget as estimated expenditures for chargeable services and improvements,

84. See Id.
85. 1971 N. Y. Laws, ch. 414. See note 66 and accompanying text supra.
86. See text following note 66 supra.
87. 1972 N.Y. Laws, ch. 966; 1973 N.Y. Laws, ch. 525; 1974 N.Y. Laws, ch. 525; 1975 N.Y. Laws, ch. 463; 1976 N.Y. Laws, ch. 98; 1977 N.Y. Laws, ch. 49; 1978 N.Y. Laws, ch. 63; 1979 N.Y. Laws, ch. 44; 1980 N.Y. Laws, ch. 42.

exclusive of those for which a special ad valorem level or special assessment is imposed, deduct (B) the total amount included in such budget as estimated revenues to be derived directly from specific services and improvements whose estimated expenditures are included in clause (A), including any state and federal aid directly attributable to, or contributed to assist the municipal corporation in providing, specific services and improvements whose estimated expenditures are so included.

(2) From (C) the total amount included in the municipal budget as estimated expenditures for all purposes other than services or improvements for which a special ad valorem level or special assessment is imposed, deduct (D) the total amount included in such budget as estimated revenues to be derived directly from specific services and improvements whose estimated expenses are included in clause (C), including any state and federal aid directly attributable to, or contributed to assist the municipal corporation in providing, specific services and improvements whose estimated expenditures are so included.

(3) Determine the percentage of the amount computed pursuant to paragraph (2) above which is represented by the amount computed pursuant to paragraph (1).

(4) Multiply the rate of tax imposed upon real property for which no exemption is allowed by the percentage computed pursuant to paragraph (3) above.

(5) The rate so produced shall be the rate to be applied to the assessed valuation of real property subject to service charges to determine the amount of such charges.

(d) Notwithstanding the provisions of any local law to the contrary, all real property owned by a corporation or association organized or conducted exclusively for religious, charitable, hospital, education or cemetery purposes, or any such property owned by the dormitory authority and leased to any such corporation or association, shall be exempt from all service charges.[88]

The above rather complicated formulation of the service charge obscures a rather simple approach. The net costs to the

88. N.Y. Real Prop. Tax § 498 (McKinney 1972).

locality of chargeable services and improvements, e.g., police services and capital improvements in the water supply system, are expressed as a fraction of the net cost of all municipal services (excluding special assessments and ad valorem levies). Net cost represents revenues the municipality itself must raise via taxation to pay for the service, i.e., it excludes revenues received from the state or federal government. This percentage is then multiplied by the tax rate, or percentage, which represents the rate at which the assessed value of exempt real property is to be charged for the specified services.

The following simple example might further clarify the derivation of the service charge on exempt real property:

Municipality X and the Service Charge Law

| | | | |
|---|---|---|---|
| Expenditures on all municipal services: | $1,000 | Expenditures on police; fire; sanitation; water supply; and street and highway construction, lighting and maintenance services: | $300 |
| − Revenues from state and federal government for all municipal services: | −500 | − Revenues from state and federal government for above services: | −100 |
| = Net cost to municipality of all services: | $500 | = Net cost to municipality of chargeable services and improvements: | $200 |

(1) (Net cost of chargeable services and improvement) ÷ (Net cost of all municipal services)

$$= \frac{\$200}{\$500} = .40$$

(2) Tax rate on nonexempt property: .20

Service charge rate on assessed value of exempt property subject to service charge: (1) × (2) = .40 × .20 = .08

As mentioned the Service Charge Law was thought to be a kind of benefit tax and consequently appropriate as a charge on exempt property. The most usual benefit tax is a specific benefit tax or a user charge.[89] User charges, in a property tax context, are amounts paid by property owners for the purchase from the government of specific goods or services exclusively benefiting the property charged. Central to this definition is the identifiability between the individual's payment for the good or service and his receipt of it. Unlike a general revenue tax, the user charge directly links the payment for and receipt of the benefit. Similar to the purchase of goods in the free market, the amount a consumer pays for such a governmentally provided good is a function of its worth to the consumer or is at least closely related to the amount and quality of the good received. A pure user charge is voluntary; those who choose not to use the particular government service financed by the user charge will not be charged for it.[90] In effect user charges are public prices. In circumstances in which user charges are appropriate this method of financing is advantageous both because it is equitable and efficient.

Equity considerations are met by user charges because the consumers pay for what they get, or in the parlance of public-finance economics, user charges follow the benefit principle. This principle reasonably asserts that it is equitable to align payments for benefits with those who receive the benefits, just as the private market does.[91]

To understand why user charges are efficient it is important to realize that many of the goods produced in the public sector are public goods, i.e., once they are produced, it is very difficult

89. See Musgrave, supra note 78, at 196.

90. Edwin Seligman developed a set of criteria for analyzing the characteristics of public revenues over 85 years ago. His approach was to measure the degree of volunteerism or compulsion in the payment of the fee or tax and the degree of private or public benefits received in the purchase of a good or service. The more voluntary the payment and the more private the benefit, the more closely the good resembles a private good, hence, the greater is the potential for the imposition of a user charge as a source of public revenue. R. Seligman, Essays in Taxation, ch. XIV (1893).

91. This is in contrast to the ability-to-pay principal, which disregards the benefit side of public expenditures, but considers equity only in terms of how revenues are raised with respect to the individual's ability to pay the costs of supporting government.

to exclude their use from any member of the community where they are produced, thus making it impossible to charge for them. In addition, public goods are frequently nonrival, i.e., their use by one person does not preclude their use by another. When considering the efficiency of user charges, the excludable or nonexcludable nature of a good is key. Many of the goods produced by the public sector are excludable, e.g., the use of a municipal parking lot or public tennis courts. As a result, it is possible for the public sector to imitate the private market and charge a price for the good or service being provided. Charging a price has obvious implications for efficiency. Consumers who are confronted with a price will ration their use of the good or service in accordance with its price and the benefit they derive from it. Output of the good or service will reach an amount consistent with the public's demand for the good. If financed by user charges a good or service provided by the government will not be overproduced, and waste will be prevented.

The Service Charge Law is not a pure user charge because it is compulsory. Thus the advantages of equity and efficiency derived from the voluntary nature of a user charge could not result from the Service Charge Law. This is particularly true of efficiency considerations since the compulsory nature of the charges eliminates the possibility of a good financed by this system being provided at or near the level it would be if it were a function of individuals' preferences.

As mentioned many goods and services produced in the public sector are public goods. As will be shown below important aspects of the services covered by the Service Charge Law have important public goods aspects. To the extent that the services covered by the Service Charge Law partake of the nature of a public good the system fails as a user charge. Financing public goods must take account of the free-rider phenomenon. Because once a public good is provided by someone paying for it, many will benefit from it and, because once the good has been provided others cannot be excluded from partaking of its benefits, rationally self-interested individuals may decide not to pay for it. They will tend to free-ride on the purchase of the good by others. In these circumstances it is likely that the good will not be produced at an optimum level. It follows that to the extent that the services covered by the Service Charge Law are public goods it would be inappropriate to charge for their financing by a user charge system. Consequently, public goods are normally financed by the compulsory system of general revenue taxes.

While some police services may be related directly to the protection of property, most of the services provided by local police forces are of a public good nature and therefore cannot fairly be financed by user charges. It would be very difficult to exclude from protection those members of a community who choose not to pay for police protection. Furthermore, because police are able to prevent crime, not only are property and the would-be victims of crime protected, but the community as a whole is better off. Fewer murders or muggings reduce the level of anxiety in the community as a whole. The services provided by police protection, then, are often invisible and cannot be charged for on a *quid pro quo* basis. Similar considerations apply to fire protection. Sanitation services also have a public good nature in that there definitely exist external benefits to the community beyond those received by each customer. Even ignoring the aesthetic aspects, the health problems posed to a community would be significant if trash removal were voluntary. Similar public good aspects to the other services covered by the Service Charge Law make them equally inappropriate for financing by a user charge system.

There are compulsory levies, however, that are grounded on benefit principles, e.g., charges upon property owners to pay for services rendered specifically to property. These charges are distinguishable from a general revenue tax because of the element of special benefit. Such a charge might be called a benefit tax and would have at least some of the equitable advantages of a user charge since property owners would be paying for what they received. The Service Charge Law also fails to qualify as a benefit tax, however, because there is little if any relation between the amount that a unit of property would be charged for service and the value to the property owner of the service provided. It would be only a fortuity if the "price" charged for the service, based as it would be on the assessed value of the property, bore any relationship to the worth of the services provided to the property owner. For example, it is extremely unlikely that the worth of police services provided to a piece of property would bear any relationship to a tax levied to finance that service based upon the assessed value of the property. This problem was very clearly seen by the Temporary State Commission on State and Local Finances in its 1975 report:

The proposition that real property which receives a direct municipal service should in some way pay for that service is one which has widespread support and with which we do not disagree. However, the concept of determining the amount to be paid for specified services regardless of benefit received and on the basis of assessed valuation is inherently inaccurate and inequitable.

The complex manner in which the service charge tax rate is determined has been set forth in the preceding section. Part of the reason for the complexity of this formula is that the service charge law is based upon the concept of the general tax levy. Namely, the computation of liability is made by multiplying a tax rate times an assessed valuation. This concept is certainly valid in computing amounts due to pay for the general governmental services provided to all taxpayers by their municipal governments. Significantly, however, the concept of the general tax levy and liability is inconsistent with the concept of the service charge. If property is to be made liable for specific municipal services which it receives, then such liability should be measured in accordance with the actual receipt of the services; assessed valuation cannot do this.

The service charge law as it currently exists does not provide for a determination of the receipt of services; thus, for example, despite the fact that a State prison has its own police and fire protection, the facility will also be liable for the costs of local police and fire protection. Examples of this type of liability can be easily conjured up, and, in all cases, they are absolutely inconsistent with the concept of the service charge.

The measurement of the amount of money to be paid by the benefited property should, by definition, be a direct relationship to the services rendered. Assessed valuation is simply not an adequate device for making such a computation. The proportional measurement of the costs of chargeable services set forth in the formula is partial recognition of the necessity to relate the charge to its overall costs. However, the method contained in the current law is obviously inadequate, and the net result is an attempt to charge for services on the basis of assessed valuation and tax rate.[92]

There follows a brief analysis of how the problem just described applies to the various services giving rise to tax under the Service Charge Law. To determine the appropriate tax for police protection it would first be necessary to segregate out police services devoted to the protection of property and not to individuals. Next, it would be necessary to determine whether or not there existed a consistent relationship between units of property owned and the amount of police protection used. Such a relationship is not obvious, as use may vary with other characteristics such as number of establishments and types of establishments rather than simply with units of property value. In any event, assuming cost could be determined, it would bear little, if any, relationship to the assessed value of the property protected.

Fire protection costs include extinguishing fires and maintaining constant fire protection. The value of a piece of property may bear some relationship to the latter costs, but none to the former. Even as to the maintenance costs of fire protection, property value is not necessarily related to such important determinants as the age of a structure and the material with

92. See Feeney Commission Report, supra note 83, at 132.

which it is built, the density of the neighborhood in which the property is located or its proximity to water or a fire station.

To the extent that street and highway construction, maintenance and lighting services are provided to property, they are likely to be relatively similar for all parcels of property located within a community. Only differences in frontage may be related to some differences in the level of the provision of the services to different parcels of property, but frontage bears little relationship to property value.

Similarly there is no identifiable relationship between property value and the cost of sanitation services. The fact that property owners are the main producers of trash in a community does not in any way imply that property is an appropriate base on which to place a tax for the service. And *mutatis mutandis* the same points apply to water supply services.

Enacted in response to what was perceived as a tax base erosion problem, it appears that the Service Charge Law was designed to mitigate this problem by raising revenues from exempt property. Justification for making a charge to exempt property was sought in the principles of benefit taxation—i.e., it would be appropriate to charge exempt property for services specifically rendered to it. Assessed value of property, however, was selected as the basis of the charge imposed by the Service Charge Law, and, in most instances, a charge made on this basis bears little relationship to the provision of specific services to property. Indeed, it appears that the Service Charge Law is essentially a general revenue-raising tax. Consequently the reasons adduced elsewhere in this study[93] for exempting property used for the general welfare from a general revenue levy apply with equal force to the Service Charge Law.

93. See the discussion in the Introduction and Chapter 6.

# 3

# A Century of Reports on Real Property Tax Exemptions

It is fair to say that real property tax exemptions have been of considerable interest to New York State leaders since at least the beginning of the century. Many reports on the subject have been done by legislative and constitutional convention and revision committees and commissions.[1] Indeed, each successive study has contained lengthy recitations of the earlier studies, with the most recent noting such earlier recitations. There have also been a number of private studies done on property tax exemptions.[2] These works will be reviewed briefly because of

1. Report of the Committee of the New York State Tax Association on Exemptions of Real Property, N.Y. Leg. Doc. No. 19 (1917); Report of the Special Joint Committee on Taxation and Retrenchment, N.Y. Leg. Doc. No. 72 (1922); Preliminary Report of the Special Joint Committee on Taxation and Retrenchment, Tax Exemption in the State of New York, N.Y. Leg. Doc. No. 86 (1927); Second Report of the Commission for the Revision of the Tax Law, Part Two —Report of Murray Haig, N.Y. Leg. Doc. No. 77 (1932); Fifth Report of the Commission for the Revision of the Tax Laws, A Tax Revenue Program for the State of New York, N.Y. Leg. Doc. No. 62 (1935); Report of the New York State Constitutional Convention Committee, Problems Relating to Taxation and Finance (1938); Temporary Commission on the Revision and Simplification of the Constitution, Staff Report (No. 28), On Tax Exemptions (1959); Report of the Temporary State Commission on the Constitutional Convention, Local Finance (1967); Final Report of the Joint Legislative Committee to Study and Investigate Real Property Tax Exemptions, N.Y. Leg. Doc. No. 15 (1970); and the Final Report of the Temporary State Commission on State and Local Finances, Vol. 2, The Real Property Tax (1975).

2. Westchester County Chamber of Commerce, Tax Exemptions on Real

their obvious relevance to this study. They have undoubtedly contributed to the concern over real property tax exemptions that has been present in New York over the years. A review will also serve to set out a number of important concepts and perspectives central to this study.

In 1916 bills were introduced in the New York State Senate aimed at forcing property exempt under section 4 of the Tax Law[3] to contribute to the support of government. This legislation gave rise to a wish to have the subject of tax exemptions studied. As the legislative committee designated to consider the matter had lapsed, it was suggested that a committee of the New York State Tax Association do the work. In January 1917 the committee filed its report with the Senate.[4]

The short report begins by warning that although the benefits accruing to the state from the policy of exemptions have been considerable, recently "the exemption statutes have been amended to meet special cases under general works until in many counties, cities and towns the policy of exemption as extended by the Legislature has become a burden oppressive to the taxpayer."[5] The report sets out data on the dollar amount

---

Estate, An Increasing Menance (1922); J. Saxe, Charitable Exemption From Taxation in New York State on Real and Personal Property (1933); C. Tobin, W. Hannan and L. Tolman, The Exemption from Taxation of Privately Owned Real Property Used for Religious, Charitable and Educational Purposes in New York State (1934); Citizens Budget Commission, Inc., Real Estate Exemptions in New York City—A Design For Reform (1967); D. Bickford and R. Zapke, Tax Exempt Properties . . . Sullivan County New York (1975); Economic Research Service of the New York State Institute, The Problem of Real Property Tax Exemptions: Legislative Options (1977); and League of Women Voters of New York State, Toward an Evaluation of the Property Tax System in New York (1979).

3. 1896 N.Y. Laws, ch. 498. Section 4 is the predecessor of N.Y. Real Prop. Tax § 421 (McKinney 1972).

4. Report of the Committee of the New York State Tax Association on Exemptions of Real Property, N.Y. Leg. Doc. No. 19 (1917).

5. Id. at 2. The committee was no doubt referring to legislation that had been passed in contravention to the 1901 Constitutional prohibition against granting exemptions by special bills or acts to particular organizations. See text accompanying note 61, Chapter 2 supra.

of exempt property by type for 1916 and then quotes from an article by Martin Saxe, president of the New York State Tax Commission, in which he notes that the value of tax-exempt property increased twice as fast as the value of taxable property between 1905 and 1915. The report closed with recommended amendments to the Tax Law,[6] brief summaries of which follow.[7] It was suggested that the costs resulting from exemptions given to institutions not designed to serve the need of the residents of the community in which they are situated but rather a wider community, e.g., a college, should be borne by the larger political subdivision. It was recommended that the Tax Law be amended to eliminate a number of exemptions that covered particular organizations and that, while passed in the form of general laws, were in fact special bills prohibited by the Constitutional Amendment of 1901. Another proposed amendment urged the denial of exemption to property located in any county other than that in which its principal office is located. This latter suggestion was largely in response to concern that had been developing in Westchester as a result of the purchase of property by a number of New York City charities.[8]

In 1919 a joint resolution of the legislature created the Special Joint Committee on Taxation and Retrenchment, chaired by Senator Fredrick M. Davenport. In 1922 the committee filed its report on the entire tax system of New York.[9] The report's brief consideration of exemptions began: "The problem of tax exemptions in New York is increasing in seriousness. A large and growing proportion of property and income is exempted

6. See note 3 supra.
7. Only the pertinent ones are summarized.
8. The term "charities" is used here in a broad sense. In fact the bills that gave rise to the study were submitted by a senator from Westchester. It is significant that Charles Tobin in his dissent from several of the suggestions and recommendations stated: *"The large increases in exemptions each year are public, not private."* Id. at 19.
9. Report of the Special Joint Committee on Taxation and Retrenchment, N.Y. Leg. Doc. No. 72 (1922).

from direct State taxation . . . and consequently the burden of taxation tends constantly to fall on a relatively narrowing base."[10] The report concluded recommending that "the situation has reached a point where proposals for further exemptions must be considered in a most critical spirit. There is some evidence that the public is becoming aroused concerning the state of affairs."[11] It found "much sound sense in the view that all publicly owned real estate should be subject to the real estate taxes of all governmental bodies within whose borders it lies, except the taxes imposed by that governmental body which owns the property."[12] On the subject of real property exemptions the report further opined, "The rules governing the exemption of real estate of charitable, religious, educational and cemetery associations should be more strictly drawn. It should be impossible for exemptions to cloak real estate which is being utilized for a business purpose for private gain."[13]

In 1922 the Westchester County Chamber of Commerce published Philip Adler's study of the history of tax exemptions.[14] This short work traces the development of property tax exemptions from antiquity to the time of its completion and is an able and fascinating piece for those interested in the history of this subject. Adler suggests that originally a number of helping institutions were run by the state but that over time many

10. Id. at 62. It found that the proportion of real estate exempted from taxation in different counties varied from 2.6% to 55.6% and that the three counties with the largest amount of exempt real property in 1919 were Albany with 55.6%, Clinton with 43.1% and Wayne with 30.79%. Id. at 65–66.

11. Id. at 66.

12. Id.

13. Id. at 67. On this interesting point it continued: "The committee is informed that in some cases this occurs under our present statutes—for example, that cemeteries operated as private profit-making enterprises and schools which are really profitable businesses frequently gain exemption under the law as it now stands." Id.

14. Westchester County Chamber of Commerce, Tax Exemptions On Real Estate, An Increasing Menace (1922). Part I of this study consisted of Mr. Adler's thesis: P. Adler, Historical Origin of the Exemption From Taxation of Charitable Institutions.

of these functions were taken over by private organizations with state subsidization and later financed solely by private contributions. He infers from this development that exemption from taxation was accorded to these organizations because of the services they rendered to the public. Adler's conclusions, which follow, have been of considerable interest to those who have thought about the problems of tax exemptions since he published his study over fifty years ago.

1. There is ample historical justification for the exemption from taxation of charitable institutions which perform without compensation a function which the State has, from Tudor times in England and colonial times in this country, avowedly undertaken to perform, viz., the care of the poor, sick, demented, crippled, blind, deaf, impotent, the helpless aged and young.
2. As a corollary to the first proposition, there is no historical basis for the exemption of benevolent institutions, like the Y.M.C.A., or of fraternal organizations, like the Odd Fellows, to the extent to which they perform no function which the State has ever undertaken to perform.
3. As the State progressively takes on social duties by way of workmen compensation laws, health insurance generally, there is a corresponding weakening of the historical sanction for the exemption of charitable institutions.
4. Although there was sufficient ground for the exemption of places of religious worship in colonial times, such ground, because of the disestablishment of the Church during the Revolution, now no longer exists.
5. There is sufficient historical sanction for the exemption of educational institutions, but not for parochial or religious schools.
6. Where an institution justly entitled to exemption, because of its charitable function, engages in other activities, such as renting its premises for profit, its claim for exemption not only ceases, but there is direct historical precedent for taxing such an institution.
7. When a charitable institution derives income from fees of its inmates, there seems to be no historical basis for exempting it from taxation. To prevent vagabondage and begging the state undertook to

maintain only the poor and impotent, the utterly helpless. Those in a position to pay have, therefore, no claim on state support. In housing such inmates an institution is in no way relieving the state of a burden which the latter has ever undertaken to bear.[15]

In 1927 the Special Joint Committee on Taxation and Retrenchment, at that time chaired by Senator Seabury Mastick, issued a report on tax exemptions,[16] which included a consideration not only of real property tax exemptions but also personal property exemptions and tax-exempt securities. On the topic of real estate tax exemptions the committee begins its summary of findings by conceding that the problem in New York is serious but "not as serious as many have supposed."[17] It found that the ratio of tax-exempt property to taxable property had been decreasing gradually since 1917. "It is, therefore, our first conclusion that the situation is not as serious as it first seemed."[18] A further finding of the committee was that there was no relationship between the amount of exempt property in a municipality and the cost of local government or tax rates. "In other words, many towns with large amounts of tax-exempt property have low costs of government and low tax rates, and many towns with a small amount of exempt property have high tax rates and high costs of government. Tax exemption is thus seen to be an unimportant factor in influencing these local conditions."[19] To test this conclusion the committee made a special study of twenty-one municipalities that contained an especially large amount of tax-exempt property. "This study tends to show that tax exemption as a whole does not result in serious injustices to cities, towns or villages. In all but one case, our investigators concluded that the local benefit exceeded local costs, though

15. Id. at 80, 81.
16. Preliminary Report of the Special Joint Committee on Taxation and Retrenchment, Tax Exemption in the State of New York, N.Y. Leg. Doc. No. 86 (1927).
17. Id. at 13.
18. Id.
19. Id.

there were a number of other cases in which it was felt there was justifiable grievance."[20] In the course of this special study it was found that in order to estimate the real costs of tax-exempt property to a community it was important to take into consideration that certain types of exempt property conferred direct benefits to the locality in which they are located, while "others are for the service of the state or the nation and confer little local benefit."[21] And further that, "In some cases a given kind of property entails a very distinct local burden, in other cases an institution takes care of itself and throws little burden upon the community."[22] The committee found, however, that in many cases where an institution benefitted those from outside the municipality in which it was located, the economic benefits to the community in terms of jobs, purchases by the institution, etc., was very great. "Even the smallest towns would gladly welcome the organization of a college or university in their midst."[23]

The committee concluded its summary of findings with respect to the real estate tax in the following manner:

> A consideration of the kinds of property for which exemption is granted has led us to the conclusion that there are very few classes of exempt property which do not bring greater benefit to the local community than the burden which they place upon that community for governmental services. The kinds of service required of local governments by exempt real estate are chiefly streets and sewers, and police and fire protection. In almost no cases are schools involved. Water service is paid for in most cases and a portion of street and sewer expenses can generally be assessed. The benefits conferred upon the local community differ with the types of institutions, and range from direct services rendered to indirect benefits accruing to local merchants or surrounding property.[24]

20. Id.
21. Id. at 72.
22. Id.
23. Id. at 73.
24. Id. at 13, 14.

The recommendations of the committee regarding real property tax exemptions follow:

1. We recommend that there be no further extension of real estate exemptions.

2. If, however, this proves impossible, we urge that any exemption granted be subject to local option and that it be for a limited term of years.

3. We recommend that there be no broadening of the classes of property now exempt on the plea that the new institutions closely resemble others which are now exempt.

4. We do not believe that any public or private property should be exempt from charges for water, or from special assessments for local improvements as is now the practice in some sections of the state.

5. We recommend that the state department of taxation and finance make a special effort to require the assessors to reappraise and list fairly all tax-exempt property, as is now provided by section 21 of the tax law. In some tax units large amounts of exempt property, such as the state canal, do not appear at all, and in others it is known that no effort has been made to keep the valuation of exempt property up to date. It has been suggested that the department of taxation and finance be empowered to make an appraisal of exempt property throughout the state. The proposal has much merit. In any case we believe that the valuation of state owned property should be furnished to the assessors by the state departments acting through some single department.

6. We recommend also that the listing of exempt property be made to show separately the value of land and the value of improvements. This is essential in the development of information for the guidance of the state in the preparation of any new policy of tax exemptions, and will require little additional labor on the part of the assessors.[25]

In 1930 the legislature established the New York State Commission for Revision of the Tax Laws.[26] This commission, chaired by Senator Mastick, was charged to review the entire system of taxation in New York State. In 1932 it issued a report

25. Id. at 16.
26. 1930 N.Y. Laws, ch. 726.

that contained a short section on property tax exemptions.[27] The report noted, "There is a widespread feeling . . . that too much property is exempt from taxation."[28] And that, "Apparently, public opinion is gradually crystallizing in favor of a less generous policy than has hitherto been followed."[29] It found that the value of exempt property increased 44.5% between 1925 and 1930 as compared to an increase of 49.6% for taxable property, and that about 31% of such property was government owned.[30] "Contrary to the general impression, exemptions to religious and charitable institutions do not bulk large in the aggregate figures."[31]

The commission recommended unanimously that "no further exemptions from real estate taxation should be granted to groups or classes not now exempt," that all lands acquired henceforth by a private or public body (except the United States) be taxable and that all increases in the value of land (except land held by the United States) over and above the actual value of the land at the time of the law's passage be taxable.[32] A majority of the commission recommended that the land of one government lying in another government be taxable by the other government.[33]

27. Second Report of the Commission for the Revision of the Tax Law, Part Two—Report of Murray Haig, N.Y. Leg. Doc. No. 77 (1932).

28. Id. at 120.

29. Id.

30. Id. It cautioned, however, that "not too much importance should be attached to this comparison because of the variations in cases observed by assessors involving exempt property." Id.

31. Id. at 121.

32. Id. at 21.

33. Id. Two private studies advertently in favor of charitable exemptions from property taxation were published in the mid-'30s: J. Saxe, Charitable Exemptions From Taxation in New York State on Real and Personal Property (1933) and C. Tobin, W. Hannan & L. Tolman, The Exemption from Taxation of Privately Owned Real Property Used for Religious, Charitable and Educational Purposes in New York State (1934) [hereinafter referred to as The Exemption From Taxation]. Both books summarily review the history of the exemption, the reasons underlying the several purposes exempted (e.g., religious, educational, charitable, library, etc.) and critique earlier reports. In addition The Exemption

In 1935 the commission issued another report that dealt with real property tax exemptions.[34] The commission found that the value of exempt property continued to enlarge and that the exemption of property was receiving more and more public attention.[35] In addition it found that in 1933 privately owned exempt property constituted 4.68% of the assessed value of all property in the state.[36] "Moreover, the ratio of such property to taxable property has not increased alarmingly."[37] The commission repeated its recommendations of 1932.[38]

A 1938 report by the New York State Constitutional Convention Committee dealing with taxation and finance contained a brief chapter on real property tax exemptions.[39] It observed that recent agitation to restrict future exemptions for privately owned properties had not been successful and that the list of private exemptions was still growing.[40] The committee found that, "the volume of exempt private property, however, has not increased during the past twenty years any faster than the vol-

---

From Taxation purports to assay the costs and benefits of the exemption concluding that its benefits outweigh its costs.

34. Fifth Report of the Commission for the Revision of the Tax Laws, A Tax Revenue Program for the State of New York, N.Y. Leg. Doc. No. 62 (1935).

35. Id. at 35. The report noted the following regarding the reliability of valuation figures:

> Throughout this section of the report the figures compiled by the State Tax Commission and printed in its 1932 reports are used. It should be remembered that, as compared with taxable property, the exempt property may be either overvalued or undervalued, since the fact that the property pays no tax removes the usual incentive both for the assessor to value it accurately and for the owner to protest the assessment if it is unfair. Moreover, all the assessors in the state do not value taxable property at the same proportion of true value—the proportion varies from 35 per cent in Sullivan county to 98 per cent in Allegany county, according to the Tax Commission's estimates—and it is therefore probable that the assessed value of exempt property is less in the low-valuing areas and more in the high-valuing areas than it would be if all property in the state were assessed at a uniform proportion of true value. Id. at 36.

36. Id. at 49.

37. Id.

38. Id. at 63.

39. Report of the New York State Constitutional Convention Committee, Problems Relating to Taxation and Finance, ch. X (1938).

40. Id. at 210.

ume of total assessed exempt and nonexempt."[41] It concluded its brief survey with the observation that "on the whole the policy of tax exemption has promoted the welfare of the people of the state."[42]

A report on real property tax exemptions for the Temporary Commission on the Revision and Simplification of the Constitution was prepared in 1959.[43] Its principal focus was on the 1938 Constitutional Amendment[44] restricting the legislature's power to deal with exemptions. Before analyzing the constitutional issues, the report noted that since the turn of the century the assessed valuation of exempt property "has consistently been increasing more rapidly than the assessed valuation of real property."[45] The report commented on the implications of this change:

> The continual rise in the proportion of exempt property to total property has been causing considerable concern among taxpayers and local officials during the past sixty or more years. It has been interpreted as an indication of a gradual whittling away and erosion of the local tax base through exemptions. Such a situation produces two equally undesirable results, namely: increased tax burden for the owners of properties remaining on the tax rolls and increased difficulties for local officials in raising revenue.[46]

The data upon which the report based its observations showed that

> . . . among the exempt privately owned properties, those owned by veterans and exempt private housing have increased in volume the fastest. Religious properties, on the other hand, have increased little

41. Id. at 211–212.
42. Id. at 219.
43. Temporary Commission on the Revision and Simplification of the Constitution, Staff Report (No. 28), On Tax Exemptions (1959).
44. N.Y. Const. art. XVI, § 1.
45. Id. at 14.
46. Id. at 17.

in volume; and exempt private educational and charitable properties have also increased in volume only moderately. In New York City the greatest increases have been in exempt public housing property and in exempt privately owned, limited dividend and redevelopment housing property: the first rose from $137 million in 1949–50 to $1,030 million in 1958–1959 and the second from $24 million to $162 million during the same period.[47]

A report prepared for the 1968 Constitutional Convention contains a chapter providing a balanced view of real property tax exemptions.[48] Like earlier studies, it notes that the assessed value of exempt property had been growing at a faster rate than the assessed value of taxable property. Such growth in exempt property is not closely analyzed to determine the relative growth rates of the several different kinds of exemptions, although the report does point out that of the $21.1 billion increase in exempt property since 1957, "Properties owned by municipal governments have increased most substantially by $4.0 billion."[49] Data presented also suggests that public authorities had shown marked growth.[50] The report observed that a lack of conceptual clarity continued to weaken the debate on exemptions:

> Most criticism of tax exemptions is directed against the weakening of the property tax base and adding to the tax burden. However, some uses of exempt property often increase the taxable value of surrounding properties by their nature or by the public improvements provided to such properties. Thus, at least in the aggregate, they add to the productivity of the property tax. Withdrawing these exemptions would tend to reduce expansion of such activities and the potential corre-

47. Id. at 7. A private report critical of New York City's real property tax exemptions was published by the Citizens' Budget Commission in 1967: Citizens Budget Commission, Inc., Real Estate Tax Exemption in New York City —A Design for Reform (1967).
48. Report of the Temporary State Commission on the Constitutional Convention, Local Finance, ch. 4 (1967).
49. Id. at 79.
50. Id. at 78.

sponding increase in the taxable value of surrounding property. In addition, certain categories of exempt properties do not remove taxable property from the rolls but rather encourage use of otherwise unused or unproductive land.[51]

These various studies, then, indicate that those who had cause to review the subject of real property tax exemption found that the situation was perhaps not as serious as the degree of concern suggested—almost surely the case with private exemptions. Nevertheless, concern continued to grow, and in 1969 the Joint Legislative Committee to Study and Investigate Real Property Tax Exemptions, chaired by Assemblyman Daniel Becker, was established. The "whereas" clauses of the resolution calling for the committee signaled a new level of anxiety over the problem.

WHEREAS, A growing number of properties which were an important source of taxable revenues in many municipalities of New York State are exempt from taxation as, increasingly, they have been acquired by religious, educational, charitable, fraternal and other non-profit organizations, associations, and corporations; and

WHEREAS, Municipalities more than ever face, on the one hand, ever-mounting costs and, on the other hand, a narrowing real property tax base because of such exemptions; and

WHEREAS, The exemptions are a major concern to officials of municipalities in which such exemptions are growing and to residents faced with the alternatives of accepting increases in taxes shifted to them because of the exempt status of many of their neighbors, or surrendering many essential services and improvements; and

WHEREAS, In many instances business enterprises not exempt from taxation are at an unfair disadvantage because they may be in competition with those enjoying tax exemption; now, therefore, be it . . .[52]

51. Id. at 76.

52. Final Report of the Joint Legislative Committee to Study and Investigate Real Property Tax Exemptions, N.Y. Leg. Doc. No. 15, 6 (1970).

The report of the committee is highly responsive to the tensed concern of this resolution and if anything reflects even more alarm regarding real property tax exemptions. In his foreword Chairman Becker asserts that as a result of the value of tax-exempt property growing about four times as fast as that of taxable property since 1900, there had been an erosion of one-third of the total assessed value of real property in the state. He then predicts darkly that "The findings of the staff suggest that if the growth of exempt properties described above continues at the same rate, one-half of the assessed value of all real property on municipal assessment rolls will be exempt within the next fifteen years."[53] The report concludes: "Thus, the years 1900 and 1968 represent two ends of a period which has seen the amount of exempt property increase steadily and continuously until it has eroded one-third of all real property value in the state."[54] Various statistics are given for counties, cities and towns indicating that the statewide average and median percent of the value of tax-exempt property to total valuation of all property was between 25% and 30%. No attempt is made to distinguish between government exemptions and private exemptions nor is any recognition given to the problems of comparing the data of different assessing units.[55]

Of particular significance for study is the failure of the Becker Committee to distinguish between government exemptions and private exemptions. It has been shown that a number of the earlier studies of the exemption problem indicated that in weighing the impact of all exemptions private exemptions were not a major factor.[56] By implication, at least, the suggestion is

53. Id. at 9. The report finds: "If we assume that the average annual increases described above will continue at their present rates at the end of the next 15 years we can expect that *50 percent* of the total assessed value of *all* real property in New York State will be exempt from taxation by municipal corporations." Id. at 35–36.
54. Id. at 24.
55. Id. at 24–27.
56. See note 8 supra and text at notes 31, 37, and 47 supra.

that to the extent exemptions are a problem the focus should be on government exemptions. Chapter 4 will show that for the most part it was government exemptions that provided the basis for the committee's agitated findings as to the increasing extent of exempt property. In this connection it should be noted that the first "whereas" clause of the resolution establishing the committee makes specific reference to exempt properties that "have been acquired by religious, educational, charitable, fraternal and other nonprofit organizations,"[57] and no reference at all is made here or in any other "whereas" clause to exempt properties acquired by government units. In addition to the apparently alarming data regarding the growth in value of exempt property, the committee was also concerned about the large number of laws exempting property that had been passed since the start of the century.[58]

In its consideration of the specific effects of certain exemptions the committee does concede that "the impact of privately owned properties is not as severe as that of public properties."[59] It did however, conclude this section with the following observation:

> The picture presented by this brief survey of exemptions granted to nonprofit organizations strongly suggests that the public benefit principle, as a criteria for granting mandated exemptions, is lacking in equity when measured against the resulting burden which may be imposed on a taxpayer. It is clear that the presence of such entities erodes a substantial portion of a municipal tax base and that the taxes, which could be levied on that property, or on comparable residential or commercial property, shift to some degree onto privately owned real property. Thus, in the case of any substantial fiscal impact, there is no

57. See text accompanying note 52 supra.

58. Id. at 36. It was predicted that a result of the increase in exemptions would be the narrowing of the tax base with a consequent increase in tax rates and that "individuals who are eligible for exemptions will increasingly be driven to claim them and where optional individual exemptions exist, local legislative bodies will be pressured to enact them." Id.

59. Id. at 32.

test to determine whether the entity is receiving a subsidy through exemption because it provides a service beneficial to the taxpayer or whether it is operating solely at the taxpayers' expense. Accordingly, it appears that some means of determining whether the principle of public benefit is operating in favor of the taxpayer should be established.[60]

The committee made four recommendations that relate to the subject of this study. First that section 420 of the Real Property Tax Law be amended to make the exemption of nonprofit organizations other than religious, charitable, educational, cemetery and hospital organizations optional with the local municipalities.[61] It was thought that this approach would enable local legislative bodies "to determine the cost-benefit effect of exemptions granted to certain organizations over which they previously had no control."[62] Second it recommended "for study purposes, the amendment of Article XVI, section 1, of the State Constitution, to eliminate its present prohibition against legislative alternation of exemptions for religious, charitable and educational organizations."[63] Third, it recommended "that exempt real property, other than that of religious, charitable, educational, cemetery and hospital corporations, shall be subject to taxation, assessments or levies to pay the cost of necessary 'safety' services which they require, such as fire and police protection, sewage disposal and water service.[64] And finally, "that an absolute moratorium on the enact-

60. Id. at 34.

61. Id. at 40–41. Section 420 was the predecessor of section 421 (see note 12, Chapter 2 supra), and the recommendation here noted, eventuated in the 1971 legislation bifurcating the statute. See text accompanying note 66, Chapter 2 supra.

62. Id. at 41.

63. Id.

64. Id. at 42. Three other recommendations related to the veterans exemption (that the exemption be made to apply to the full rather than assessed value of property), to property of public authorities (that such property leased to nonexempt tenants be taxable), and to state property (that such property leased back to private tenants before being used for state purposes be taxable).

ment of new exemptions must be maintained."[65]

In 1973 the Temporary State Commission on State and Local Finances was established.[66] It was chaired by Senator John J. Feeney, and in the spring of 1975 published Volume 2 of its final report.[67] Volume 2 of this report will be referred to hereafter as the Feeney Report. As indicated in Chapter 1, the Feeney Report provides an excellent general primer on the property tax system of New York State. It is divided into two parts. Part I describes the tax, its administration and theory, discusses equity considerations and provides a comprehensive examination of the assessment problem. Part II deals with exemptions from the tax and is significantly entitled: "The Diminishing Local Tax Base: Origins and Responses." In its summary at the start, the Feeney Report describes Part II as focusing "on the erosion of the local property tax base through exemptions"[68] and in its introduction to Part II states: "The granting of exemptions by the taxing authority necessarily reduces the base, which in turn affects either collections or the relative tax burden on the individual taxpayer."[69] It continues:

> Increasingly during the last fifteen years, local governments and their official representatives have expressed severe criticism of the multiplicity of exemptions and sincere concern for the continued viability of this primary source of local revenue. That exemptions, most often imposed on local governments by the State, are in fact a serious local fiscal problem, is not to be doubted.[70]

A chief concern of the Feeney Report is the proliferation of statutory exemption provisions "in an unbelievable fashion."[71] The Feeney Report concludes on this problem, "That this pro-

65. Id. at 43.
66. 1973 N.Y. Laws, ch. 100.
67. Final Report of the Temporary State Commission on State and Local Finances, Vol. 2, The Real Property Tax (1975).
68. Id. at 7.
69. Id. at 86.
70. Id. at 86.
71. Id. at 87.

liferation has diminished the potential local tax base is obvious; that it has generated vast discontent is a matter of historical record."[72]

The Feeney Report made no attempt to update the Becker Committee's findings on the extent of "erosion" caused by exemptions. In its short section on "The Impact of Tax Exempt Property" it merely reproduces some data developed in the Becker Committee's report.[73] Most of this section is devoted to a good analysis of the problems of the data used to make these "impact" studies and of the general approach these studies take. It first notes that the data used, viz., assessed valuation data is inherently inaccurate and ascribes several causes as giving rise to this problem.

> First initial assessed valuations are determined by local assessors, and, in the case of wholly exempt properties, there is generally no reason for the assessor to develop an accurate figure. Because the property will generate no revenue, the assessor will often simply estimate a value to enter on the assessment roll in fulfilling his statutory duty to assess all real property. An extremely low valuation will have no adverse effect on the local tax base or rate, while an extremely high valuation will generate no benefit other than providing evidence of additional loss or diminution of that base.[74]

This problem is compounded by the difficulty of placing a value on special use property, e.g., churches or university campuses. Furthermore, owners of exempt property are not likely to challenge an overassessment since no tax liability results from such an assessment. Related to these problems is the fact that there is little reason for an assessor to update an original estimate of value.[75]

A second major problem found in these impact studies is their

72. Id.
73. Id. at 88–92.
74. Id. at 90.
75. Id. at 90–91.

"predominant attitude of attributing a negative effect to the exemption"[76] and neglecting to consider that exempt property often makes a positive fiscal contribution to the community in which it is located in terms of "employment, retail sales, capital development and related activities."[77] Such contributions should be offset against any tax losses in making a full assessment of the impact of the exemption.[78]

The rest of Part II provides a descriptive examination of the various exemptions, government and private, whole and partial, and discusses a number of current issues with regard to these exemptions.[79] Its major conclusion on the subject of private exemptions is that the legislature in implementing the constitutional exemptions in section 421 of the Real Property Tax Law—the central focus of this study—provided no statutory definition or limitation on the terms religious, charitable and educational.

> The obvious problem is that for many years now the constitutional exemption has merely been repeated in the statute, without legislative definition. As a result, the courts have been forced to determine the application of the statute on a case-by-case basis without any further guidance from the legislature. The consequence to local governments has been an expansion of the scope of this exemption into properties traditionally associated with private, entrepreneurial activity and also traditionally subject to taxation. The mandatory exemption of these properties is both a fiscal liability to the community and a source of local irritation.[80]

76. Id. at 91.
77. Id. at 92.
78. Id.
79. Special mention is made of the concern that noncity municipalities develop over exemptions being granted to property used by nonprofit organizations for camp purposes. These properties were said to be used for recreational and resort type purposes and to compete with private commercial recreational uses. Id. at 125.
80. Id. at 120.

To deal with this problem the commission made the following recommendation:

There should be enacted statutory provisions to precisely define property exempt pursuant to paragraph (a) of subdivision 1 of § 421 (nonprofit organizations) in order to limit this exemption to properties which are used strictly for the enumerated purposes.[81]

It also recommended:

There should be consideration of returning the class of property designated as "moral and mental improvement of men, women and children" to paragraph (b) of subdivision 1 of § 421 in order to permit localities to exercise the option to tax such properties.[82]

81. Id. at 128.

82. Id. at 128. Three fairly recent private reports that deal with property tax exemptions should be mentioned. In 1975 a report was prepared for the Sullivan County Environmental Management Council: D. Bickford and R. Zapke, Tax-Exempt Properties . . . Sullivan County New York (1975). This report provides a layman's explanation of the real property tax system and an analysis of tax exemptions in the several towns of Sullivan County. It is generally critical of exemptions and focuses particularly on holdings of private nonlocal organizations many of which are used for recreational purposes of people from outside the town in which the properties are located. To set the problem in an historical context, it reproduces the alarmist findings of the Becker committee. In 1977 a report was prepared at the request of Senator Joseph L. Galiber: Economic Research Service of the New York State Institute, The Problem of Real Property Tax Exemptions: Legislative Options (1977). Relying upon the findings of prior studies it decries the proliferation of property tax exemptions and suggests several options for legislative consideration, including bringing exemptions into municipalities' budgets in a tax-expenditure section, taxing public authorities and church property and having local governments reimbursed by the federal and state governments for the use of their land. Lastly, in 1979 the League of Women Voters published a report: League of Women Voters of New York State, Toward an Evaluation of the Property Tax System in New York (1979). This report offers a good primer on the real property tax in New York and examines the effect of the property tax on education, housing, land and economic development. Its chapter on tax exemptions provides a balanced summary of the issues. No specific recommendations regarding exemptions are made.

# 4

# The Impact of Charitable Real Property Tax Exemptions

Chapter 2 indicates that much of the concern about tax exemptions stems from fears that the granting of exemptions causes an erosion of the tax base. Indeed, this concern has been the major motive behind the many studies of the exemption question that have been made during the past seventy-five years. As noted in Chapter 3, a joint legislative committee of the New York State Legislature in 1970 predicted that, if the rate of growth of exempt property continued to outpace the rate of growth of taxable property at the same relative rate at which it had apparently been growing, by 1985 50% of all the property in New York would be tax exempt.[1] Alarmed by this prophecy, as noted in Chapter 2, the legislature in 1971 amended subdivision 1 of section 421 giving municipalities the right to subject to the property tax property used for a number of purposes that theretofore had been exempt purposes.[2] Furthermore, the Court of Appeals in two cases decided in the early 1970s, denying the application of the exemption to certain organizations,

1. Final Report of the Joint Legislative Committee to Study and Investigate Real Property Tax Exemptions, N.Y. Leg. Doc. No. 15, 9 (1970) [hereinafter cited and referred to as the Becker Committee Report]. See note 53 and accompanying text, Chapter 3 supra.
2. See text accompanying note 66, Chapter 2 supra.

made reference to these dire findings by the Becker Committee Report in apparent support of their holdings.[3]

This chapter examines the extent of the exemption problem in terms of the amount of assessed value of property that is exempt as compared to the assessed value of all property and shows what the trends have been. The examination is divided into two parts. The first part covers New York City, and the second part covers all the remaining municipalities referred to in the aggregate as the Upstate municipalities. The New York City Tax Commission has been gathering and annually publishing data regarding the assessed value of different categories of real property since before the turn of the century. On the other hand, the State Board of Equalization and Assessment has been collecting comprehensive information on Upstate municipalities only since the early 1970s.[4] Accordingly, while data is available for a fairly long historical view of New York City's circumstances regarding its property tax base, such is not the case for Upstate municipalities. Furthermore, this data is not classified in the same manner as the City data, so the comparisons made in the two parts will not be exactly the same. There are two points to be made about this division. First, the City has always had most of the tax exempt property in New York State—about 66% by assessed value as of 1978—and, as well, a large portion of the assessed value of all taxable property—about 54% in 1978.[5] Secondly, as will be seen below, it seems likely that the concern over the tax base problem arose largely out of observing New York City developments. Thus, it is fortunate

3. See text accompanying notes 94–95 infra.
4. See Section B infra.
5. In 1978 all property in New York City was assessed at an aggregate value of \$64,309,901 and all property in the State of New York at an aggregate value of \$118,416,964. In 1978 exempt property in New York City was assessed at an aggregate value of \$25,698,096 and exempt property in the State of New York at an aggregate value of \$39,207,572. New York State Comptroller, Special Report on Municipal Affairs, table 4 (at 124), table 3-1 (at 52) and table 3 (at 46), N.Y. Leg. Doc. No. 92 (for fiscal year ending 1978).

that data for New York City covers a longer period.

The data used in this chapter is assessed value data, i.e., the assessed value of different types of property at different periods. Chapter 1 describes the many problems with the assessment process in New York. This suggests the problems that inhere in assessed value data used in this chapter's examination, problems covered by the broad rubric "differential assessment problems." Different types of property are assessed at different fractions of actual full market value. Under the best of circumstances assessing property necessarily has a large subjective element to it. Some jurisdictions only revalue property when it is sold. Some jurisdictions (few it seems) regularly revalue all property within their boundaries, whether sold or not.[6] And some jurisdictions revalue only some of the property within their boundaries that has not been sold. Moreover, it is not known how exempt property is assessed as compared to taxable property, i.e., for instance, whether it is assessed at a higher or lower fraction of actual full value than taxable property. For these reasons, the comparisons of the kind made below may involve comparing dissimilar values. For example, if a comparison is made of a museum and a large home, both with actual values of $1,000,000, and the museum is assessed at 80% of actual value and the home is assessed at 40%, a comparison of assessed values will produce misleading data. There is no actual evidence that suggests, however, that exempt property is assessed at a substantially different ratio than taxable property. In any event, no claim is made for the validity of the data presented in this chapter. It may or may not reflect what actually exists, yet it probably does give a fair indication of the overall situation and some fairly reliable trend indications. The data is all that is available and given the nature of the assess-

6. With respect to New York City, one writer characterized "the semblance of systematic, periodic reassessment" as a "fantasy." R. Kuttner, Revolt of the Haves, 122 (1980).

ment problem may be as good as can ever be obtained. With these strong caveats on the record the examination proceeds.

## Section A—New York City

Data in this section was obtained from various editions of the *Annual Report of the Tax Commission,* presented each year to the Mayor of the City of New York by the New York City Tax Commission.[7] In the examination of New York City data, comparisons are made of changes over time in the percent that the value of Exempt property makes up of the value of all property. Among different types of Exempt property, a major division is made between Private Exempt property and Public Exempt property. Further, Public Exempt property is divided between five subcategories: Federal, State, City, Public Authorities and Housing, and Private Exempt property is divided between two subcategories: Charitable and Private Miscellaneous Exempt. The five subcategories of Public Exempt property include six categories of exemptions listed in the *Annual Reports* under the general head Governmental.[8] They are: New York City, Public Authorities, Housing, U.S. Government, New York State and Foreign Governments.[9] The *Annual Reports* categories

7. The Tax Commission reviews and corrects assessments of real property made for taxation purposes and rules on applications for tax exemptions, and the Annual Report sets forth statistics on the taxable and exempt status of all real estate in the five boroughs of the City. See City of New York, Annual Report of the Tax Commission to the Mayor of the City of New York for the Fiscal Year 1979–80, 5 (1980) [hereinafter referred to as 1979–80 Annual Report].

8. The *Annual Reports* make a major distinction of exempt properties between Governmental and Non-Governmental. See 1979–80 Annual Report, supra note 7, at 32. The category Governmental is equivalent to the category Public Exempt used here and Non-Governmental is equivalent to the category Private Exempt.

9. In the 1979–80 Annual Report the following subcategories are listed under each of these larger categories:

*City of New York*—Borough Presidents, Armories, Public Safety, Education, Environmental Protection, Economic Development, Airfields (Leased to Port of New York Authority), Municipal Services Administration, Department of Social Services, Parks and Recreation, Health Services Administration, Transportation Administration, Hous-

U.S. Government and Foreign Governments have been included here under the subcategory Federal. Private Exempt property, classified in the *Annual Reports* under the category Non-Governmental, lists in the *1979–80 Annual Report* the following categories: Religious, Parsonages, Clergy, Hospitals, Charitable, Educational (Privately Owned), Cemeteries, Exemption Railroads, Alterations,[10] Fall-Out Shelters, Veterans, Senior Citizens, Non-Profit Medical and Dental Indemnity and Hospital Service Corporations, Environmental Protection, Telephone and Telegraph Ceiling Equipment, New Industrial or Commercial Building Exemption, and Altered Industrial or Commercial Building Exemption.[11] The *Annual Report's* categories Exemption Railroads, Alterations, Fall-Out Shelters, Veterans, Senior Citizens, Environmental Protection, Telephone and Telegraph Ceiling Equipment, New Industrial or Commer-

---

ing and Development Administration, Urban Renewal (Commercial), N.Y.C. Public Development Corporation, N.Y.C. Educational Construction Fund, N.Y.C. Industrial Development Agency.
*Public Authorities*—Port of New York Authority, P.A.T.H., Triborough Bridge and Tunnel Authority (MTA), N.Y.C. Transit Authority (MTA), Commuter Railroads (MTA), Municipal Railroads, Power Authority of State of New York, N.Y. Job Development Authority.
*Housing*—Federal Aided, State Aided, City Aided, Dwellings Acquired From Federal Government, Miscellaneous (State Assisted), Housing Development Fund Companies, Limited Dividend, Redevelopment, Limited Profit (Mitchell-Lama), New Multiple Dwellings, New One and Two Family Dwellings, Redevelopment Companies (Phase-out exemptions).
*U.S. Government*—Armed Forces, Post Offices, Lighthouses, Cemeteries, Hospitals, Government Land and Buildings.
*New York State*—Military, Hospitals, State Land and Buildings, Public Works, State Urban Development Corporation, Dormitory Authority.
*Foreign Governments,*—Foreign Government (Consulates), United Nations Headquarters, Mission to the United Nations, United Nations Development Corp.
See 1979–80 Annual Report, supra note 7, at 33–34.

10. Alterations presumably refers to the exemptions provided to increases in assessed valuation due to alterations and improvements to multiple dwellings under section 489 of the Real Property Tax Code and section J51-2.5 of the Administrative Code of the City of New York. See 1979–80 Annual Report, supra note 7, at 9-10.
11. See 1979–80 Annual Report, supra note 7, at 34.

**Table 1: Exempt and Taxable Property in New York City (millions of current dollars). 1910, 1920, 1930, 1940, 1950, 1960, 1970 and 1979**

| | 1910 | 1920 | 1920/10 Growth[1] | 1930 | 1930/20 Growth | 1940 | 1940/30 Growth | 1950 | 1950/40 Growth | 1960 | 1960/50 Growth | 1970 | 1970/60 Growth | 1979 | 1979/70 Growth |
|---|---|---|---|---|---|---|---|---|---|---|---|---|---|---|---|
| Public Exempt | $1,042.5 | $1,908.3 | 6.2% | $3,337.8 | 5.8% | $4,189.2 | 2.3% | $5,349.1 | 2.5% | $9,423.9 | 5.8% | $15,133.2 | 4.8% | $22,595.2 | 4.1% |
| Federal[2] | 70.6 | 116.4 | 5.1 | 171.8 | 4.0 | 242.1 | 3.5 | 355.3 | 3.9 | 506.4 | 3.6 | 698.9 | 3.3 | 810.0 | 1.5 |
| NYS | 1.8 | 8.7 | 17.1 | 39.8 | 16.4 | 109.1 | 10.6 | 54.1 | −6.8 | 148.7 | 10.6 | 395.3 | 10.3 | 684.8 | 5.6 |
| NYC | 970.1 | 1,783.2 | 6.3 | 3,126.2 | 5.8 | 3,817.6 | 2.0 | 4,312.6 | 1.2 | 5,506.9 | 2.5 | 8,450.3 | 4.4 | 12,268.1 | 3.8 |
| Public Authorities | NA[3] | NA | NA | NA | NA | NA | NA | 149.0 | NA | 1,868.1 | 28.8 | 3,013.0 | 4.9 | 4,478.4 | 4.0 |
| Housing | NA | NA | NA | NA | NA | 20.4 | NA | 478.1 | 37.1 | 1,393.8 | 11.3 | 2,575.7 | 6.3 | 4,353.9 | 5.4 |
| Private Exempt | 316.6 | 413.3 | 2.7 | 864.2 | 7.7 | 929.4 | 0.7 | 981.3 | 0.5 | 1,768.9 | 6.1 | 3,509.6 | 7.1 | 4,408.5 | 2.3 |
| Charitable | NA | NA | NA | NA | NA | NA | NA | 948.3 | NA | 1,561.6 | 5.1 | 2,855.5 | 6.2 | 3,346.1 | 1.6 |
| Miscellaneous | NA | NA | NA | NA | NA | NA | NA | 33.0 | NA | 207.3 | 20.2 | 654.1 | 12.2 | 1,062.4 | 5.0 |
| Total Exempt | 1,359.0 | 2,321.6 | 5.5 | 4,202.0 | 6.1 | 5,118.6 | 2.0 | 6,330.4 | 2.2 | 11,192.9 | 5.9 | 18,642.8 | 5.2 | 27,003.7 | 3.8 |
| Taxable | 7,044.2 | 8,626.1 | 2.0 | 18,203.5 | 7.8 | 16,553.4 | −0.9 | 18,396.1 | 1.1 | 24,944.4 | 3.1 | 35,329.4 | 3.5 | 38,056.8 | 0.8 |
| Total[4] | 8,403.2 | 10,947.7 | 2.7 | 22,405.5 | 7.4 | 21,672.0 | −0.3 | 24,726.5 | 1.3 | 36,137.3 | 3.9 | 53,972.3 | 4.1 | 65,060.5 | 1.9 |

Source: 1910, 1920, 1930, 1940, 1950, 1960, 1970 and 1979 City of New York Annual Reports of the Tax Commission to the Mayor of the City of New York.

1. Growth rates are compound growth rates.
2. The subcategory "Federal" includes the Annual Reports' categories "U.S. Government" and "Foreign Governments."
3. N.A., Data not available.
4. Totals may not add due to rounding.

cial Building Exemption and Altered Industrial or Commercial Building Exemption have been included here under the subcategory Private Miscellaneous Exempt. The remaining Non-Governmental categories of the *Annual Reports* are included here under the subcategory Charitable. Over the years there have been some changes in the listings under these various categories as new forms of exemptions were created. Furthermore, the category Public Authorities did not exist until 1920 and was included under the category Non-Governmental in 1930. The terms used in the listings under the category Non-Governmental changed quite substantially between 1960 and 1970, but it appears that while the terms may have changed the kinds of property in fact included under the Non-Governmental category have remained very similar. In instances where types of property were listed under one category of property in an earlier year and under another category in a later year, adjustments were made to assure the consistency between categories over time. Of course, it is almost surely the case that the kinds of property listed under the various categories are not the same for each year, but there does appear to be a considerable degree of consistency in these reports and, given the difficulties with the data mentioned above, this caveat is a rather minor one.

Table 1 sets forth data on the assessed value of Exempt property (broken down into the categories Public Exempt and Private Exempt and their subcategories) and Taxable property at ten-year intervals between 1910 and 1970 and for 1979, the last year for which data was available at the time of this writing.

Much of the following analysis is based upon a comparison among the years 1910, 1950 and 1979 of the percents of the value of all assessed property, listed as Total in Table 1, that are constituted by the assessed values of property listed in Table 1 under the categories Exempt, Public Exempt (and its subcategories) and Private Exempt (and its subcategories). Table 2, which follows, lists these percents.

**Table 2: Exempt and Taxable Property in New York City as a Percent of Assessed Value of All Property. 1910, 1920, 1930, 1940, 1950, 1960, 1970 and 1979**

| | 1910 | 1920 | 1930 | 1940 | 1950 | 1960 | 1970 | 1979 |
|---|---|---|---|---|---|---|---|---|
| Public Exempt | 12.4% | 17.4% | 14.9% | 19.3% | 21.6% | 26.1% | 28.0% | 34.7% |
| Federal | 0.8 | 1.1 | 0.8 | 1.1 | 1.4 | 1.4 | 1.3 | 1.2 |
| State | 0.02 | 0.08 | 0.1 | 0.5 | 0.2 | 0.4 | 0.7 | 1.1 |
| City | 11.5 | 16.3 | 14.0 | 17.6 | 17.4 | 15.2 | 15.6 | 18.8 |
| Public Authorities | NA | NA | NA | NA | 0.6 | 5.2 | 5.6 | 6.9 |
| Housing | NA | NA | NA | 0.09 | 1.9 | 3.8 | 4.8 | 6.7 |
| Private Exempt | 3.8 | 3.8 | 3.8 | 4.3 | 4.0 | 4.9 | 6.5 | 6.8 |
| Charitable | NA | NA | NA | NA | 3.8 | 4.3 | 5.3 | 5.1 |
| Miscellaneous | NA | NA | NA | NA | 0.1 | 0.6 | 1.2 | 1.6 |
| Total Exempt | 16.2 | 21.2 | 18.8 | 23.6 | 25.6 | 31.0 | 34.5 | 41.5 |
| Taxable | 83.8 | 78.8 | 81.2 | 76.4 | 74.4 | 69.0 | 65.5 | 58.5 |

Source: Table 1.

Between 1910 and 1950 in New York City the assessed value of Taxable property grew about 1½ times,[12] while the assessed value of Exempt property grew over 3½ times.[13] As a result the assessed value of Taxable property, which constituted 83.8% of all property in 1910,[14] fell to 74.4% in 1950,[15] and the assessed value of Exempt property, which constituted 16.2% of all property in 1910,[16] increased to 25.6% of all property in 1950,[17] an increase of 9.4%. Nearly all of the growth in Exempt property, however, occurred in the public (government) sector. In 1910 the assessed value of Public Exempt property constituted over 12% of all property.[18] By 1950 Public Exempt property share had grown to over 21%.[19] In contrast, the assessed value of Private Exempt value stood at 3.8% of all property in 1910[20] and had increased to 4.0% in 1950.[21]

Between 1950 and 1979 the value of Exempt property increased somewhat over three times,[22] while the value of Taxable property increased a little over once.[23] As a result, by 1979 Exempt property had come to constitute 41.5% of all property,[24] and the value of Taxable property had dropped to

12. $18,396.1 ÷ $7,044.2 = 2.611. The $ figures which are presented in this note and the following notes are from Table 1.
13. $6,330.4 ÷ $1,359.0 = 4.658
14. $7,044.2 ÷ $8,403.2 = .838
15. $18,396.1 ÷ $24,726.5 = .744
16. $1,359 ÷ $8,403.2 = .162
17. $6,330.4 ÷ $24,726.5 = .256
18. $1,042.5 ÷ $8,403.2 = .124.
19. $5,349.1 ÷ $24,726.5 = .216. The value of Public Exempt property as a fraction of all value increased 9.2% from 12.4% in 1910 (see note 18 supra) to, as noted, 21.6% in 1950. Most of this growth occurred in the subcategories City, which grew from 11.5% of all value in 1910 ($970.1 ÷ $8,403.2 = .115) to 17.4% in 1950 ($4,312.6 ÷ $24,726.5 = .174) and Housing, which was not an exempt category in 1910 and which constituted 2% of all value in 1950 ($478.1 ÷ $24,726.5 = .019).
20. $316.6 ÷ $8,403.2 = .038
21. $981.3 ÷ $24,726.5 = .040
22. $27,003.7 ÷ 6,330.4 = 4.26
23. $38,056.8 ÷ $18,396.1 = 2.07
24. $27,003.7 ÷ $65,060.5 = .415

58.5%.[25] Thus, the value of Exempt property as a fraction of the value of all property increased about 16% between these two years.[26] Most of this 16% increase is attributable to the growth in the value of Public Exempt property, rising 13.1% between these two years from 21.6% of all value in 1950[27] to 34.7% in 1979.[28] In contrast, the value of Private Exempt property as a fraction of the value of all property increased by about 2.8%, rising from 4.0% in 1950[29] to 6.8% in 1979.[30]

As is evident from the above figures, growth in Public Exempt property dominated this period and accounts for most of the increase in the portion of Exempt property as a percent of all property. Extraordinary growth occurred in the subcategories Public Authorities and Housing. Between 1950 and 1979 the value of property in the subcategory Public Authorities increased about twenty-nine times[31] and in Housing about eight times.[32] As a result, these two subcategories of property came to amount to over 13½%[33] of the value of all property and accounted for 11.1%[34] of the 16%[35] increase in the value of Exempt property as a fraction of all property. (Of the 16% increase Public Exempt counted for 13.1%—i.e., in addition to the 11.0% increase occasioned by increases in the subcategories Public Authorities and Housing, the portion of all value made up by the remaining subcategories of Public Exempt increased 2.1%.[36])

25. \$38,056.8 ÷ \$65,060.5 = .585
26. In 1950 the value of Exempt property constituted 25.6% of the value of all property (see note 17 supra); by 1979 this figure had increased to 41.5%. See note 24 supra.
27. See note 19 supra.
28. \$22,595.2 ÷ \$65,060.5 = .347
29. See note 21 supra.
30. \$4,408.5 ÷ \$65,060.5 = .068
31. \$4,478.4 ÷ \$149.0 = 30.06
32. \$4,353.9 ÷ 478.1 = 9.11
33. In 1979 property in the subcategory Public Authorities constituted 6.9% of the value of all property (\$4,478.4 ÷ \$65,060.5 = .069) and Housing property 6.7% (\$4,353.9 ÷ \$65,060.5 = .067).
34. In 1979 Public Authorities and Housing property constituted 6.9% and 6.7% respectively (see note 33 supra) of all property as compared to .6% (\$149.0 ÷ \$24,726.5 = .006) and 2% (\$478.1 ÷ \$24,726.5 = .019) respectively in 1950, an increase of 6.3% and 4.7% respectively or a total of 11.0%.
35. See note 26 supra.
36. Federal property decreased .2% (Federal property constituted 1.4% of

It has been shown that the value of Exempt property as a fraction of all property increased 16% between 1950 and 1979[37] and that Public Exempt property accounted for about 13.1% of this increase. Private Exempt property accounted for the remaining 2.8% increase, rising from 4.0% in 1950[38] to 6.8% in 1979.[39] The most notable growth occurred in the Private Miscellaneous Exempt subcategory, which increased thirty-one times between 1950 and 1979.[40] Charitable Property, in contrast, increased only 2½ times[41] during this period. As a result, Private Miscellaneous Exempt property, which constituted only .1% of total value in 1950,[42] came to comprise 1.6% of all value in 1979,[43] and Charitable property, which constituted 3.8% of all value in 1950,[44] increased to 5.1% of all value in 1979.[45] Thus, in the long period from 1910 to 1979 the value of subcategory Charitable property as a fraction of all property increased only 1.3%, from 3.8% in 1910[46] to 5.1% in 1979. Table 1 indicates that in 1970 the value of all property in the subcategory Charitable made up 5.3%[47] of all value. This is some indication then that more recently this subcategory has been decreasing as a percent of all value.[48]

---

the value of all property in 1950—$355.3 ÷ $24,726.5 = .014—and 1.2% in 1979—$810 ÷ $65,060.5 = .012), State property increased .9% (State property constituted .2% of the value of all property in 1950—$54.1 ÷ $24,726.5 = .002—and 1.1% in 1979—$684.8 ÷ $65,060.5 = .011) and City property increased 1.4% (City property constituted 17.4% of the value of all property in 1950—$4,312.6 ÷ $24,726.5 = .174—and 18.8% in 1979—$12,268.1 ÷ $65,060.5 = .188) for a net increase of 2.1%.

37. See note 26 supra.
38. See note 21 supra.
39. See note 30 supra.
40. $1,062.4 ÷ $33.0 = 32.19
41. $3,346.1 ÷ $948.3 = 3.53
42. $33.0 ÷ $24,726.5 = .001
43. $1,062.4 ÷ $65,060.5 = .016
44. $948.3 ÷ $24,726.5 = .038
45. $3,346.1 ÷ $65,060.5 = .051
46. See note 20 supra.
47. $2,855.5 ÷ $53,972.3 = .053
48. A news release of the Department of Finance of the City of New York dated January 29, 1981 reports that the final total assessed valuation of all taxable real estate in the City of New York as of May 26, 1980 was $39,-495,654,887 and that the tentative total assessed valuation of all taxable real estate in the City as of January 31, 1981 was $43,435,654,887. See N.Y. Times, January 30, 1981, at 1, col. 1. Consequently there was as of January 1981 a

There follows a summary recapitulation of the above description of the development of exempt property from 1910 to 1979. In 1910 the value of Exempt property as a percent of the value of property stood at 16.2%, of which Private Exempt property made up 3.8%[49] of all value as against 12.4%[50] for Public Exempt. Between 1910 and 1950 the portion that Exempt property made up of all property increased 9.4% from 16.2% in 1910[51] to 25.6% in 1950.[52] Nearly all of this 9.4% increase, viz., 9.2% is attributed to Public Exempt property, which increased from 12.4% of all value in 1910[53] to 21.6% in 1950,[54] and most of this increase occurred in the subcategories City and Housing.[55] Only nominal growth took place in Private Exempt property between 1910 and 1950, with Private Exempt property increasing from 3.8%[56] to 4.0%.[57] Between 1950 and 1979 Exempt property as a fraction of all property increased 15.9%, from 25.6% in 1950 to 41.5% in 1979. In this period also Public Exempt property accounted for the largest share of the growth, viz., 13.1% of the 15.9%, increasing from 21.6% in 1950 to 34.7% in 1979. Private Exempt property increased also, but its

---

tentative increase in the total assessed valuation of property in New York City (all subsequent figures in this note are in millions of current dollars) of $5,378.9 between the years 1979–80 and 1981–82, viz., $43,435.7—$38,056.8, an increase of about 14%. No comprehensive figures are given for exempt property in the news release, but it is extremely unlikely that exempt property increased anywhere near this much. (The report indicates a net increase in all exempt property of $447.7 between 1980–81 and 1981–82. Using the 1979–80 figure of total exempt property of $27,003.7 this would suggest an increase in exempt property of about 1½% from one year to the next or a compound increase of a little over 3% for two years.) If this is so the value of exempt property as a percent of all property will drop between these two years and very likely the subcategory Charitable will also drop.

49. See note 20 supra.
50. See note 18 supra.
51. See note 16 supra.
52. See note 17 supra.
53. See note 18 supra.
54. See note 19 supra.
55. See note 19 supra.
56. See note 20 supra.
57. See note 21 supra.

impact on the increase of all Exempt property as a fraction of all property was not nearly as great as Public Exempt property. Private Exempt property accounted for only about 2.8% of the 15.9% increase as a result of its increase from 4.0% in 1950 to 6.8% in 1979. Significantly for this report, the subcategory Private Miscellaneous Exempt property became an important factor during this period.

While the subcategory Charitable property increased somewhat as a percent of all value between 1910 and 1979, viz., 1.3%, it was a relatively small increase. Most of it occurred between 1950 and 1979, but in the latter part of this period Charitable property appeared to become a less significant factor. Indeed, in 1910 the subcategory Charitable property constituted 23.3%[58] of all Exempt property and this fraction dropped to 15% in 1950[59] and to 12.4% in 1979.[60]

## Section B—Upstate New York

Data for Upstate New York municipalities is based on information collected by the State Board of Equilization and Assessment from 991 municipalities for the years 1973 and 1978. According to representatives from the State Board, available data on exempt property prior to 1973 is not useable due to inaccuracies in the methods employed by local assessors to identify the owner and use of each parcel. Particular difficulties inhered in the identification of use. Collection of this data was not assumed by the State Board until 1970, and it took until 1973 before sufficient confidence in the quality of its reports had developed to support their use for the kind of analysis made here.

58. 316.6 ÷ $1,359.0 = .233
59. $948.3 ÷ $6,330.4 = .149
60. $3,346.1 ÷ $27,003.7 = .124

For each municipality the percent of the assessed value of all property made up by the assessed value of All Exempt property, all Private Wholly Exempt property, and all Public Wholly and Partially Exempt property (which includes private and public property) was determined.[61] This was done for both 1973 and 1978.

In 1973 the average of the percentages[62] of All Exempt property to all property[63] for the 991 municipalities was 21.46%; in 1978 it was 20.41%.[64] Before going further an excursus on methodological problems that arise because of the nature of the data is needed. Averaging the percentages of individual municipalities produces a different percent than would be derived by computing a percent whose numerator is the total value, for example, of All Exempt property (calculated by adding the values of All Exempt property for each municipality) and whose denominator is the total value of all property (calculated by adding the values of all property for each municipal-

61. Three fractions were developed for each municipality whose numerators were (1) the assessed value of All Exempt property, (2) the assessed value of all Private Wholly Exempt property and (3) the assessed value of all Public Wholly Exempt and Partially Exempt property, and whose denominators were, in each case, the assessed value of all property, both taxable and exempt, within the municipality. The fractions were reduced to produce percents. The first fraction produces a percent sometimes called the "Total Exempt Percent," the second fraction a percent sometimes called the "Private Wholly Exempt Percent" and the third fraction a percent sometimes called the "Public Wholly and Partially Exempt Percent." An appendix at the end of this chapter sets out the types of property that fit under these three categories and the sections of the Real Property Tax Law or other laws that exempt them.

62. The Total Exempt Percents.

63. When reference is made here and below to the percent that (some category of) exempt property makes up of all property, it should be recognized that what is meant is the percent that the assessed value of (some category of) exempt property makes up of the assessed value of all property. To facilitate expression from time to time reference to "assessed value" is dropped.

64. State Aid Unit, New York State Board of Equalization and Assessment, Exempt Property Related to All Property, table 3 (n.d.) (Arrays: Wholly Exempt as Percent of All Property, Rolls completed in 1973 and 1978) (computer printouts available from State Aid Unit, New York State Board of Equalization and Assessment).

ity).[65] This is because those municipalities with a large amount of assessed value would have a much stronger effect in determining the average percentage than when, as computed here, the individual percentages are averaged and each municipality is given the same weight regardless of amounts of assessed value. The latter approach, however, would not be appropriate because, as noted, municipalities assess property at different fractions of actual full value[66] so that to add individual municipalities values would involve adding noncomparable values, rendering the totals meaningless. Moreover, the method used here by which each municipality is given equal weight is consistant with the focus of this study on the impact of exemption on particular taxing units rather than attempting a statewide aggregate analysis.

Implicit in the approach used here is the assumption that exempt property is assessed at the same ratio of actual full value as taxable property and further that each class of property within these two categories is assessed at the same ratio, i.e., that all property in a municipality regardless of class is assessed at the same ratio of actual full value. As suggested in Chapter 1, this is almost certainly not the case. Also as noted above there is no evidence to suggest, however, that exempt property is uniformly assessed at a substantially different ratio than taxable property. Furthermore, an anlysis similar to the one that follows of all 991 municipalities is made below of the 61 municipalities that have recently gone to full value (and which presumably assess all property at the same ratio of full actual market value, viz., 100% or close to 100%) shows that this smaller sample parallels fairly closely the results of the data taken from all 991 municipalities. This suggests that the differential assessment

65. The same point developed here for Wholly Exempt property applies for Private Wholly Exempt property and for Public Wholly and Partially Exempt property.

66. See Chapter 1 for a discussion of how real property is assessed in New York and of the differential assessment problem.

problem should not invalidate the general findings made here. Finally, in comparing the percentages of exempt to taxable values in 1973 with 1978 to see whether more or less property (assessed value of property) has become exempt during this five-year period, the differential assessment problem would not seem to be of major concern as it is not very likely that material changes in assessment ratios were made during this time. In any event, as in the case of the examination of the New York City data, the data cited here are the only data available. The findings made seem supportable but given the nature of the data and the differential assessment problem these findings must be regarded with some caution.

As noted the average of the percentages of all the assessed value of All Exempt property to the assessed value of all property for the 991 Upstate municipalities[67] was 21.46% in 1973 and 20.41% in 1978.[68] Figures 1 and 2 present histogram graphs showing for 1973 and 1978 respectively the numbers and percents of the total number of Upstate municipalities falling within various categories that have been set with the purpose of showing the extent of exempt property. Each category indicates a range of percents of the assessed value of All Exempt property to the assessed value of all property, both taxable and exempt.[69] For example, Figure 1 shows that in 1973, 70.3% (or 697) of all municipalities had 25% or less of all value made up by the value of exempt property and Figure 2 shows that in 1978, 74% (or 733) of all municipalities fell within this category.

These tables indicate that during this five-year period on a municipality-by-municipality basis the amount of all assessed value constituted by All Exempt property decreased, i.e., more

67. The Total Exempt Percents. See note 61 supra.
68. See note 64 supra.
69. Id.

**Figure 1: Percent and Number of All Upstate Municipalities Which Had Exempt Property by Assessed Value Making Up Between 0–25%, 26–50%, 51–75% and 76–100% of the Assessed Value of All Property as of December 1, 1973. (Values in parentheses at top of column reflect the number of municipalities within each group).**

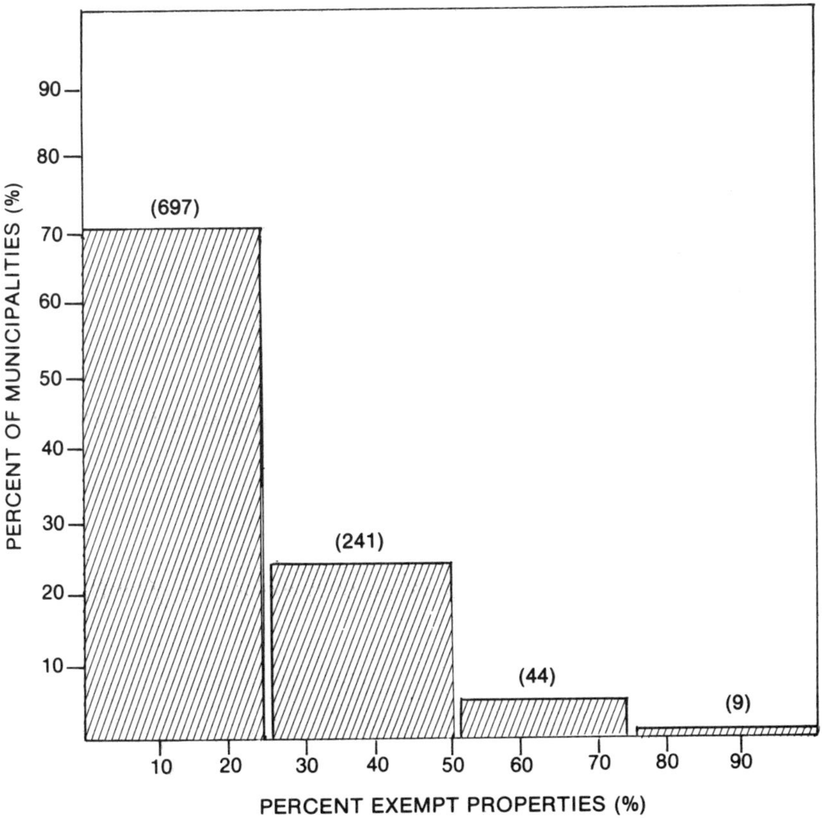


Source: See note 64 supra.

**Figure 2: Percent and Number of All Upstate Municipalities Which Had Exempt Property by Assessed Value Making Up Between 0–25%, 26–50%, 51–75% and 76–100% of the Assessed Value of All Property as of December 1, 1978. (Values in parentheses at top of column reflect the number of municipalities within each group).**

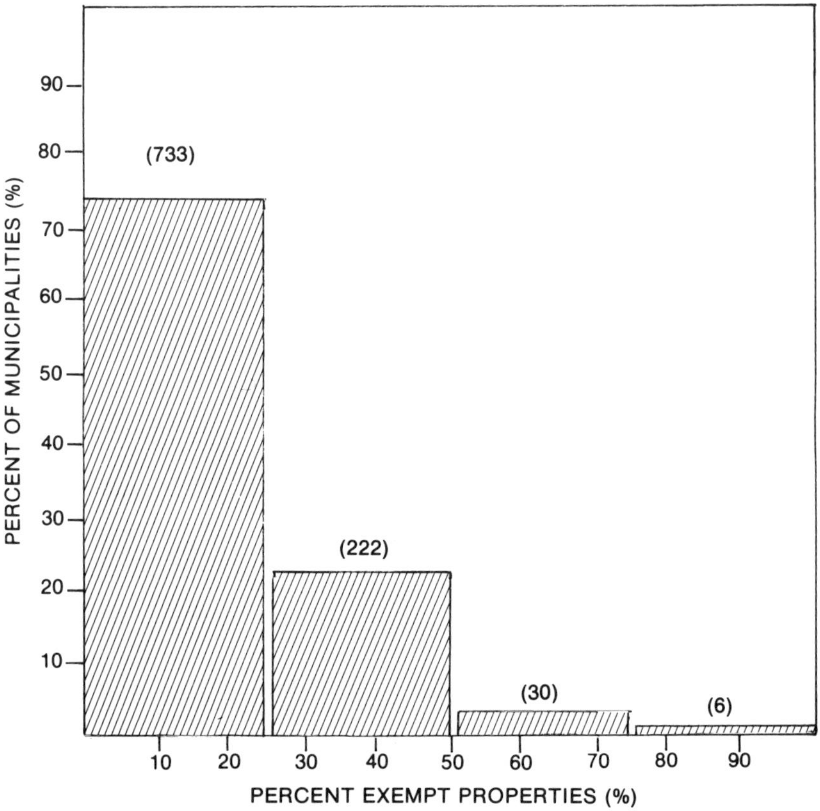


Source: See note 64 supra.

**Figure 3: Percent and Number of All Upstate Municipalities Which Had Exempt Property by Assessed Value Making Up Between 0–5%, 6–10%, 11–15%, 16–20% and 21–25% of the Assessed Value of All Property as of December 1, 1973. (Values in parentheses at top of column reflect the number of municipalities within each group).**

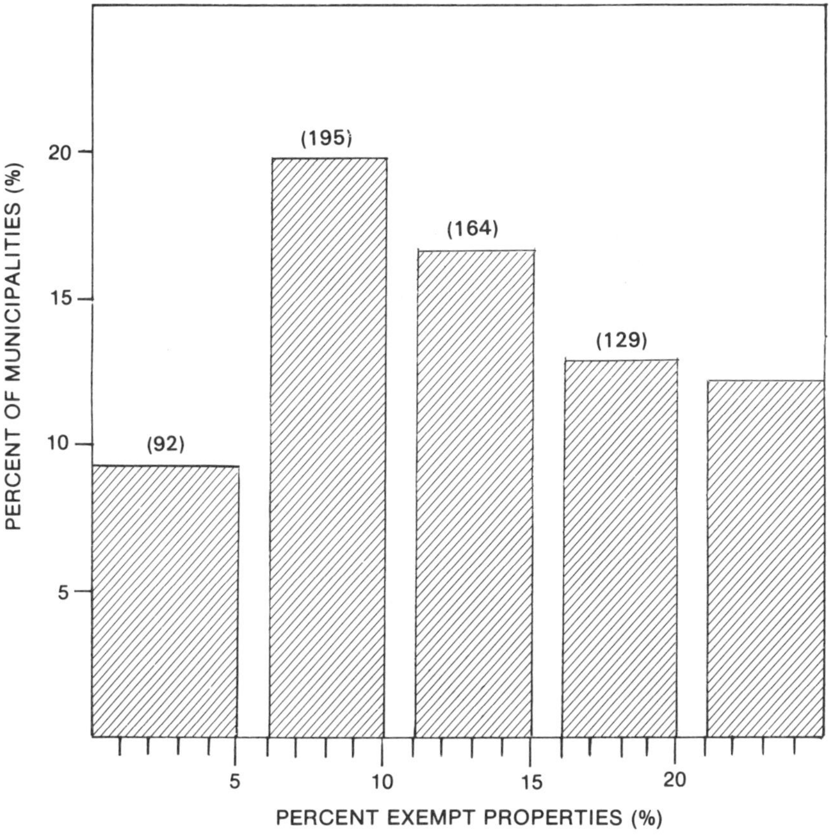


Source: See note 64 supra.

**Figure 4: Percent and Number of All Upstate Municipalities Which Had Exempt Property by Assessed Value Making Up Between 0–5%, 6–10%, 11–15%, 16–20% and 21–25% of the Assessed Value of All Property as of December 1, 1978. (Values in parentheses at top of column reflect the number of municipalities within each group).**

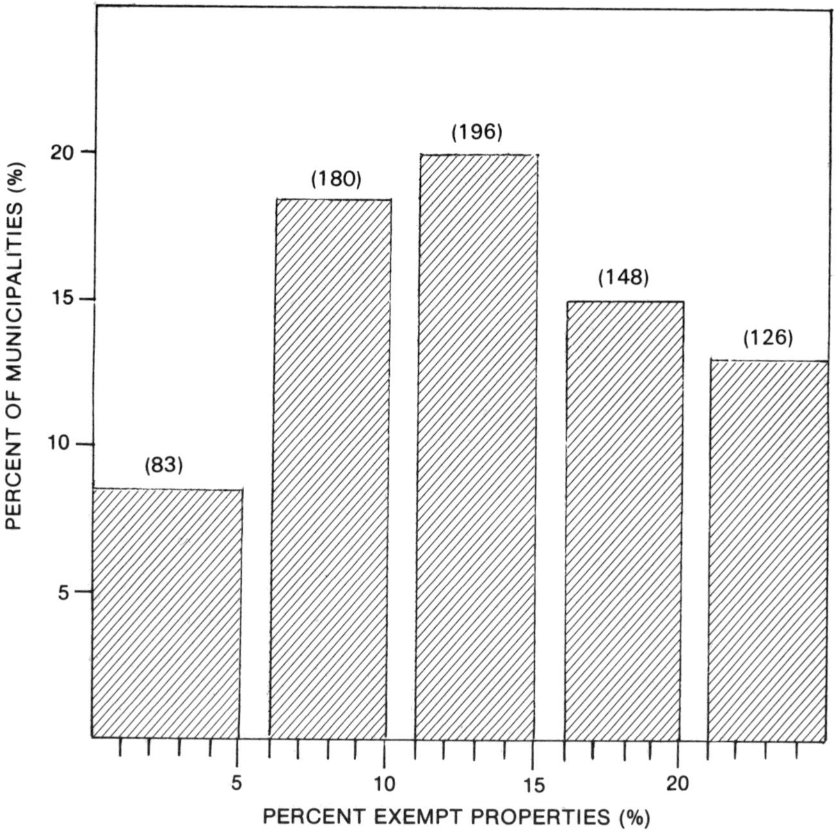


Source: See note 64 supra.

municipalities had smaller percents of exempt property at the end of the period than at the beginning. This is consistent with the decrease in the average of all Total Exempt Percents from 21.46% to 20.41%.[70]

Figures 3 and 4 for 1973 and 1978 respectively show for municipalities within the 0–25% categories of Figures 1 and 2 a more differentiated breakdown among smaller percent categories, viz., 0–5%, 6–10%, 11–15%, 16–20% and 21–25%. Only small changes in the proportionate distribution of municipalities among these smaller percent categories took place between 1973 to 1978, although the total number of municipalities that fall within the 0–25% range increased by about 5%. These figures indicate that most of the municipalities that have exempt property in the 0–25% range[71] (which Figures 1 and 2 indicate make up a very large majority of all municipalities—on the order of 70%) have less than 15% of exempt property. In 1973 over 45% of all municipalities (or 65% of all municipalities within this 0–25% range) had 15% or less of the assessed value of all property made up of exempt property, and in 1978 over 46% of all municipalities (or 63% of all municipalities within this 0–25% range) had 15% or less of the assessed value of all property made up of exempt property.

The ominous Becker Committee prediction in 1970 that if the relative rates of growth in exempt property and taxable property remained constant, by 1985 one-half of the value of all property in the state would be exempt[72] is hardly supported for Upstate municipalities[73] by the above data. In 1978 only 36 of 991 municipalities (somewhat less than 4%) had exempt property in excess of 50% of all value.

Whether or not exemptions constitute a tax base erosion

70. See note 64 supra.

71. I.e., the assessed value of wholly exempt property constitutes between 0 and 25% of the assessed value of all property.

72. See text accompanying note 1 supra.

73. The New York City situation is discussed above in the preceding section.

**Figure 5: Percent and Number of All Upstate Municipalities Which Had Private Wholly Exempt Percents by Assessed Value Making Up Between 0–25%, 26–50%, 51–75% and 76–100% of the Assessed Value of All Property as of December 1, 1973. (Values in parentheses at top of column reflect the number of municipalities within each group).**

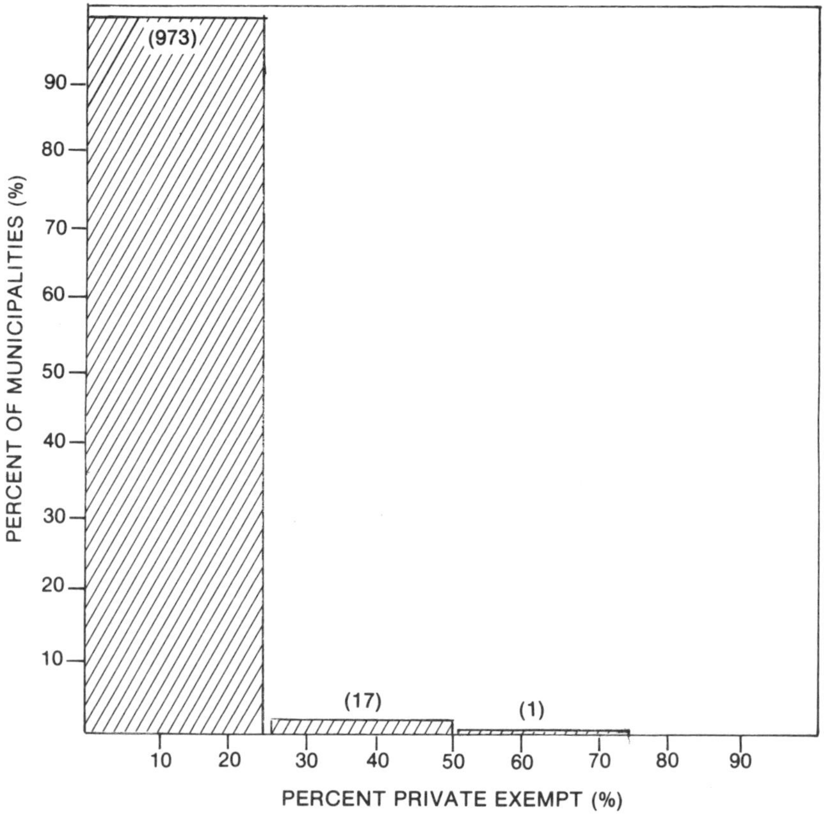


Source: See note 64 supra.

**Figure 6: Percent and Number of All Upstate Municipalities Which Had Private Wholly Exempt Percents by Assessed Value Making Up Between 0–5%, 6–10%, 11–15%, 16–20% and 21–25% of the Assessed Value of All Property as of December 1, 1973. (Values in parentheses at top of column reflect the number of municipalities within each group).**

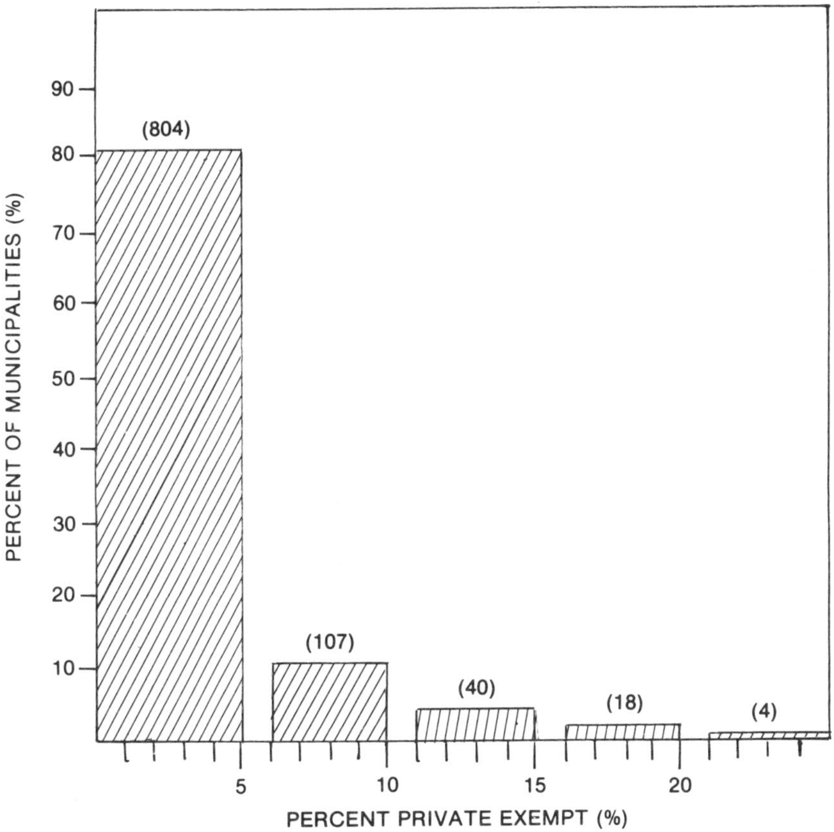


Source: See note 64 supra.

**Figure 7: Percent and Number of All Upstate Municipalities Which Had Private Wholly Exempt Percents by Assessed Value Making Up Between 0–25%, 26–50%, 51–75% and 76–100% of the Assessed Value of All Property as of December 1, 1978. (Values in parentheses at top of column reflect the number of municipalities within each group).**

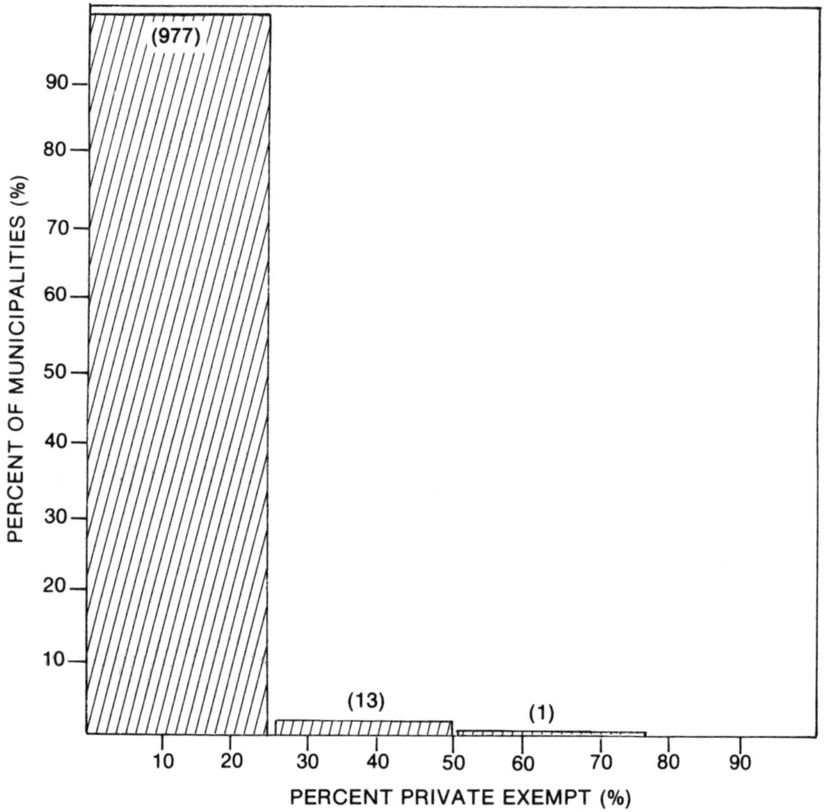


Source: See note 64 supra.

**Figure 8: Percent and Number of All Upstate Municipalities Which Had Private Wholly Exempt Percents by Assessed Value Making Up Between 0–5%, 6–10%, 11–15%, 16–20% and 21–25% of the Assessed Value of All Property as of December 1, 1978. (Values in parentheses reflect the number of municipalities within each group).**

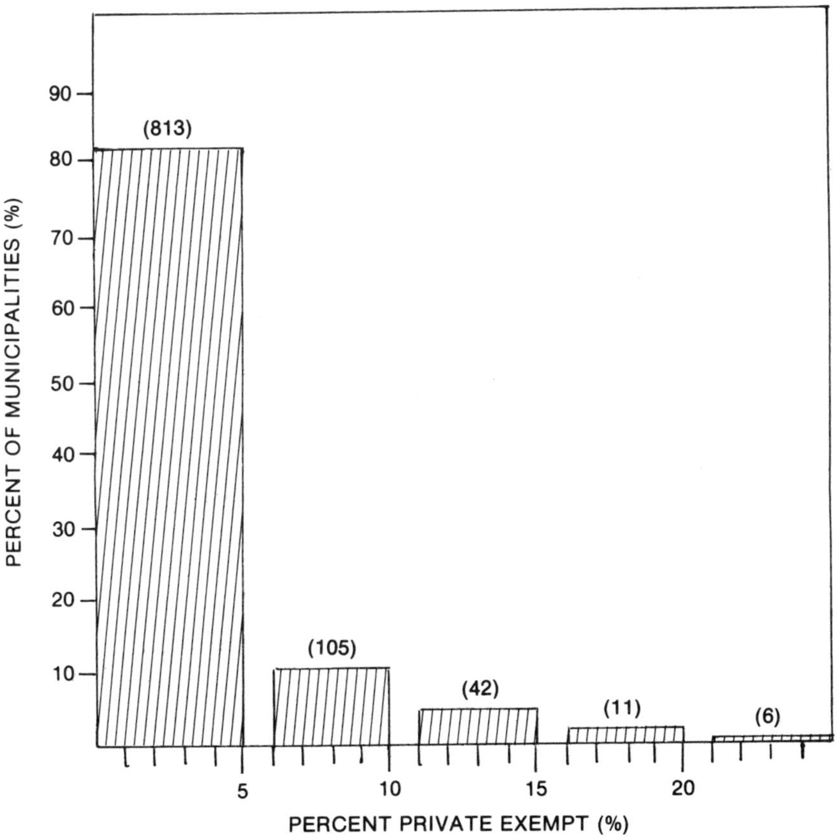


Source: See note 64 supra.

problem for Upstate municipalities, and the data strongly suggests that this is not the case, exemptions to Private Wholly Exempt property do not. In 1973 the average of 991 Upstate municipalities Private Wholly Exempt percents (i.e., the percents that the assessed value of private exempt property made up of the assessed value of all property for each municipality) was 4.04%; by 1978 the average had dropped to 3.7%.[74] Figures 5 and 6 present histogram graphs, similar to those above, showing the distribution of the 991 Upstate municipalities' Private Wholly Exempt Percents among various percent ranges. Figures 7 and 8 show the same data for 1978.

Figure 8 shows that only 17 municipalities (or about 1½% of the total) had Private Wholly Exempt Percents in excess of 15% in 1978, down from twenty-two (or about 2% of the total) in 1973 as Figure 6 shows. One can conclude from these figures that for the overwhelming proportion of Upstate municipalities tax base erosion attributed to Private Wholly Exempt property is not a problem and that the changes between 1973 and 1978 suggest a trend toward decreasing levels of private exempt property. As Private Wholly Exempt property is a more embrasive category than the charitably exempt[75] property (using the term "charitably" in the broad sense used throughout this study), i.e., the category charitably exempt property is a part of the larger category Private Wholly Exempt property, it follows *a fortiori* that an excessive amount of charitably exempt property, the focus of this study, is not a concern for Upstate municipalities. To the extent that there are grounds for concern with exemptions in Upstate municipalities, the difficulty would

74. See note 64 supra.

75. The Appendix at the end of this chapter lists the numerous exemptions included under the category Private Wholly Exempt. In addition to property exempt under N.Y. Real Prop. § 421 (McKinney 1972) twenty-five other exemptions are included under this category. Available data do not distinguish between these various categories. It is believed, however, that the § 421 exemptions are by far the most predominant type of private wholly exempt property exemptions.

lie with the nonPrivate Wholly Exempt property—i.e., Public Wholly and Partially Exempt property,[76] and not with Private Wholly Exempt property. In 1973 the average of 991 Upstate municipalities Public Wholly and Partially Exempt Percents[77] (i.e., the percents that the assessed value of nonPrivate Wholly Exempt property makes up of the assessed value of all property) for each municipality was 17.42% as compared to 4.04%, as noted, for Private Wholly Exempt property.[78] The same figures for 1978 were 16.71% for nonPrivate Wholly Exempt property and 3.7% as noted, for Private Wholly Exempt property.[79] Table 3 below presents for 1978 the average of Private Wholly Exempt percents[80] and Public Wholly and Partially Exempt[81] percents of municipalities with Total Exempt Percents[82] within six categories of percent ranges. Thus, for example, of the 261 municipalities which had Total Exempt Percents between 0%

**Table 3: Average Private Wholly Exempt Percent and Public Wholly and Partially Exempt Percent for Municipalities With Total Exempt Percents Between 0–10%, 11–20%, 21–30%, 31–40%, 41–50% and 51% and Greater**

| | Total Exempt | | | | | |
|---|---|---|---|---|---|---|
| | *0–10%* | *11–20%* | *21–30%* | *31–40%* | *41–50%* | *≥ 51%* |
| Private Wholly Exempt | 1.51 | 3.14 | 4.46 | 6.47 | 7.43 | 8.20 |
| Public Wholly and Partially Exempt | 5.74 | 12.39 | 20.56 | 28.97 | 35.09 | 55.41 |
| Number of Municipalities | 261 | 338 | 197 | 117 | 41 | 36 |

Source: See note 64 supra.

76. For a description of the kinds of exemptions that are included within these two categories, see Appendix at end of this chapter.
77. See note 64 supra.
78. Id.
79. See Id.
80. See note 61 supra.
81. Id.
82. Id.

**Table 4: Number of Municipalities With Total Exempt Percents Between 21–30%, 31–40%, 41–50% and 51% and Greater Distributed on the Basis of Private Wholly Exempt Percents Between Less Than 10%, 11–15%, 16–20%, 21–30%, 31–40%, 41–50% and 51% and Greater.**

| | Private Wholly Exempt Percent | | | | | | |
|---|---|---|---|---|---|---|---|
| *Total Exempt Percents* | *≤ 10%* | *11–15%* | *16–20%* | *21–30%* | *31–40%* | *41–50%* | *≥ 51%* |
| 21–30% | 177 | 15 | 3 | 2 | 0 | 0 | 0 |
| 31–40% | 95 | 11 | 4 | 5 | 2 | 0 | 0 |
| 41–50% | 27 | 5 | 2 | 5 | 1 | 1 | 0 |
| ≥ 51% | 29 | 2 | 1 | 1 | 0 | 2 | 1 |
| Total Number of Municipalities | 328 | 33 | 10 | 13 | 3 | 3 | 1 |

Source: See note 64 supra.

**Table 5**
**Average of the Percent That the Assessed Value of Private Wholly and Public Wholly and Partially Exempt Property Made Up of All Assessed Value for All Upstate Municipalities and a Sample of Full Value Upstate Municipalities—1973–1978**

| | 1973 | | 1978 | |
|---|---|---|---|---|
| | 991 Municipalities | Full-value Sample of 21 | 991 Municipalities | Full-value[1,2] Sample of 61 |
| Private Wholly Exempt | 4.4% | 3.8% | 3.7% | 3.3% |
| Public Wholly and Partially Exempt | 17.42% | 10.3% | 16.71% | 13.7% |

Source: For the data relating to all 991 municipalities, see note 64 supra. For the data relating to the full-value samples, see Full Value Programs, supra note 85: State Aid Unit, New York State Board of Equalization and Assessment, Exempt Property Related to All Property, table 3 (n.d.) (Arrays: Wholly Exempt as Percent of All Property, Rolls Completed in 1973 and 1978) (computer printouts available from State Aid Unit, New York State Board of Equalization and Assessment) [hereinafter cited as Percent Wholly Exempt].

1. Confidence intervals were determined using a two-tailed 5% significance level for the 1973 sample private averages. The intervals are:

| | *1973* | *1978* |
|---|---|---|
| True Private Average Ranges Between: | 1.6% and 6% | 1.6% and 5% |

2. As will be shown later, see text accompanying note infra, thirteen of these sixty-one municipalities went to full value in 1978. The Private Wholly Exempt average for these thirteen was 2.2% and the Public Wholly plus Partial Exempt level was 13.8% in 1978.

and 10%, their average Private Wholly Exempt percent in 1978 was 1.51% and their average Public Wholly and Partially Exempt percent was 5.74%.

Table 3 shows that nonPrivate Wholly Exempt property constitutes to a very considerable degree a far larger amount of assessed value than Private Wholly Exempt property. As indicated in Table 4 of the 391 municipalities in 1978 with Total Exempt Percents in excess of 20%, 328 (or about 84%) had Private Wholly Exempt percents below 10%. This pattern occurred in the high ranges as well as the low. Thus of the thirty-six municipalities with Total Exempt Percents of 50% or more, twenty-nine (or 81%) had Private Wholly Exempt percents below 10%. Of the forty-one municipalities with Total Exempt Percents between 41% and 50%, twenty-seven (or 66%) had Private Wholly Exempt percents below 10%, and of the 117 municipalities with Total Exempt Percents between 31% and 40%, ninety-five (or 81%) had Private Wholly Exempt percents below 10%. In sum, in those relatively few municipalities where there is a fair to large amount of exempt property, it is almost all made up by nonPrivate Wholly Exempt property, i.e., Public Wholly and Partially Exempt property, and only to a small extent by Private Wholly Exempt property.

An examination was made of those municipalities assessing at full value in 1973 and 1978. 1973 full value municipalities assessing at a rate less than 70% by 1978 were eliminated from consideration. Full value municipalities were selected only if they were assessing in 1978 at a rate between 94% and 106%.[83] This method of selection was used to focus on those municipalities that appeared to be making a genuine effort in their full value assessment programs. Twenty-one municipalities met the

83. New York State Division of Equalization and Assessment, Full Value Programs During the 1970s (1979) [hereinafter cited as Full Value Programs].

1973 criterion[84] and sixty-one met the 1978 criterion.[85] All of the 1973 municipalities went to full value in 1973. Approximately 80% of the 1978 full value municipalities went to full value from 1976 through 1978. The result appears in the following table.

The above supports the results found when dealing with all 991 municipalities and appears to indicate that municipalities tend to overvalue rather than undervalue exempt properties. It will also be noted that whether in dealing with the full value sample or with all 991 municipalities, private exempt property on average does not constitute a significant amount of the total property of municipalities.

As demonstrated above, when all 991 municipalities are considered, most municipalities have private exempt levels in the 1% to 5% range. This also holds true for the full value sample of municipalities used here. A few municipalities with very high private exempt levels tend to pull the entire private exempt average up considerably. For example, if the two highest private exempt towns are eliminated in the 1978 full value sample, and the private exempt average for the remaining fifty-nine is computed, the average is 2% rather than 3.3% as found above.[86]

The contention that municipalities did not revalue exempt property in the above sample when going to full value and that therefore the above results are invalid can be easily dismissed. Table 6 presents the thirteen municipalities of the 1978 sample

84. These municipalities are: Avoca, Barrington, Brutus, Covert, Decatur, Fayette, Italy, Junius, Kinderhook, Lewisboro, Little Falls, Lodi, Milo, Montour, Ogden, Ovid, Ramapo, Seneca Falls, Tyre, Varich and Waterloo.

85. These municipalities are: Alexander, Alfred, Allegany, Almond, Barrington, Batavia, Beekmantown, Bethany, Byron, Chatham, Cincinnatus, Clinton (Clinton County), Cortlandville, Cato, Cugler, Danby, Eaton, Elba, Ellenburg, Enfield, Freetown, Galen, Greene, Groton, Harford, Hillsdale, Homer, Huron, Islip, Lloyd, Lapeer, Marathon, Montour, Nassau, New Hudson, Norwich, Oakfield, Oneonta, Pembroke, Piercefield, Pitcher, Plymouth, Preston, Ramapo, Rochester, Scott, Sherburne, Smithfield, Smyrna, Solon S. Valley, Stafford, Taylor, Torrey, Tuxedo, Virgil, Wallkill, West Almond, Western, Woodstock and Watertown.

86. The two towns are Alfred (52% private exempt) and Allegany (32% private exempt).

**Table 6**
**1977 and 1978 Private Exempt Levels and State Equalization Rates for Municipalities Which Went to Full Value in 1978**

| | Equalization Rates | | Percent Private Exempt | |
|---|---|---|---|---|
| *Municipality* | *1977* | *1978* | *1977* | *1978* |
| Beekmantown | 17 | 100 | 0 | 1 |
| Clinton | 13 | 102 | 7 | 2 |
| Danby | 33 | 105 | 2 | 2 |
| Eaton | 38 | 105 | 2 | 1 |
| Ellenburg | 17 | 97 | 3 | 4 |
| Enfield | 39 | 103 | 1 | 1 |
| Groton | 41 | 106 | 4 | 4 |
| Islip | 11 | 105 | 1 | 1 |
| Nassau | 6 | 97 | 3 | 2 |
| Piercefield | 44 | 102 | 15 | 8 |
| W. Almond | 10 | 97 | 0 | 0 |
| Western | 16 | 99 | 1 | 1 |
| Watertown | 37 | 96 | 4 | 2 |
| Averages: | 24.8 | 101.1 | 3.3% | 2.2% |

Source: New York State Comptroller, Special Report on Municipal Affairs, table 4, N.Y. Leg. Doc. No. 92 (1979) (for local fiscal year ended in 1978); Full Value Programs, supra note 83; notes to table 5 supra.

that went to full value in 1978. Data on their exempt levels and equalization rates just prior (1977) to their going to full value are also presented. These data strongly suggest that revaluation did occur for the exempt property in these municipalities.[87] Of the thirteen municipalities, eight municipalities either remained the same or increased their level of private exempt property between 1977 and 1978, a period in which the average equalization rate[88] jumped from 24.8 to 101.1 for the group. Of the five municipalities that decreased in terms of the private exempt level, no municipality had a private exempt decrease as great as the equalization rate increase. This, of

87. This assumes there was not an extraordinary jump in exempt property for these municipalities between 1977 and 1978, clearly a fair assumption.

88. As explained in Chapter 1, the equalization rate indicates on the average the percent of full actual market value at which municipalities assess their property. See text accompanying note 31, Chapter 1 supra.

course, implies that private exemptions were revalued for these municipalities as well.

## Section C—An Evaluation of the Becker Committee Report

As noted above the Becker Committee in its 1970 report[89] prophesied that for all of New York State by 1985 "one-half of the assessed value of all real property on municipal assessment rolls will be exempt."[90] The above data show this is not going to happen. On the basis of a municipality-by-municipality average, the percent of assessed value of all Upstate municipalities' real property made up by the value of exempt property stood at about 20% in 1978, having decreased from about 21% in 1973. (As noted it would be meaningless to determine an aggregate percent of all exempt property as a fraction of all property because of the differential assessment problem).[91] A more troubling situation exists in New York City. New York City—putting aside for a moment the differential assessment problem—contains about 54% of all value in the state.[92] As noted below New York City has a higher equalization rate than most Upstate municipalities—which means it assesses its real property at a higher percent of actual market value than most Upstate municipalities do. Thus, taking account of the differential assessment problem, it is likely that New York City contains less than 54% of all state value. Consequently, if one regards the totality of New York State, even conceding an alarming growth rate of exempt property in New York City, it is quite impossible that anything close to 50% of the assessed value of all real property on all New York State municipal assessment rolls will be exempt by 1985.

Previously cited data show that by 1979 exempt property as

89. See note 1 supra.
90. Id. at 9.
91. See text accompanying note 66 supra.
92. See note 5 and accompanying text supra.

a percent of all property in New York City had come to equal about 41½%, up from about 25½% in 1950. This is a substantial growth but as shown above the overwhelming preponderance of this growth occurred in properties that are publicly exempt, particularly Housing and Public Authorities exemptions, and the category referred to above as Private Miscellaneous Exempt. It is also likely that in the years remaining until 1985 because of the rapid growth in the value of taxable property, that the percent of all value made up by exempt value in New York City will diminish.

In any event, as noted, if a serious tax base erosion problem is endemic to New York City, it involves for the most part public exemptions and not what have been called charitable exemptions. A similar finding is made for the Upstate municipalities (although the overall exemption problem Upstate is not as severe as in the City), i.e., where there is a high proportion of a municipality's value taken up by exempt property it is usually property that is publicly exempt. The Becker Committee, however, in making its dire predictions, does not distinguish between public and private exemptions. And yet, as noted in Chapter 2, the principal legislative response to the Becker Committee Report was to restrict the charitable exemptions of section 421 of the Real Property Tax Law. Indeed, the enactment effecting this change made implicit reference to the Becker Committee Report.[93] Significant also is the fact that the two Court of Appeals decisions, viz., *Association of the Bar of New York v. Lewisohn*[94] and *American Bible Society v. Lewisohn,*[95] in interpreting the 1971 amendment so as to further narrow the charitable exemption, both made express reference to the legislative finding, and the *Association of the Bar* opinion

93. 1971 N.Y. Laws, ch. 414 § 1. Section 1 is prefaced "Legislative findings and intent," and as shown in Chapter 2 the legislative findings are those of the Becker Committee Report.
94. 34 N.Y. 2d 143, 313 N.E.2d 30, 356 N.E.2d 555 (1974).
95. 40 N.Y.2d 78, 351 N.E.2d 697, 386 N.Y.S. 2d 49 (1976).

also made express reference to the Becker Committee Report.[96]

There are several technical difficulties with the Becker Committee Report. A serious problem lies in the use of aggregate values. This method adds the assessed value of all municipalities and compares aggregates. No account is taken of the fact that different municipalities assess their properties at different percents of actual market value. In this connection, one of the findings of the Becker Committee Report that may have startled people anxious about the real property tax base problem was that as of 1967 approximately 30% of the total assessed valuation of real property in New York State was exempt.[97] This figure was based upon a statewide aggregate. Since, however, municipalities generally assess their real property at different percents of actual market value, a conclusion based on statewide aggregates is uncertain. For example, if those municipalities with a higher proportion of exempt property assess their property at a higher percent of actual market value than those municipalities with a lower proportion of exempt property, a finding based upon an aggregate figure will be skewed.

An examination of 1978 assessed value and State Equalization Rate[98] data for cities and towns reveals that this is not merely a hypothetical issue. New York State cities had an average State Equalization Rate of 49.6%, while towns had an average rate of 36.6%.[99] Cities, however, also had a higher average level of

96. 34 N.Y. 2d 143, 155, 313 N.E.2d 30, 35, 356 N.Y.S. 2d 555, 563 (1974). A recent trial court case upholding the denial of an exemption to a building used for the production of cultural performances on a nonprofit basis, cites the legislative findings of the 1971 enactment in its entirety as providing support for its holding. The Symphony Space, Inc. v. Tishelman, 185 N.Y.L.J., March 4, 1981, at 12 col. 2 (Sup. Ct. February 20, 1981).

97. See Becker Committee Report, supra note 1, at 24.

98. As explained in Chapter 1, the State Equalization Rate indicates on the average the percent of full actual market value at which municipalities assess their property. See text accompanying note 31, Chapter 1 supra.

99. New York State Comptroller, Special Report on Municipal Affairs, tables 3, 3–1 and 4, N.Y. Leg. Doc. No. 92 (1979) (for local fiscal year ending in 1978). Table 3–1 shows that in 1978 New York City had a State Equalization Rate of

exempt property of 35.5%, compared to the average for towns of 19.5%.[100] Thus, cities with their high levels of exempt property would receive an unjustifiably higher weight than low level exempt towns in a method based upon a statewide aggregation such as that used in the Becker Committee Report. Furthermore, municipalities may change from year to year the percent of actual market value at which they assess their properties. Thus one group of municipalities, say, cities, might over time increase the percent of actual market value at which they assess property within their jurisdiction because of, e.g., an increasing need for revenues, while another group, say, towns, might over time keep the percent of actual market value at which they assess value constant (or even drop it). If, as has been shown, cities have a larger proportion of exempt property than towns to start off with, statistics on the relative growth rate of taxable and exempt property based on aggregate data would also be seriously skewed. On these grounds alone the prediction that one-half of all property in the state would be exempt by 1985 must be seriously questioned.

Even ignoring this serious problem, there are several other technical difficulties with the Becker Committee Report. First, the basis for the finding that 50% of the value of all property would be exempt by 1985 was an asserted relative growth rate of 8% for exempt property, compared to 3% for taxable property.[101] While such a relative growth rate would indeed produce the prophesied results, on the figures apparently used by the Becker Committee to determine the rate, it appears that

---

50½%, fully taxable property of $38,611,805,862 and wholly exempt property of $25,698,096,819.

100. State Aid Unit, New York State Board of Equalization and Assessment, Exempt Property Related to All Property, table 3 (n.d.) (Arrays: Wholly Exempt as Percent of All Property, Rolls completed in 1973 and 1978) (Computer printouts available from State Aid Unit, New York State Board of Equalization and Assessment); New York State Comptroller, Special Report on Municipal Affairs, tables 3 and 3–1, N.Y. Leg. Doc. No. 92 (1979) (for local fiscal year ending in 1978).

101. Becker Committee Report, supra note 1, at 8–9.

exempt property would only increase at a rate of 5%.[102]

Secondly, an enormous period of time is used, viz., 1900–1967, to establish a relatively recently developed trend. Such an analysis is necessarily based on comparisons of widely disparate values. Furthermore, given the differential assessment problem discussed above, this problem, inherent in any data taken from such long periods of time, is greatly exacerbated.

Finally, the Becker Committee Report notes a 3,000% increase in exempt property between 1900 and 1967,[103] an alarming figure, but this figure was based on current dollar comparisons and consequently no account is taken of what must have been an enormous change in price levels between those two years.

In sum, it has been seen that a significant narrowing of the scope of charitable exemptions from property taxation resulted in considerable part from the Becker Committee Report. The response, however, was to legislate in an area that the facts underlying the report and which have since developed show is not a problem. That is, the tax base erosion problem, to the extent it exists, has to do with governmentally exempt property, particularly in New York City, and only very little, if at all, with

102. The Becker Commission Report states that in 1900 there was $723,-345,000 of assessed value of exempt property in New York State and in 1967 there was $22,703,000,000 of exempt property. Id. at 24. It also states that 11.14% of all property in 1900 was exempt (Id.), which implies that $5,769,-878,000 was taxable in 1900. It further states that in 1967, $52,600,000,000 was the assessed value of taxable property. Id. For the 67 year period, these data imply an annual compound growth rate of 5.3% for exempt property or a 3.3% rate for taxable property. Thus, while the data apparently used by the Becker Committee do support a growth rate of taxable property of about 3% it shows a growth rate of exempt property of about 5% and not 8%. It is interesting to note that on the basis of the data used in the Becker Committee Report, however, private exempt property grew at nearly the same 3% rate as taxable property. The Becker Committee Report reveals that the assessed value of exempt real property owned by private nonprofit organizations increased approximately nine fold between 1905 and 1967 to a level of $3,562,000,000 implying a 1905 nonprofit exempt level of $395,777,000. Id. at 33. For the 62 year period, this implies an annual compound growth rate of 3.6%.

103. Becker Committee Report, supra note 1, at 24.

charitably exempt property. Furthermore, the data and methods used in the report give rise to serious questions about its validity.

## Appendix

This appendix sets out the type of exemptions that are included under the three major categories used in the preceding chapter, viz., 1. Private Wholly Exempt property; 2. Public Wholly Exempt property and 3. Partially Exempt property. The listings came from the State Board's memo on exemption codes,[104] which lists the types of property falling under each category and the law under which each type is exempt. The listings are set forth just as they are in the State Board's memo. "RPTL" indicates Real Property Tax Law.[105] "PUB. AUTH. LAW" indicates Public Authorities Law.[106] "GEN. MUNY L" indicates General Municipal Law.[107] "PUB. HSG L" indicates Public Housing Law.[108] "P.H. FI. L" indicates Private Housing Finance Law.[109] "CORP LAW" indicates Not-For-Profit Corporation Law.[110] "INS. LAW" indicates Insurance Law.[111] "COUNTY LAW" indicates County Law.[112] "AGRIC-MKTS L" indicates Agricultural and Markets Law.[113] And "GML" indicates General Municipal Law.[114] "UCON" indicates Unconsolidated Laws.[115]

104. State Board of Equalization And Assessment, Real Property Exemption Codes (1980) [hereinafter cited as Real Property Exemption Codes].
105. N.Y. Real Prop. (McKinney 1972).
106. N.Y. Pub. Auth. (McKinney 1970).
107. N.Y. Gen. Mun. (McKinney 1979).
108. N.Y. Pub. Hous. (McKinney 1955).
109. N.Y. Priv. Hous. Fin. (McKinney 1976).
110. N.Y. Not-For-Profit Corp. (McKinney 1970).
111. N.Y. Ins. (McKinney 1966).
112. N.Y. County (McKinney 1972).
113. N.Y. Agric. & Mkts. (McKinney 1972).
114. N.Y. Gen. Mun. (McKinney 1979).
115. N.Y. Unconsol. Laws (McKinney 1979).

| Description of Exemption | Section of Law |
|---|---|
| *Private Wholly Exempt*[116] | |
| RESIDENTIAL PROPERTY OF RELIGIOUS CORPORATIONS | RPTL 462 |
| NON-PROFIT, CONSTITUTIONALLY PROTECTED | RPTL 421-1-A |
| NON-PROFIT, HOSPITALS AND CEMETERIES | RPTL 421-1-A |
| ALL OTHER NON-PROFIT | RPTL 421-1-B |
| FRATERNAL ORGANIZATIONS | RPTL 428 |
| NON-PROF MED. OR DENTAL INDEMN. OR HOSP. SERV. CORP. | INS. LAW 251-3 |
| NON-PROFIT MEDICAL CORPORATION | RPTL 486-A |
| INFANT HOMES | RPTL 440 |
| AGRICULTURAL SOCIETIES | RPTL 450 |
| VETERANS ORGANIZATIONS | RPTL 452 |
| INCORPORATED ASSOCIATION OF VOLUNTEER FIREMEN | RPTL 464 |
| HISTORICAL SOCIETIES | CORP. LAW 190 |
| INTERDENOMINATIONAL CENTERS | RPTL 430 |
| FIRE PATROL AND SALVAGE CORPORATIONS | RPTL 468 |
| RAILROAD REAL PROPERTY—SUBSIDIZED | RPTL 489-DD |
| CEMETERIES | RPTL 446 |
| RETIREMENT SYSTEMS | INS. LAW 200-7 |
| NOT FOR PROFIT HOUSING COMPANIES | RPTL 422 |
| PROPERTY OF COMMUNITY DEVELOPMENT CORPORATIONS | P.H.FI. L260 |
| NON-PROF. CORP. IMPROV. HSG. IND. AND/OR RES. FAC. | UCON. C172L68[117] |
| INST. FOR INSTRUCTION OF WOMEN AND GIRLS IN TRADES | RPTL 425 |
| OPERA HOUSES | RPTL 426 |
| HOSPITALS FOR THE BENEFIT OF A CITY | RPTL 438 |
| TRUSTEES OF HOSP., PLAYGROUNDS, OR LIB. FOR BENE. CITY | RPTL 438 |
| ACADEMIES OF MUSIC | RPTL 434 |
| PERFORMING ARTS BUILDINGS | RPTL 427 |
| PASSENGER STATIONS > 1,000,000 POPULATION | RPTL 476-A |
| SOLDIER MONUMENT CORPORATIONS | CORP. LAW 162 |

| Description of Property | Section of Law |
|---|---|
| *Public Wholly Exempt*[118] | |
| NEW YORK STATE | RPTL 404-1 |
| EMPLOYEE RETIREMENT SYSTEM | RPTL 404-2 |
| TEACHERS RETIREMENT SYSTEM | RPTL 404-3 |
| PUBLIC AUTHORITIES—STATE | PUB. AUTH. LAW |
| COUNTY OWNED WITHIN COUNTY | RPTL 406-1 |
| CITY OWNED WITHIN CORPORATE LIMITS | RPTL 406-1 |
| TOWN OWNED WITHIN CORPORATE LIMITS | RPTL 406-1 |
| VILLAGE OWNED WITHIN CORPORATE LIMITS | RPTL 406-1 |
| SCHOOL DISTRICTS | RPTL 408 |
| BOCES | RPTL 408 |
| SPECIAL DISTRICTS | RPTL 410 |
| PUBLIC AUTHORITIES—LOCAL | PUB. AUTH. LAW |
| PROPERTY OWNED BY TWO MUNICIPALITIES | RPTL 406 |
| USA | RPTL 401 |
| FOREIGN GOVERNMENTS | RPTL 418 |
| INDIAN RESERVATIONS | RPTL 454 |
| U.N. | RPTL 416 |
| PROP. OF HEALTH & MENTAL HYGIENE FACILITIES CORP. | UCON.C359 L1968[119] |
| INDUSTRIAL DEVELOPMENT AGENCIES | GEN. MUNY. L874 |
| MUNICIPALLY ACQUIRED PROPERTY FOR URBAN RENEWAL | GEN. MUNY. L506 |
| PROPERTY OF MUNICIPAL RENEWAL AGENCIES | GEN. MUNY. L555 |
| CITY AND FEDERALLY AIDED HOUSING | PUB. HSG. L52-3 |
| MUNY, ACQUIRED FROM LIMITED PROFIT HOUSING COMPANY | P.H.FI, L36-A-2 |
| PROPERTY OF NYS HOUSING AND FINANCE AGENCY | P.H.FI. L53 |
| UDC PROPERTY—NO PROFIT HSG, CO, SUBSIDIARIES | P.H.FI, L33-1-C |
| UDC PROJ.—HSG, DEVEL. FUND CO. SUBSID., NON-PROFIT | P.H.FI. L577-3 |
| UDC—INDUSTRIAL, LAND USE IMPRV & CIVIC PROJECTS | UCON. 6272 |
| MUNICIPAL RAILROADS | RPTL 456 |

| Description of Property | Section of Law |
|---|---|
| *Partially Exempt*[120] Limited Exemption (Private) | |
| VETERANS | RPTL 458-1 |
| SUBSCRIPTION VETS | RPTL 458-2 |
| PARAPLEGIC VETS | RPTL 458-3 |
| CLERGY | RPTL 460 |
| OFFICERS OF RELIGIOUS DENOMINATIONS | RPTL 436 |
| AGRICULTURAL BUILDINGS—5 YEAR EXEMPTION | RPTL 483 |
| AGRICULTURAL DISTRICTS (STATE FORMED) | AGRIC-MKTS L305 |
| AGRICULTURAL DISTRICTS (COUNTY FORMED) | AGRIC-MKTS L305 |
| AGRICULTURAL DISTRICTS (INDIVIDUAL APPLICATION) | AGRIC-MKTS L305 |
| PERSONS OVER 65—ALL PURPOSES | RPTL 467 |
| PERSONS OVER 65—COUNTY & CITY/TOWN | RPTL 467 |
| PERSONS OVER 65—COUNTY | RPTL 467 |
| PERSONS OVER 65—CITY/TOWN | RPTL 467 |
| PERSONS OVER 65—SCHOOL | RPTL 467 |
| PERSONS OVER 65—COUNTY & SCHOOL | RPTL 467 |
| PERSONS OVER 65—CITY/TOWN & SCHOOL | RPTL 467 |
| LOVE CANAL—ALL PURPOSES | RPTL ART 17 |
| LOVE CANAL—COUNTY & CITY/TOWN PURPOSES | RPTL ART 17 |
| LOVE CANAL—COUNTY PURPOSES ONLY | RPTL ART 17 |
| OPEN SPACE RESTRICTION | GML 247 |
| DENTAL SOCIETIES IN CITIES > 175,000 POP. | RPTL 474 |
| DENTAL SOCIETIES IN CITIES > 175,000 POP. | RPTL 474 |
| DENTAL SOCIETIES IN CITIES > 175,000 POP. | RPTL 474 |
| PHARMACEUTICAL SOC. IN CITIES > 175,000 POP. | RPTL 472 |
| PHARMACEUTICAL SOC. IN CITIES > 175,000 POP. | RPTL 472 |
| PHARMACEUTICAL SOC. IN CITIES > 175,000 POP. | RPTL 472 |
| IMPROVEMENTS TO MULTIPLE DWELLINGS | RPTL 489-1 |
| RAILROAD REAL PROPERTY—AMOUNT EXCEEDING CEILING | RPTL 489-D |
| NEWLY OR RECONSTRUCTED RAIL FACILITIES | RPTL 476-B |
| RAIL BRIDGES, VIADUCTS & STRUCTURES CONST—HGY LAW | RPTL 476-C |
| FISHER ACT REFORESTED LANDS | RPTL 480 |
| PRIVATE FOREST LANDS | RPTL 480-A |
| ELIG. BUS. FACIL. CERT. BY NYS JOB INCENTIVE BOARD | RPTL 485 |
| ELIG. BUS. FACIL. CERT. BY NYS JOB INCENTIVE BOARD | RPTL 485 |
| ELIG. BUS. FACIL. CERT. BY NYS JOB INCENTIVE BOARD | RPTL 485 |
| ELIG. BUS. FACIL. CERT. BY NYS JOB INCENTIVE BOARD | RPTL 485 |
| ELIG. BUS. FACIL. CERT. BY NYS JOB INCENTIVE BOARD | RPTL 485 |
| ELIG. BUS. FACIL. CERT. BY NYS JOB INCENTIVE BOARD | RPTL 485 |
| ELIG. BUS. FACIL. CERT. BY NYS JOB INCENTIVE BOARD | RPTL 485 |
| STEEL MFG PROP IN CITIES < 50,000 POP. | RPTL 485A |
| BUSINESS INCENTIVE—ALL PURPOSES | RPTL 485-B |
| BUSINESS INCENTIVE—COUNTY & CITY/TOWN | RPTL 485-B |
| BUSINESS INCENTIVE—COUNTY | RPTL 485-B |
| BUSINESS INCENTIVE—CITY/TOWN | RPTL 485-B |
| BUSINESS INCENTIVE—SCHOOL | RPTL 485-B |
| BUSINESS INCENTIVE—COUNTY & SCHOOL | RPTL 485-B |
| BUSINESS INCENTIVE—CITY/TOWN & SCHOOL | RPTL 485-B |
| FALLOUT SHELTER FACILITIES | RPTL 479 |
| TELEPHONE STATION EQUIPMENT | RPTL 470 |
| SCENIC EASEMENTS | 000 |
| AIR POLLUTION CONTROL FACILITIES | RPTL 481 |
| AIR POLLUTION CONTROL FACILITIES | RPTL 481 |
| AIR POLLUTION CONTROL FACILITIES | RPTL 481 |
| AIR POLLUTION CONTROL FACILITIES | RPTL 481 |
| AIR POLLUTION CONTROL FACILITIES | RPTL 481 |
| AIR POLLUTION CONTROL FACILITIES | RPTL 481 |
| AIR POLLUTION CONTROL FACILITIES | RPTL 481 |
| URBAN DEVELOPMENT ACTION AREA—ALL PURPOSES | GML 696 |
| URBAN DEVELOPMENT ACTION AREA—COUNTY & CITY | GML 696 |
| URBAN DEVELOPMENT ACTION AREA—COUNTY | GML 696 |

| Description of Property | Section of Law |
|---|---|
| *Partially Exempt*[120] Limited Exemption (Private) | |
| URBAN DEVELOPMENT ACTION AREA—CITY | GML 696 |
| URBAN DEVELOPMENT ACTION AREA—CITY & SCHOOL | GML 696 |
| MUNICIPALLY SOLD—PRIVATE HOUSING COMPANY | PUB. HSG. L58 |
| PROPERTY LIMITED PROFIT HOUSING COMPANY | P.H.FI. L33-1-A |
| UDC PROPERTY SUCCESSOR LTD. PROF. HSG. COMPANY | P.H.FI. L33-1-C |
| DWELLING IN PROJ. LEASED TO HSG. AND FINANCE AGENCY | P.H.FI. L33-2 |
| DWELLING IN PROJ. LEASED TO MUNY. HSG. AGENCY | P.H.FI. L33-3 |
| PROJECT OF APPROVED MUTUAL COMPANY—(CO-OPS) | P.H.FI. L33-4 |
| MUNY PROJ. SOLD TO LIMITED PROFIT HOUSING COMPANY | P.H.FI. L36-A-4 |
| PROPERTY OF LIMITED DIVIDEND HOUSING COMPANY | P.H.FI. L93-4 |
| UDC PROJECT SUCCESSOR LTD. DIVIDEND HSG. COMPANY | P.H.FI. L93-6 |
| PROJECTS OF REDEVELOPMENT COMPANIES | P.H.FI. L125 |
| PROJECTS OF HOUSING DEVELOPMENT COMPANIES | P.H.FI. L577-1 |
| UDC PROJECT SUCCESSOR HSG. DEVELOPMENT FUND COMPANY | P.H.FI. L577-3 |
| LIMITED PROFIT NURSING HOME COMPANIES | PUB. HEL. L2864 |
| THEATRICAL CORPORATIONS—BY AN ACT OF CONGRESS | RPTL 432 |
| CEMETERIES IN CERTAIN COUNTIES | RPTL 448 |
| QUARANTINED LANDS | RPTL 482 |
| SOLAR & WIND ENERGY SYSTEMS | RPTL 487 |
| CONSERVATION IMPROVMTS TO CERTAIN RESIDENTIAL PREMISES | RPTL 487-A |
| OFFSTREET PARKING WITH UNDERGROUND SHELTER | RPTL 478 |
| INDUSTRIAL WASTE TREATMENT FACILITIES | RPTL 477 |

| Description of Property | Section of Law |
|---|---|
| *Partially Exempt* Limited Exemption (Public) | |
| STATE OWNED REFORESTATION | RPTL 534 |
| STATE OWNED LAND (TAXABLE FOR SCHOOL ONLY) | RPTL 536 |
| COUNTY TAX SALE | RPTL 406-5 |
| COUNTY TAX SALE | RPTL 406-5 |
| COUNTY OWNED OUTSIDE CORPORATE LIMITS | RPTL 406-3 |
| COUNTY OWNED OUTSIDE CORPORATE LIMITS | RPTL 406-3 |
| COUNTY OWNED OUTSIDE CORPORATE LIMITS | RPTL 406-3 |
| COUNTY OWNED OUTSIDE CORPORATE LIMITS | RPTL 406-3 |
| COUNTY OWNED OUTSIDE CORPORATE LIMITS | RPTL 406-3 |
| COUNTY OWNED OUTSIDE CORPORATE LIMITS | RPTL 406-3 |
| COUNTY OWNED OUTSIDE CORPORATE LIMITS | RPTL 406-3 |
| COUNTY OWNED REFORESTATION LAND | COUNTY LAW 219 |
| CITY TAX SALE | RPTL 406-5 |
| CITY TAX SALE | RPTL 406-5 |
| CITY OWNED OUTSIDE CORPORATE LIMITS | RPTL 406-3 |
| CITY OWNED OUTSIDE CORPORATE LIMITS | RPTL 406-3 |
| CITY OWNED OUTSIDE CORPORATE LIMITS | RPTL 406-3 |
| CITY OWNED OUTSIDE CORPORATE LIMITS | RPTL 406-3 |
| CITY OWNED OUTSIDE CORPORATE LIMITS | RPTL 406-3 |
| CITY OWNED OUTSIDE CORPORATE LIMITS | RPTL 406-3 |
| CITY OWNED OUTSIDE CORPORATE LIMITS | RPTL 406-3 |
| TOWN TAX SALE | RPTL 406-5 |
| TOWN OWNED OUTSIDE CORPORATE LIMITS | RPTL 406-3 |
| TOWN OWNED OUTSIDE CORPORATE LIMITS | RPTL 406-3 |
| TOWN OWNED OUTSIDE CORPORATE LIMITS | RPTL 406-3 |
| TOWN OWNED OUTSIDE CORPORATE LIMITS | RPTL 406-3 |
| TOWN OWNED OUTSIDE CORPORATE LIMITS | RPTL 406-3 |
| TOWN OWNED OUTSIDE CORPORATE LIMITS | RPTL 406-3 |
| TOWN OWNED OUTSIDE CORPORATE LIMITS | RPTL 406-3 |
| VILLAGE TAX SALE | RPTL 406-5 |
| VILLAGE OWNED OUTSIDE CORPORATE LIMITS | RPTL 406-3 |
| VILLAGE OWNED OUTSIDE CORPORATE LIMITS | RPTL 406-3 |

| Description of Property | Section of Law |
|---|---|
| *Partially Exempt* | |
| Limited Exemption (Public) | |
| VILLAGE OWNED OUTSIDE CORPORATE LIMITS | RPTL 406-3 |
| VILLAGE OWNED OUTSIDE CORPORATE LIMITS | RPTL 406-3 |
| VILLAGE OWNED OUTSIDE CORPORATE LIMITS | RPTL 406-3 |
| VILLAGE OWNED OUTSIDE CORPORATE LIMITS | RPTL 406-3 |
| VILLAGE OWNED OUTSIDE CORPORATE LIMITS | RPTL 406-3 |
| STATE AIDED HOUSING | PUB. HSG. L52-4 |
| MUNICIPAL LEASED PROJECT TO PRIVATE HOUSING COMPANY | PUB. HSG. L58 |
| UDC PROPERTY—LIMITED PROF. HSG. CO. SUBSIDIARIES | P.H.FI. L33-1-C |
| MUNY, LEASED PROJ. LTD. PROFIT HOUSING COMPANY | P.H.FI. L36-A-4 |
| UDC PROJECT—LIMITED DIVIDEND HOUSING COMPANY SUSID. | P.H.FI. L93-6 |
| PROPERTY OF URBAN REDEVELOPMENT CORPORATION | P.H.FI. L211 |
| UDC PROJ. HSG. DEVEL. FUND CO. SUBSID.—OTHER | P.H.FI. L577-3 |

116. Real Property Exemption Codes 2.
117. 1968 N.Y. Laws, ch. 172.
118. Real Property Exemption Codes 1.
119. 1968 N.Y. Law, Ch. 35a
120. Real Property Exemption Codes 3, 4 and 5.

# 5

# An Analysis of Charitable Purposes Qualifying for Real Property Tax Exemptions

Real property tax exemptions in New York are granted to property owned by corporate entities[1] organized or conducted exclusively for one or more of a number of enumerated purposes and used exclusively for one or more of such purposes. This chapter analyzes the law in New York on the meaning of the terms that designate the purposes for which exemptions are granted,[2] and examines the inherent difficulties of the constitutional and statutory scheme providing the exemptions, making their application uncertain and problematical. Within this critique, a restatement of the law of New York on the meaning of certain key terms is attempted based on an examination of cases interpreting them.

Law in New York regarding tax exemptions for property used for charitable and like purposes is confused. It rests on a statu-

1. Corporate entities include corporations, associations and trusts. Mohonk Trust v. Board of Assessors of Gardiner, 47 N.Y.2d 476, 482–483, 392 N.E. 2d 876, 879, 418 N.Y.S. 2d 763, 766 (1979).

2. In Chapter 2 a general description of the law on exemptions is provided covering various tests that have to be met to be recognized as tax exempt in addition to the "purposes" criterion discussed in this chapter. See generally Note, New York's Real Property Tax Exemptions For Religious, Educational, And Charitable Institutions: A Critical Examination, 44 Alb. L. Rev. 488 (1980).

tory scheme inherited from the nineteenth century that provides little illumination as to the meaning of its terms. Only adding to the confusion was the 1971 bifurcation mandating that property used for some purposes must be exempt while property used for other purposes may be exempt or taxable at the option of the local taxing district.[3] Interpretations by the courts have provided little clarity and there are some decisions that appear to be contradictory to one another. Compounding the confusion is a body of administrative law established by the State Board of Equalization and Assessment (SBEA) through a series of published opinions of counsel. These opinions are highly influential with local assessors who make the important initial determination of the exemption of an organization. In New York City, which contains well over half of all the exempt property in the state,[4] a powerful Tax Commission operates as a quasi-judicial body in initially determining exemption questions.

## *Background and Principal Issues*

In 1938 an amendment to the New York State Constitution was adopted authorizing the legislature to alter and repeal then existing exemptions to the property tax except for those exempting property used exclusively for religious, educational or charitable purposes as defined by law if such properties are owned by any nonprofit corporate entities organized or conducted exclusively for one or more such purposes.[5] The statute granting exemptions, which preexisted Article XVI by many

3. See note 66 and accompanying text, Chapter 2 supra.
4. See note 5 and accompanying text, Chapter 4 supra.
5. N.Y. Const. art. XVI § 1. This section provides in part:

> Exemptions from taxation may be granted only by general laws. Exemptions may be altered or repealed except those exempting real or personal property used exclusively for religious, educational or charitable purposes as defined by law and owned by any corporation or association organized or conducted exclusively for one or more of such purposes and not operating for profit.

years,[6] enumerated twenty purposes qualifying for exemption,[7] including the three purposes specified in Article XVI. No definition of any of these purposes was provided in the statute. As noted in Chapter 2 the nineteenth-century history of the statute's origins suggests that the reason for so many purposes being enumerated is the likelihood that the original drafters simply selected a number of the purposes that had theretofore received exemption through special bills, gave these purposes fairly general descriptive terms, and listed them in the statute.[8] The method used was one of extension or denotation, listing all the specific purposes to be exempt, rather than one of intention or connotation, which would attempt to provide a generalized definition to encompass the essential characteristics of all these purposes.

With so many enumerated purposes it is not surprising that many early cases would find particular activities as evincing several exempt purposes, e.g., charitable, moral or mental improvement of men and women, and patriotic.[9] Clear lines did not have to be drawn between the various purposes and in many cases the courts may have thought that some of the terms were included in the meaning of other terms. The situation

6. See text accompanying notes 5–6, Chapter 2 supra.

7. N.Y. Tax Law art. 4 § 6 (McKinney 1943) in effect at the time of the amendment, provided in part:

> 6. The real property of a corporation or association organized exclusively for the moral or mental improvement of men and women, or for religious, bible, tract, charitable, benevolent, missionary, hospital, infirmary, educational, public playground, scientific, literary, bar association, library, patriotic, historical or cemetery purposes, or for the enforcement of laws relating to children or animals, or for two or more such purposes, and used exclusively for carrying out thereupon one or more of such purposes.

8. This is not to assert that the nineteenth-century codifiers were indiscriminate in their collection. On the contrary, it appears they were faced with a very large number of exempt purposes, most of which had been granted through special bills or charters and that they probably selected from this large number those purposes which seemed particularly appropriate for exemption. Chapter 2 traces the history of the statute.

9. See, e.g., National Navy Club of New York v. City of New York, 122 Misc. 89, 203 N.Y.S. 114 (Sup. Ct. 1923).

changed decisively in 1971 when the legislature bifurcated[10] the twenty enumerated purposes so some became the basis of mandatory exemptions that municipalities must recognize (those enumerated in 421(1)(a) and hereinafter referred to as "paragraph (a) purposes") and some became the basis of exemptions that could be accorded at the municipalities' option (those presently enumerated in section 421(1)(b) and hereinafter referred to as "paragraph (b) purposes").[11] In the latter case the municipality by local law could remove the exemption theretofore provided to these (b) purposes. The distinction between paragraph (a) and paragraph (b) purposes is of critical importance for those jurisdictions having exercised the option. In such a jurisdiction, for example, if a particular activity is found to be covered by the purpose "religious," a paragraph (a) purpose, it would be exempt. On the other hand if it is found to be covered by the purpose "bible," a paragraph (b) purpose, it would not be exempt.[12]

Section 421(1)(a) enumerates the three purposes required to be be exempt under Article XVI § 1 of the Constitution and in addition lists "hospital," "moral or mental improvement of men, women or children" and "cemetery" purposes.[13] Apart from a further constitutional amendment, the religious, educational and charitable purposes cannot be altered or repealed by the legislature by, e.g., making any of these purposes (b) purposes. Consequently, the definition of these three terms is of singular importance.

There is some ambiguity about the meaning of the clause prescribing that exemptions for these purposes "as defined by

10. 1971 N.Y. Laws, ch. 414.

11. N.Y. Real Prop. Tax § 421 (McKinney 1972). See text accompanying notes 13–14, Chapter 2 supra.

12. See text accompanying notes 16–17 infra.

13. The purpose "moral or mental improvement of men, women or children" was originally included in paragraph (b). 1971 N.Y. Laws, ch. 414. The following year it was shifted to paragraph (a). 1972 N.Y. Laws, ch. 529. See text accompanying notes 150–153 infra.

law" cannot be altered or repealed. It might mean as defined by the legislature and interpreted by the courts as of the time of the amendment. Or it might mean that the legislature is empowered to refine or alter the definitions of these terms from time to time. The latter is the construction that the Court of Appeals appears to have had in mind when at the close of *Mohonk Trust v. Board of Assessors of Gardiner* it noted:[14]

> It is, of course, within the power of the Legislature to establish and modify tax exemptions, subject only to constitutional limitations. Thus, where the Legislature has chosen to create only limited exemptions for particular activities which might otherwise be deemed to fall within the somewhat broader absolute exemptions provided by section 421 (subd 1, par. [a]), those distinctions must be given full effect by the courts (see *Matter of American Bible Soc. v. Lewisohn,* 40 N.Y.2d 78; *Matter of Swedenborg Foundation v. Lewisohn,* 40 N.Y.2d 87).[15]

It might also simply refer to the courts' inherent power to define these terms as they came before them in litigated disputes. In any event it is clear that while the legislature may be authorized to define these terms, and perhaps to modify and refine these definitions, it cannot prescribe definitions that would alter the essential meanings these terms have for the Constitution, i.e., what the people of New York thought these terms to mean when Article XVI § 1 was approved.

As noted, however, the legislature has not defined these three terms (or any of the other terms for that matter)—except perhaps by enumerating along with them a number of other terms

14. 47 N.Y. 2d 476, 392 N.E. 2d 876, 418 N.Y.S. 2d 763 (1979).

15. Id. at 484–485, 392 N.E. 2d at 880, 418 N.Y.S.2d at 767–768. This may also have been the view of the Staff of the Temporary Commission on the Revision and Simplification of the Constitution when it opined that the clause "as defined by law" was added " so as to give the Legislature the power to clarify these terms which otherwise could be subjected to different interpretations." It appears from the debates on the amendment that the words "as defined by law" were added to in response to a suggestion "that the term probably should be more clearly defined." See N.Y.S. Constitutional Convention, 2 Revised Record (1938) (remarks of Mr. Saxe and Mr. Rennalt). This, of course, does not suggest who should do the defining.

which may suggest that the meaning of these "other" terms is not included within the meaning of the constitutional terms. For example, in *American Bible Society v. Lewisohn,*[16] the court held that the activities of the Society, consisting primarily of the distribution of the Bible by an organization not directly associated with an organized religious denomination, were conducted primarily for bible rather than religious purposes. The property involved was located in New York City, a municipality that had taken advantage of the 1971 legislation by withdrawing the exemption of organizations covered by paragraph (b). In discussing the legislation the court concluded that "it was intended to distinguish between 'religious' and 'bible' purposes and to expose the latter to taxation."[17] And in *Association of the Bar of New York v. Lewisohn,*[18] the court held under the same statute that the Explorers Club, which promoted geographic exploration and research in the earth sciences, was conducted primarily for "scientific" purposes under paragraph (b) rather than "educational" purposes under paragraph (a). The court noted that it is not "to be overlooked that for some years the Legislature has chosen to classify scientific organizations separately, obviously conceiving a distinction between an organization conducted primarily for scientific purposes and one conducted primarily for charitable and educational purposes, as those terms accord with common usage."[19] These decisions are understandable given the statutory scheme they were applying. Nonetheless the meaning of "educational" becomes uncertain when "scientific," "literary" and "library" purposes are removed from its reach. Similarly, the meaning of "religious"

16. 40 N.Y. 2d 78, 351 N.E. 2d 697, 386 N.Y.S. 2d 49 (1976).
17. Id. at 86, 351 N.E. 2d at 701, 386 N.Y.S. 2d at 53.
18. 34 N.Y. 2d 143, 313 N.E. 2d 30, 356 N.Y.S. 2d 555 (1974).
19. Id. at 155, 313 N.E. 2d at 36, 356 N.Y.S. 2d at 563. This case also found that the Bar Association of the City of New York was not organized primarily for charitable or educational purposes of paragraph (a) but rather primarily for bar association purposes of paragraph (b).

is strained when "bible," "tract" and "missionary" are put outside of its ambit.[20]

As suggested, the statutory scheme itself generates confusion. No definitions of terms are offered, and terms that would normally be conceived as including certain activities do not seem to as these activities are listed separately. As a consequence of the lengthy enumeration the terms in the law of charities may have come to have some special and narrow meaning for purposes of New York State real property exemptions.

It does not seem likely that a conscious legislative choice was made to give these terms special and narrow meanings. Indeed, it is very unlikely that the nineteenth-century codifiers of the statute sought to give the terms a special meaning substantially different from the meaning given to those terms under the law of charities, but unfortunately the method they chose to reach their aims, i.e., the long enumeration, serves as a basis for such a construction.

In the following analyses of the terms "charitable," "educational" and "religious" two objectives are sought to be

20. This kind of confusion was not new to the law of New York. In 1905 the legislature bifurcated the transfer tax exemption provisions to: a) exempt all property which was transferred to institutions organized for religious, educational, charitable, missionary, benevolent, hospital and infirmary purposes and to institutions organized exclusively for bible and tract purposes; and to b) exempt personal property other than money and securities transferred to organizations organized exclusively for the following purposes: moral or mental improvement of men and women, scientific, literary, library, patriotic, cemetery, historical and laws relating to children and animals. (1905 N.Y. Law 6, ch. 368). Prior to this split all these purposes had been listed together in a provision that did not provide an exemption to monetary transfers. To shield a monetary bequest to the YMCA from the transfer tax, the Appellate Division in 1910 held that the Y fell within the definition of educational. In In re Moses' Estate, 138 A.D. 525, 530, 123 N.Y.S. 443, 447 (2d Dept. 1910), it is recognized that:

> In a sense it is certainly a corporation for the moral improvement of men, that is, the objects of this corporation can be said, speaking to the result, the moral improvement of men. But so it can be said of a religious corporation, a missionary corporation, a Bible or a tract corporation.

The court found, however, that a monetary bequest to the Brooklyn Society for the Prevention of Cruelty to Children was not exempt.

achieved. First, to continue the critical examination of the constitutional and statutory scheme and second, to restate the law in New York with respect to the more important paragraph (a) purposes. In this last regard a brief examination will be made of the "moral or mental improvement" purpose. No consideration will be given to the more or less self-evident purposes "hospital" and "cemetery." No serious interpetative problems appear to have developed around these terms.[21]

### *Charitable*

"Charitable" has traditionally had a broad and embracing meaning in the law of charities. Its classic statement was given by Lord Macnaghten in *Commissioners for Special Purposes of Income Tax v. Pemsel,*[22] where he states:

> "Charity" in its legal sense comprises four principal divisions: trusts for the relief of poverty; trusts for the advancement of education; trusts for the advancement of religion; and trusts for other purposes beneficial to the community, not falling under any of the preceding heads.[23]

Bogert has said that this formulation has come to be "considered a restatement of the preamble to the Statute of Charitable Uses in modern terms."[24] The Restatement of Trusts (Second) definition of charitable purpose closely parallels Lord Macnaghten's formulation. Section 368 (What Purposes Are Charitable) provides:

21. No examination is made of paragraph (b) purposes. There is very little law interpreting these terms. They are pivotal only for jurisdictions that have not exercised the option to make them nonexempt purposes, and at least in terms of the case law, it has often been fairly self-evident as to whether a particular activity was within their ambit. In those jurisdictions that have exercised the option, as indicated above, they are defined in cases holding that a particular purpose is a paragraph (b) purpose rather than a paragraph (a) purpose. The leading cases of this type have been discussed.

22. (1891) A.C. 531.

23. Id. at 583.

24. G. Bogert, The Law of Trusts and Trustees § 369 at 64 (rev. 2d ed. 1977) [hereinafter cited as Bogert].

Charitable purposes include (a) the relief of poverty; (b) the advancement of education; (c) the advancement of religion; (d) the promotion of health; (e) governmental or municipal purposes; (f) other purposes the accomplishment of which is beneficial to the community.[25]

Finally it might be noted that the regulations under section 501(c)(3) of the Internal Revenue Code of 1954, as amended, which provides an exemption from federal income taxes to enterprises organized and operated exclusively for religious, charitable or educational (and certain other) purposes, define "charitable" as follows:

(2) *Charitable defined.* The term "charitable" is used in section 501(c)(3) in its generally accepted legal sense and is, therefore, not to be construed as limited by the separate enumeration in section 501(c)(3) of other tax-exempt purposes which may fall within the broad outlines of "charity" as developed by judicial decisions. Such a term includes: relief of the poor and distressed or of the underprivileged; advancement of religion; advancement of education or science; erection or maintenance of public buildings, monuments or works; lessening the burdens of government; and promotion of social welfare by organizations designed to accomplish any of the above purposes.[26]

"Charitable" under the formulations just mentioned is very much an embracive term even going as far as to encompass the two other Article XVI § 1 purposes, viz., "educational" and

25. Restatement (Second) of Trusts § 368 (1958).

26. Treas. Reg. § 1.501(c)(3)–1(d)(2)(1959). Bogert simply says: "A charitable trust may be briefly defined as one which is for the public benefit." Bogert, supra note 24, § 369 at 65. Scott states: "Certain purposes are clearly charitable. These include the relief of poverty, the promotion of education, the advancement of religion. So, too, it is well settled that the promotion of health is a charitable purpose. So are governmental or municipal purposes, such as the erection of public buildings, the laying out of highways, the erection of bridges, and the like. In addition to these purposes there must be added a more general and indefinite category, a general catch-all, to include the vast number of miscellaneous purposes which are held to be charitable. Perhaps these can best be included under the heading of other purposes, the accomplishment of which is beneficial to the community. This category is, indeed, broad enough to cover all charitable purposes, including those more specifically enumerated above." A. Scott, 4 The Law of Trusts § 368, at 2853 (3d ed. 1967).

"religious." For what follows it is important to note that "purposes beneficial to the community" is a key concept in these definitions of the term "charitable." Indeed the Restatement of Trusts (Second) identifies the promotion of the public welfare as the central notion underlying the concept of "charitable."[27] There are sound policy reasons for giving the term "charitable" a broad and flexible meaning. New charitable purposes emerge in response to new societal problems. By keeping the term broad recognition can be given to these new purposes.

Under section 421[28] of the New York statute the term "charitable" is listed alongside a number of purposes, which would almost certainly be included within the meaning of "charitable" as used in other contexts, including (from paragraph (a)) the purposes "hospital," "moral or mental improvement of men, women or children," "cemetery" (and from paragraph (b)), "benevolent," "infirmary," "public playground," "medical society," "patriotic" and "for the enforcement of law relating to children or animals."[29] As suggested, the removal of these purposes from the purpose "charitable" might be construed as giving the term "charitable" for purposes of section 421 a special meaning unattached to the generally accepted meaning that has developed over the years in the common law of trusts or, for example, that has evolved in resolving questions about

27. In Comment a after section 368 (What Purposes Are Charitable), the reporter notes that "the general scope of charitable purposes is that they are designed to accomplish objectives which are beneficial to the community." Comment b (The Nature of Charitable Purposes) begins: "A purpose is charitable if its accomplishment is of such social interest to the community as to justify permitting the property to be devoted to the purpose in perpetuity." Restatement (Second) of Trusts § 368, Comments a and b (1959).

28. N.Y. Real Prop. Tax § 421 (McKinney 1972).

29. The statutory scheme is further confused by the coverage under separate sections of certain types of organizations that would normally be considered charitable or educational, e.g., opera houses (section 426), performing arts buildings (section 427), interdenominational centers (section 430), academies of music (section 434). See N.Y. Real Prop. Tax §§ 426, 427, 430 & 434 (McKinney 1972) and Chapter 2. There are special conditions to some of these provisions making some of them appear to be the special bills.

exemptions under federal income, estate and gift taxes. That such a departure might have been considered is suggested by *Association of the Bar of New York v. Lewisohn,*[30] where the Court of Appeals noted that although the Bar Association and the Explorers Club conferred a public benefit, public benefit is not the test of qualification for exemption.

> To be sure, the Association confers a public benefit, and a great one, through its laudable activities in the screening of judicial candidates, rooting out the unauthorized practice of law, processing of grievances against lawyers, and timely commenting on issues of broad public concern, to name but a few. But public benefit is not the test of qualification for exemption, as the legislative history of section 421, discussed hereinafter, makes so abundantly clear.[31]

The legislative history referred to was the 1970 Report of the Joint Legislative Committee to Study and Investigate Real Property Tax Exemptions,[32] which predicted that were exemptions to continue at the then current rate by 1985 one-half of all real property would be exempt. The Court noted that:

> Against this background, the Legislature enacted chapter 414 of the Laws of 1971. Its purpose was clear—to stem the erosion of municipal tax bases by permitting local governments to terminate exemptions for nonprofit organizations other than those conducted exclusively for religious, educational, charitable, hospital or cemetery purposes.[33]

And yet as noted above "public benefit" is at the center of the traditional definition of charitable purpose. Shortly after the *Association of the Bar* decision, this point was picked up by Justice Ventiera in holding that the Bedford-Stuyvesant Restoration Corporation (BSRC) was not exempt from the property

30. 34 N.Y. 2d 143, 313 N.E. 2d 30, 356 N.Y.S. 2d 555 (1974).
31. Id. at 154, 313 N.E. 2d at 35, 356 N.Y.S. 2d at 562.
32. Final Report of the Joint Legislative Committee to Study and Investigate Real Property Tax Exemptions, N.Y. Leg. Doc. No. 15 (1970).
33. 34 N.Y.2d 143, 155–156, 313 N.E. 2d 30, 36, 356 N.Y.S. 2d 555, 563–564 (1974).

tax as an organization devoted to charitable purposes.[34] BSRC had been formed and operated to restore and rehabilitate certain sections of Brooklyn that had deteriorated to a very great degree. And in 1976 the Court of Appeals reaffirmed its position in *Swedenborg Foundation, Inc. v. Lewisohn:*[35] "Again we say that 'public benefit is not the test of qualification for exemption.' "[36] Citing *Association of the Bar,* Counsel for the SBEA has also rested on this proposition in ruling that real property belonging to a Little League organization is not entitled to exemption pursuant to section 421 because a public benefit purpose is not the test for qualification of exemption.[37] In this ruling Counsel concluded that pre-*Association of the Bar* "cases suggesting that organizations devoted to generally good or beneficial purposes are entitled to exemption under section 421 have little or no relevance to current questions of exempt status."[38] Most recently, a trial court upheld the New York City Tax Commission denial of an application for exemption from the real property tax made by the Symphony Space, Inc., an organization formed to make possible musical, theatrical and dance performances and related educational activities on a nonprofit basis. After noting that prior case law had "developed a flexible definition" of the term "charitable," the court concluded, "Notwithstanding here public benefit is not the test of exemption (*Association of the Bar v. Lewisohn,* 37 N.Y. 2d 173 at 155)."[39]

The rejection of the public benefit test may have been prompted by the 1971 bifurcation since many, if not all, of the

34. Bedford-Stuyvesant Restoration Corp. v. Lewisohn, 172 N.Y.L.J., August 1, 1974, at 11, col. 2 (Sup. Ct. July 31, 1974), aff'd mem., 50 A.D. 2d 815, 376 N.Y.S. 2d 912 (2d Dept. 1975). See note 75 infra.

35. 40 N.Y. 2d 87, 351 N.E. 2d 702, 386 N.Y.S. 2d 54 (1976).

36. Id. at 95, 351 N.E. 2d at 707, 386 N.Y.S. 2d at 59.

37. 6 Op.Counsel SBEA No. 17 (1977). In an earlier ruling involving a civic air patrol group the same point was made. 3 Op. Counsel SBEA No. 115 (1974).

38. 6 Op. Counsel SBEA No. 17 (1977).

39. The Symphony Space, Inc. v. Tishelman, 185 N.Y.L.J., March 4, 1981, at 12, col. 2 (Sup. Ct. February 20, 1981). See note 81 infra.

purposes listed in paragraph (b), e.g., "benevolent," "infirmary," "public playground," "library," etc., surely confer a public benefit. Nevertheless, as noted this result sharply opposes what many courts and informed observers have taken to be a principle element of the concept of "charitable," viz., the promotion of the general welfare.[40] Indeed two early New York Court of Appeals cases clearly regard public benefit as an important part of the concept of "charitable." In *In re MacDowell's Will,*[41] the Court in dealing with the question of the definition of "charitable," for purposes of charitable trust law, noted that: "Many definitions of a charitable trust have been formulated, but all definitions that have been attempted carry the implication of public utility in its *purpose.*"[42] *Untermeyer v. McGregor,*[43] holding land exempt under the predecessor of section 421, which land was devoted to use as a public park and garden, found that such "public" purposes were charitable. *MacDowell* is probably the lead case defining the term "charitable" in New York. It is a charitable trust case and not a real property tax exemption case and as such may have limited precedential value for property tax cases. It has, however, been cited in a number of property tax and transfer tax cases.[44] Moreover a clear distinction has never been drawn between charita-

40. The Supreme Court in Ould v. Washington Hospital for Foundlings, 95 U.S. 303, 311, (1877) stated that, "A charitable use, where neither law nor public policy forbids, may be applied to almost anything that tends to promote the well-doing and well-being of social man." (citation omitted).

41. 217 N.Y. 454, 112 N.E. 177 (1916).

42. Id. at 460, 112 N.E. at 178 (citations omitted). The court then continues with its oft-quoted definition: "If the purpose to be attained is personal, private, or selfish, it is not a charitable trust. When the purpose accomplished is that of public usefulness unstained by personal, private, or selfish considerations, its charitable character insures its validity." Id.

43. 295 N.Y. 237, 66 N.E. 2d 292 (1946).

44. See Church Home of the Protestant Episcopal Church in the City of Rochester v. Wagner, 58 A.D. 2d 972, 974, 397 N.Y.S. 2d 478, 479–480 (4th Dept. 1977), In re Rockefellers Estate, 177 A.D. 786, 791, 165 N.Y.S. 154, 158 (1st Dept. 1917), American-Russian Aid Association, Inc. v. City of Glen Cove, 41 Misc. 2d 622, 626, 246 N.Y.S. 2d 123, 127 (Sup. Ct. 1964), aff'd, 23 A.D. 2d 966, 260 N.Y.S. 2d 589 (2d Dept. 1965).

ble trust and tax cases; interpretations made under one type of case are frequently used in the other type. Indeed, as shown above, for federal income tax purposes the definition of "charitable" is established by reference to "its generally accepted legal sense" which has been construed to mean the law of charitable trusts.[45] Section 421 itself contains a suggestion that "charitable" should be construed broadly and may be used to cover many of the more particular purposes. Paragraph (d) of subdivision 1, which eliminates the exemption of real property otherwise exempt under paragraphs (a) and (b) if anyone receives pecuniary profit from the operations of such real property, except payments made in "reasonable compensation for services in effecting one or more of such purposes [presumably referring to the purposes enumerated in paragraphs (a) and (b)], or as proper beneficiaries of *its strictly charitable purposes.*" (emphasis supplied).

If the statutory scheme from its inception has caused confusion, the 1971 legislation bifurcating section 421 made matters worse.[46] It resulted in some narrow interpretations of terms that traditionally have been broadly defined. These interpretations appear to have been largely motivated by concern over tax base erosion, a concern articulated in the legislative findings of the 1971 enactment. These findings in turn were based upon the Final Report of the Joint Legislative Committee to Study and Investigate Real Property Tax Exemptions.[47] As shown in Chapter 4, however, the data upon which this report based its conclusions bear little, if any, pertinence to the charitable exemption. To the extent that tax base erosion attributable to exemptions is correctly identified by the report, the problem lies with exemptions granted to property held by the government, especially in New York City, and not to exemptions

45. Rev. Rul. 67–325, 1967-2 C.B.113 and Rev. Rul. 71–447, 1971– 2 C.B230. See also text accompanying note 26 supra.
46. 1971 N.Y. Law, ch. 414.
47. See note 32 and accompanying text supra.

granted to property held for charitable uses.[48] In sum, a significant narrowing of the scope of charitable purposes under the statutory and constitutional scheme for exemption from property taxes resulted in response to a perceived problem that if read and correctly analyzed suggest solutions having virtually nothing to do with charitable exemptions. This narrowing of the meaning of charitable purposes has been unfortunate since it undercuts important policy reasons for keeping the concept broad and flexible. As society evolves, new problems arise to which new charitable solutions develop in response. A broad interpretation of "charitable purposes" permits recognition of these new solutions. On the other hand, a narrow view of the meaning of "charitable" seriously obstructs the possibility of a dynamic response to emerging problems.

Recently, however, it appears that the Court of Appeals has retreated from its apparent extrusion in *Association of the Bar* of public benefit as a criterion for exemption.[49] In *Mohonk Trust v. Board of Assessors of Gardiner,*[50] the Court held exempt 5,000 acres of undeveloped wilderness devoted to environmental purposes. In considering the property the Court stated: "We conclude that it is . . . used primarily for an assortment of 'charitable . . . educational, [and] moral improvement of men, women or children' purposes, for we see no reason why these categories should not encompass lands used for environmental and conservation purposes which are necessary to the public good."[51]

48. See notes 27–36 and accompanying text, Chapter 4 supra. Furthermore, the data used is of questionable value and the most alarmist finding appears to have been made on the basis of a mathematical error.

49. See text accompanying note 31 supra.

50. 47 N.Y. 2d 476, 392 N.E. 2d 876, 418 N.Y.S. 2d 763 (1979).

51. Id. at 484, 392 N.E. 2d at 880, 418 N.Y.S. 2d at 767 (citation omitted). Public benefit was again recognized by the court in North Manursing Wildlife Sanctuary, Inc. v. City of Rye, 48 N.Y. 2d 135, 140, 397 N.E. 2d 693, 695, 422 N.Y.S. 2d 1,3 (1979), holding that land held for the purpose of providing a sanctuary for wild birds constituted an exempt purpose under paragraph (a). "For property to be entitled to an exemption on the ground that it is be-

It would appear then that the Court has worked itself back to a more tenable position in its interpretation of the term "charitable" in section 421 by including the criterion of "public benefit" as central to a finding that a particular purpose is charitable. Perhaps the only effect of the specific removal from paragraph (a) of the purposes listed in paragraph (b), which might otherwise be included within the term "charitable," is to remove these fairly discrete purposes from its coverage.[52] This is quite a different general interpretation of section 421 than one which, as suggested above, would hold that the 1971 bifurcation operated to substantially change the traditional meaning of the term "charitable" by narrowing its ambit in some quite unspecified way. This latter way of viewing the statute may have been moved toward in *Association of the Bar* with its rejection of the public benefit criterion, but *Mohonk* and *North Manursing Wildlife Sanctuary Inc. v. City of Rye*[53] suggest an approach more consistent with viewing charitable purposes as broad in their coverage and definable within the mainstream of their development under various laws in various jurisdictions. It may be that the 1971 bifurcation will ultimately facilitate the clear adoption of this latter approach since prior to that time all of the purposes, both those of paragraph (a) and paragraph (b), were considered uniformly.[54]

---

ing used for a charitable purpose, it must a fortiori be used for a public purpose."

52. This conclusion fits easily enough with all the terms enumerated in paragraph (b) with the possible exception of the term "benevolent." Indeed, for some purposes "benevolent" has been interpreted to be broader than "charitable." In re Altman's Estate, 87 Misc. 255, 149 N.Y.S. 601 (Sur. Ct. 1914); In re Watkin's Estate, 118 Misc. 645, 194 N.Y.S. 342 (Sur. Ct. 1922). There is hardly any current law on the meaning of the term "benevolence." 4 Op. Counsel SBEA No. 95 (1975) quotes from a North Carolina case that benevolence is " 'the doing of a kind, helpful action toward another under no obligation except an ethical one' (State v. Dunn, 134 N.C. 663, 46 S.E. 949)."

53. 48 N.Y. 2d 135, 397 N.E. 2d 693, 422 N.Y.S. 2d 1 (1979).

54. It would be a nice irony if an amendment originating in a pragmatic concern involving a fear of tax base erosion ended up supporting a more principled and coherent treatment of the exemption problem. This point is suggested in an early transfer tax case, In re Moses' Estate, 138 A.D. 525, 123 N.Y.S. 443

In any event, the confusion resulting from lengthy enumeration as the basis for the property tax charitable exemption system could easily be cured by reducing the number of terms defining charitable purposes to the few that have been traditionally used in the law of charities (if not to the single current "charitable"), and by giving to these few terms the broad and flexible interpretation that the law of charities has traditionally accorded to them. Such a change would make possible the evolution of a charitable system able to respond dynamically to societal changes with no added threat of tax base erosion.

There follows an examination of some further New York decisions construing the term "charitable," a large number of which have involved residential facilities or facilities used for people coming together. Of two recent appellate division cases, one found the activity at issue exempt as serving a charitable purpose, while the other ruled against exemption.

In *Church Home of the Protestant Episcopal Church in the City of Rochester v. Wagner,*[55] a home that provided nursing care for people residing in the vicinity of Rochester was held to be exempt. Residents were admitted regardless of their ability to pay. The home operated at substantial losses and received subsidies by way of private contributions from churches and individuals. The Court, citing *MacDowell,*[56] found that "the

(2d Dept. 1910), classifying a bequest after section 221 had been bifurcated. See note 20 supra. There, in disclosing the intent of the legislature in making the split, (the opinion writer) Judge Jenks noted: "I think it may be said that the objects and purposes of religious, educational, missionary, benevolent, hospital, infirmary, bible or tract corporations are more closely articulated with the functions of government for the amelioration of society . . . than are scientific, literary, library, paternal, cemetery, historical or moral and mental improvement of men and women. Praiseworthy as are the objects of the latter class, such corporations would not devote money or securities as directly to the benefit of people as would the organizations enumerated in the exemption." Id. at 528, 123 N.Y.S. at 446.

55. 58 A.D. 2d 972, 397 N.Y.S. 2d 478 (4th Dept. 1977).

56. In re MacDowell's Will, 217 N.Y. 454, 112 N.E. 177 (1916). MacDowell was a will construction case. The question at issue was whether a trust to operate a home for gentlewomen of limited means was a charitable trust and so immune from the rule against perpetuities. The court held that the trust was

rendering of health and nursing services to persons in genuine need of such care on a nonprofit basis"[57] was a charitable purpose. *Presbyterian Residence Center Corporation v. Wagner*[58] involved an apartment complex that leased to those over 62 years of age. The buildings were intended to be self-sustaining but not profit-making. The Court found that it was "indistinguishable from a commercial apartment complex having appurtenant recreational facilities except that it houses elderly tenants, is designed and constructed with safety features and amenities appropriate to their age and involves a health facility as an integral part of the complex."[59] It held that the center was not exempt as a charitable organization, noting that: "The purposes for which petitioner is organized are indistinguishable from the purposes of commercial real estate corporations generally, with the one exception that petioner's complex is intended to serve elderly persons . . . [but the] . . . operation of a housing project for the elderly does not, per se, qualify the property as an exempt charitable use."[60] While the point was not made explicit it appears that a significant fact in this case was that the residents of the complex were not penurious. Admission fees ranging from $8,500 to $33,500 were charged and tenants were required to pay rental fees from between $495 and $730 a month.[61]

Property used as a large recreational facility was denied exemption in *Valeria Home, Inc. v. Cook.*[62] While the home ope-

---

charitable and in the course of the opinion noted that public utility was inherent in all definitions of charity. See text accompanying note 41 supra.

57. 58 A.D. 2d 972, 974, 397 N.Y.S. 2d 478, 486 (4th Dept. 1977).

58. 66 A.D. 2d 998, 411 N.Y.S. 2d 765 (4th Dept. 1978), aff'd mem., 48 N.Y. 2d 885, 400 N.E. 2d 1348, 424 N.Y.S. 2d 896 (1979).

59. Id. at 999, 411 N.Y.S. 2d at 766–767.

60. Id. at 999, 411 N.Y.S. 2d at 767 (citations omitted).

61. Although the certificate of incorporation of the corporation owning the complex called for the creation of an endowment to subsidize tenants unable to pay standard fees, at the time of the decision no fund had yet been settled. Id. at 998, 411 N.Y.S.2d at 766.

62. 22 N.Y. 2d 388, 239 N.E. 2d 631, 292 N.Y.S. 2d 882 (1968).

rated at a loss, the owning corporation earned a considerable profit through its investments; and while the will establishing the home contemplated that it would be run as a convalescent home, it was in fact operated as a recreation center offering golf, tennis, hiking, boating and indoor recreational and social facilities to its users. No one in ill health was ever admitted to it. That the home was used in a manner contrary to that called for by the will was significant in the Court's decision but it noted as well that "the manner in which the home is run would not bring it within the generally understood definition of a charitable and benevolent institution."[63] In *Good Will Club of Amsterdam v. City of Amsterdam,*[64] a facility used as a club was held not to be exempt as a charitable organization even though it awarded a few very small scholarships each year.[65]

In sum, organizations providing residential and health services to persons unable to afford such services have been found to be charitable and accordingly exempt, while those organizations providing either residential opportunities to the nonpenurious or services of a nature that might be characterized as nonessential, such as recreation or opportunities for fellowship to a relatively limited class (which appeared also to include the nonpenurious), were found not to be charitable and accordingly subject to tax. The former, charitable category furnished a public good benefiting all of society in the sense that, for

63. Id. at 393, 239 N.E. 2d at 634, 292 N.Y.S. 2d at 886 (citation omitted).
64. 31 Misc. 2d 1096, 222 N.Y.S. 2d 896 (Sup. Ct. 1961).
65. See also Great Neck Section National Council of Jewish Women v. Board of Assessors of Nassau, 21 Misc. 2d 142, 189 N.Y.S. 2d 623 (Sup. Ct. 1959), where the court found that, although the organization in question provided a number of beneficial services, its essential purpose was to promote fellowship among American Jewish women; and Mount Tremper Lutheran Camp v. Board of Assessors of Shandaken, 70 A.D. 2d 984, 417 N.Y.S. 2d 796 (3d Dept. 1979), holding that the organization and operation of summer camps for recreative purposes was not an exempt purpose. See also 4 Op. Counsel SBEA 42 (1979), holding that a fraternal lodge is not exempt, and 1 Op. Counsel SBEA 61 (1972), holding that a community center used primarily for social and recreational purposes is not exempt.

example, providing residential or nursing facilities to the poor relieves society of a burden it would otherwise be forced to undertake.

Few additional New York laws exist to help give a sense of what "charitable" means for section 421. An early case held a grant-making philanthropy to be charitable.[66] As noted *Mohonk Trust v. Board of Assessors of Gardiner*[67] held that lands used for environmental and conservation purposes are covered by the terms "charitable," "educational" and "moral or mental improvement." Finally a free voluntary ambulance service has been held to be charitable.[68] Coming down against a finding of charitableness are *Chamber of Commerce of New York v. Mills* [69] and *Bedford-Stuyvesant Restoration Corp. v. Lewisohn.*[70] *Chamber of Commerce* involved property used to promote commerce. The court held that while the aims of the Chamber of Commerce were worthy such worthy actions and aims did not bring it within the provisions of the exemption statute, citing *Medical Society of Kings County v. Neff.*[71] *The Medical Society* case involved the Medical Society of the County of Kings formed for the purpose of regulating the practice of physic and surgery in New York and for mental improvement and certain educational and charitable purposes. The court denied the exemption noting that the society "is, in effect, a medical club house"[72] founded for the promotion of the individual development of its members as much as for the benefit of the

66. In re Rockefeller's Estate, 177 A.D. 786, 165 N.Y.S. 154 (1st Dept. 1917), aff'd mem., 223 N.Y. 564 (1918).

67. 47 N.Y. 2d 476, 392 N.E. 2d 876, 418 N.Y.S. 2d 763 (1979).

68. Wantagh-Levittown Community Ambulance Corps. v. Board of Assessors of Nassau, 56 Misc. 2d 545, 289 N.Y.S. 2d 330 (Sup. Ct. 1968) and 3 Op. Counsel SBEA No. 111 (1974).

69. 188 Misc. 593, 65 N.Y.S. 2d 231 (Sup. Ct. 1946).

70. 172 N.Y.L.J., Aug. 1, 1974, at 11, col. 2 (Sup. Ct. July 31, 1974), aff'd mem., 50 A.D. 2d 815, 376 N.Y.S. 2d 912 (2d Dept. 1975).

71. 34 A.D. 83, 53 N.Y.S. 1077 (2d Dept. 1898).

72. Id. at 89, 53 N.Y.S. at 1081.

public at large. In this connection the Court of Appeals in *Association of the Bar v. Lewisohn,*[73] holding that the association was not entitled to an exemption under section 421(a) noted that the association was not organized and conducted primarily for charitable or educational purposes. "It is an association of professionals organized for traditional Bar Association purposes and primarily concerned with the professional interests of its members. While it has functions and attributes properly characterizable as educational and . . . as charitable, these are incidental and peripheral only."[74]

At issue in the *Bedford-Stuyvesant* case was an organization designed to restore a blighted neighborhood. In denying the exemption the court found that the taxpayers' primary purpose was "the restoration and rehabilitation of housing for all persons in these areas, whether indigent or not, and that the alleviation of poverty is, at best, an incidental offshoot of such restoration and rehabilitation."[75] Such purpose was held not to be charitable.

These cases also suggest that a critical element for a finding of charitableness is an activity's provision of a broad public good rather than a good that benefits a relatively small segment of society comprised of those who are not in need of special help.

### *Educational*

The law interpreting the meaning of "educational purposes" is towered over by the 1976 Court of Appeals decision *Swedenborg Foundation, Inc. v. Lewisohn.*[76] The Swedenborg Foundation was a nonprofit corporation whose activities were aimed at

73. 34 N.Y. 2d 143, 313 N.E. 2d 30, 356 N.Y.S. 2d 555 (1974).
74. Id. at 153, 313 N.E. 2d at 35, 356 N.Y.S. 2d at 562.
75. Bedford-Stuyvesant Restoration Corp. v. Lewisohn, 172 N.Y.L.J., August 1, 1974, at 11, col. 2 at col. 5 (Sup. Ct. July 31, 1974), aff'd mem., 50 A.D. 2d 815, 316 N.Y.S. 2d 912 (2d Dept. 1975).
76. 40 N.Y. 2d 87, 351 N.E. 2d 702, 386 N.Y.S. 2d 54 (1976).

disseminating as widely as possible the writings of the Swedish philosopher Emanuel Swedenborg. Publications were sold at or below cost or given away. In holding that the foundation was not organized and conducted exclusively for educational purposes, the court stated:

We think education, at least within the contemplation of subdivision 1 of section 421, refers to the development of faculties and powers and the expansion of knowledge by teaching, instruction or schooling. We distinguish the very much broader process of the communication of facts and ideas. . . . It cannot be said that the foundation is itself directly affiliated with any recognized educational institution nor does any significant portion of its activities form part of an organized instructional program . . . significant are the facts that the foundation was not chartered by the Board of Regents and it is not classified as an educational institution by the Department of Education.[77]

This case may have suggested for some the rule that for an activity to be educational it must involve formal schooling. This appears to have been the interpretation of the Counsel for the SBEA: "Thus it has been held that educational organizations, to be exempt as such, must maintain a curriculum, schedule of classes, and a roster of qualified instructors, and an otherwise somewhat formalized system of instruction."[78] SBEA opinions

77. Id. at 94–95, 351 N.E. 2d at 706, 386 N.Y.S. 2d at 58.

78. 4 Op. Counsel SBEA No. 45, 75 (1975); 4 Op. Counsel SBEA No. 105, 194 (1975) and 3 Op. Counsel SBEA No. 115, 177 (1974). The formulation continues: "Without such restrictions the exemption might become available to an infinite number of organizations or organized pressure groups which the Legislature never intended to exempt." Id. The emphasis on formal education may have its roots in In re De Peyster's Estate, 210 N.Y. 216, 104 N.E. 714 (1914). This was a transfer tax case deciding whether the New York Historical Society was "educational" for purposes of that part of section 221 prescribing an exemption for any property transferred to institutions organized for such purposes or whether it was "scientific, literary, library, patriotic or historical" for that part of section 221 defining the exemption to transfers of money and securities to institutions organized for such purposes. In holding that the bequest in question was not exempt the court noted: "A corporation or association organized for scientific, literary, library, patriotic or historical purposes . . . is necessarily to some extent educational in its nature. . . . The legislature in including educational corporations in the first part of the statute . . . intended corporations

of counsel also frequently demand that an organization claiming exemption as educational must be properly registered with the Commission of Education or chartered by the Board of Regents.[79] The recent trial court decision mentioned above,[80] upholding the denial of a real property tax exemption to the Symphony Space, Inc., which used an old movie house on the Upper West Side of New York City to offer various cultural (music, dance, theater) performances on a nonprofit basis, seems to rest on a similar view in finding that the uses were not primarily educational.[81]

*Swedenborg* can be limited to its facts so that all that is surely removed from the meaning of "educational" is the dissemination of writings alone. The mere communication of facts and ideas is suggestive of activities designed to influence opinion for political and similar purposes, a type of action which has been sharply set off from educational under many exemption statutes.[82] Nevertheless, there remains the clear implication that for a purpose to be educational the education involved must be accomplished "by teaching, instruction and schooling." Some of the problems with this limitation of the notion of education are brought out in *Trustees of Columbia University v. Orange-*

---

engaged in something more than incidental education which necessarily derived from corporations organized for scientific, literary, library, patriotic or historical purposes." Id. at 221, 104 N.E. at 715.

79. 4 Op. Counsel SBEA No. 45, 75 (1975); 4 Op. Counsel SBEA No. 105, 194 (1975).

80. See note 39 and accompanying text supra.

81. The Symphony Space, Inc. v. Tishelman, 185 N.Y.J.L., March 4, 1981, at 12, col. 2 (Sup. Ct. February 20, 1981).

82. For example, for federal income tax purposes the Treasury Regulations in defining the term "educational" under section 501(c)(3) of the Internal Revenue Code state that: "An organization may be educational even though it advocates a particular position or viewpoint so long as it presents a sufficiently full and fair exposition of the pertinent facts as to permit an individual or the public to form an independent opinion or conclusion." Treas. Reg. §1.501(c)(3)-1(d)(3)(i)(b) (1959). This provision is clearly aimed at indicating how far an educational organization can go before it runs afoul of the statute's rules about influencing legislation.

*town,*[83] involving Columbia's Lamont-Dougherty Geological Observatory. Orangetown had argued that the observatory was organized for scientific purposes under paragraph (b) of section 421 rather than for educational purposes under paragraph (a).[84] It would have been very odd, indeed, to have found that the observatory was not educational since it was a part of a major, degree-awarding university. Nevertheless it is also clear from the opinion that the observatory is essentially an organization engaged in scientific research. In the course of its opinion the court noted: "that basic scientific research is an inherent part of the learning process, essential for the fulfillment of the educational mission of the research university. . . . Education, as that term is used in the statute, necessarily requires that the corporation commit itself to two fundamental educational responsibilities. One is the communication of existing knowledge to the next generation through the teaching of students and the other is the development of new knowledge through research and scholarship."[85] And, "the University is not limited solely to pedagogy. In order to carry out its function and purpose, to expand and transmit the knowledge of man, the university encourages scientific investigation and experimentation and these are an integral part of the overall university educational function."[86]

The status of museums, art galleries, "unpopular" theater, dance and music organizations is perhaps the most significant question raised by restricting the concept of education to teaching, instruction, or schooling. Early, pre-*Swedenborg* New York law suggests that such organizations should be exempt. In *In re*

83. 93 Misc.2d 261, 402 N.Y.S.2d 899 (Sup. Ct., 1976), aff'd, 60 A.D.2d 582, 399 N.Y.S.2d 708 (2d Dept. 1977).

84. As a technical matter, the court found the local law attempting to take advantage of the 1971 bifurcation defective but nevertheless addressed the substantive issue of whether or not the observatory was covered by the term "educational."

85. Id. at 265, 402 N.Y.S. 2d at 903.

86. Id. at 266, 402 N.Y.S. 2d at 903.

*Mergentime*[87] the objectives of the Metropolitan Museum of Art were held to be educational for purposes of the transfer tax. In the course of the opinion the author stated:

I do not suppose that it is essential to constitute an educational corporation that there should be furnished a regular corps of teachers, with regular classes of students. A corporation which is organized for the purpose of supplying instruction to those who are willing to accept the facilities or opportunities supplied, it seems to me, is organized for an educational purpose.[88]

*In re Arnot*[89] held that a bequest to an art gallery was exempt since the gallery was devoted to educational purposes. The court found that the testator

had a well-defined scheme in mind to benefit, improve, and educate the citizens of his native city by directing their attention to works of art, and giving them an opportunity for forming and cultivating such a taste. . . . Certainly a study by any person or persons with a love for art and a desire to create such a love of the pictures alone bequeathed by this testator could not but be an education.[90]

These cases suggest a much broader conception of education than one that is limited to teaching, instruction and schooling and one that is more in line with the interpretation of "educational" made for other purposes as, for example, exemption from federal income taxes and for trust law purposes.[91] One of

87. 129 A.D. 367, 113 N.Y.S. 948 (1st Dept. 1908), aff'd mem., 195 N.Y. 572, 88 N.E. 1125 (1909).

88. Id. at 371–372, 113 N.Y.S. at 951.

89. 145 A.D. 708, 130 N.Y.S. 499 (3d Dept. 1911).

90. Id. at 716–717, 130 N.Y.S. at 504.

91. The Treasury Regulations define the term "educational" in part as "the instruction and training of the individual for the purpose of improving or developing his capacities." Treas. Reg. §1.501(c)(3)—1(d)(3)(i)(a) (1959). That such instruction does not have to occur in the context of formal schooling is made clear by one of the examples given under the definition, viz., "Museums, zoos, planetariums, symphony orchestras, and other similar organizations." Treas. Reg. §1.501(c)(3)—1(d)(3)(ii) Example (4)(1959). The Restatement of Trusts (Second) simply states: "A trust for the advancement of education is charitable." Restatement (Second) of Trusts §370 (1959). The broad nature

the broadest definitions of "education" was given in *In re Wolfe,*[92] interpreting a will provision that established a trust for the education of testator's brother in order to determine the duration of the trust. The court found education to culminate in Newman's illative sense: an awareness of the interrelatedness of all experience and the development of a special power of discernment enabling one "to distinguish the true from the false in cases where a plausible argument may be made as well for wrong as for right."[93] "To reach this goal there is needed more than schooling; which is a principal reason for declining to identify school and education."[94]

In a property tax exemption case[95] the property of a nonprofit community theater was held to be exempt under the educational and moral and mental improvement categories. In addressing the argument that the theater's purposes were not "educational" the court stated:

> While it is true that strictly speaking the actual performance of the play after weeks of rehearsal may not in and of itself fulfill all of the corporate purposes of the petitioner and probably redounds to the amusement and pleasure of the audience, it also serves as a vehicle for concentrated training and education in the art of dramatics and stage management to those participating therein. The play itself is the culmination of all of the work and effort comprising the educational program of the petitioner and must be construed as a part and parcel thereof just as a high school valedictory address is the reward for the

---

intended for the term "education" is suggested in Comment *a.* Methods of Advancing Education: "Trusts for the promotion of education include trusts to establish or maintain schools, colleges or other educational institutions; . . . to establish or maintain public libraries, art museums or other museums; to promote the advancement of knowledge by research; to promote the dissemination of knowledge or of beliefs by the publication of books and pamphlets or the delivery of lectures." Restatement (Second) of Trusts §370, Comment a (1959).

92. 164 Misc. 504, 299 N.Y.S. 99 (Sur. Ct. 1937).

93. Id. at 506, 299 N.Y.S. at 101.

94. Id.

95. Little Theatre of Watertown Inc. v. Hoyt, 7 Misc. 2d 907, 165 N.Y.S. 2d 292 (Sup. Ct. 1956).

successful culmination of four years of academic study and education rather than a part of the educational curriculum.[96]

*Swedenborg*[97] itself can be reasonably read to support a broad interpretation of education. In its above-quoted key formulation of the meaning of "education" emphasis is given to "the development of faculties and powers,"[98] and "teaching" and "instruction" certainly do not have to be interpreted as exclusively meaning formal education, particularly as they are listed disjunctively with the term "schooling."

Finally, education was given a broad construction, and one that extends far beyond formal schooling, in the *Mohonk* case,[99] where a 500-acre nature preserve was found to be used for an assortment of charitable, educational and moral or mental improvement purposes.[100]

96. Id. at 911, 165 N.Y.S. 2d at 296.

97. Swedenborg Foundation, Inc. v. Lewisohn, 40 N.Y. 2d 87, 351 N.E. 2d 702, 386 N.Y.S. 2d 54 (1976).

98. See text accompanying 77 supra.

99. Mohonk Trust v. Board of Assessors of Gardiner, 47 N.Y.2d 476, 392 N.E.2d 876, 418 N.Y.S.2d 763 (1979).

100. From the perspective taken here there is some very unfortunate dicta in the recent Symphony Space case mentioned above (See notes 39 & 81 supra) The Symphony Space, Inc. v. Tishelman, 185 N.Y.L.J., March 4, 1981, at 12, col. 2 (Sup. Ct. February 20, 1981). The Supreme Court noted that "the appreciation and enjoyment of the performing arts, valuable in itself as a broadening and life enhancing experience, is not primarily educational as contemplated by RPTL section 421(1)(a). It lies in the realm of communication of facts and ideas through the performing arts." Id. This is a very narrow view of education. It is one which is at odds with the more usual interpretation of the term "educational." See note 91 supra. It is also one which a reading of Swedenborg Foundation, Inc. v. Lewisohn, 40 N.Y.2d 87, 351 N.E.2d 702, 386 N.Y.S.2d 54 (1976) does not compel.

The weight given to formal instruction in some of these cases sometimes produces questionable results. In American Management Associations v. Assessor of Madison, 63 A.D.2d 1102, 406 N.Y.S.2d 583 (3d Dept. 1978), aff'd mem., 47 N.Y.2d 841, 392 N.E.2d 571, 418 N.Y.S.2d 584 (1979), an organization devoted to the promotion of entrepreneurial goals that used the property in question to provide continuing education to businessmen was found to be exempt as educational. It is clear that the court was very much influenced by the formal nature of the instruction, e.g., classroom-type courses were given

*Religious*

New York case law on the question of what is a religious purpose is still in the early stages of formation. The appellate courts have not yet approached the difficult issues surrounding efforts to determine the nature of "religion," such as whether a belief in a supreme being is necessary. Most of the cases have assumed that the organization seeking tax exemption is religious and have addressed instead such questions as whether a particular use made of property by such an organization is primarily a religious use.[101] For example, in *Mount Tremper Lutheran Camp, Inc. v. Board of Assessors of Shandaken,*[102] the exemption was denied where 25% of the taxpayer's income was derived from renting idle portions of its campsite for nonexempt uses. But in *Order Minor Conventuals v. Lee,*[103] land preserved in its natural state and used for solitary prayer was exempt, and in *Shrine of Our Lady of Martyrs of Auriesville v. Board of Assessors of Glen,*[104] parking lots and food and lodging facilities were held exempt because the nearest facilities were five miles away and were inadequate to serve visitors to the shrine.

---

over regular intervals by instructors. The dissent, however, found that AMA "is a trade organization providing services as consultant for its members and non-member subscribers, and only minimally conducts educational programs." Id. at 1105, 406 N.Y.S.2d at 587. And after quoting at length from Association of the Bar, the dissent concludes: "Similarly, petitioner is an association of business executives organized for business management purposes, and is primarily concerned with the business interest of its members." Id. at 1105–1106, 406 N.Y.S.2d at 588.

101. This issue is similar to a large amount of litigation that has occurred involving other exempt purposes. For example, it might be conceded that an organization is organized and created exclusively for charitable or educational uses but its use of a particular piece of property might nonetheless be found not to be in furtherance of such purposes. See text accompanying notes 27–28, Chapter 2 supra.

102. 70 A.D.2d 984, 417 N.Y.S.2d 796 (3d Dept. 1979).

103. 64 A.D.2d 227, 409 N.Y.S.2d 667 (3d Dept. 1978).

104. 40 A.D.2d 75, 337 N.Y.S.2d 786 (3d Dept. 1972), aff'd, 33 N.Y.2d 713, 304 N.E.2d 563, 349 N.Y.S.2d 993 (1973).

New York courts have moved gingerly in the area of defining "religious purpose," no doubt constrained by the free-exercise and nonestablishment clauses in the First Amendment of the United States Constitution. There are, however, two Court of Appeals and several lower court decisions that deal with the substantive issue regarding the nature of religious purpose. *Peace Haven, The House of the New Commandment, R.F.M.M. Retreat Inc. v. Geiger*[105] involved the dedication of the country residence of William Vanderbilt to an organization formed to provide a retreat for the study of metaphysics. It is not entirely clear whether "metaphysics" for Peace Haven meant followers of the occult or professional philosophers. In any event, the Court was impressed that the quarters were, "somewhat luxurious; that various athletic and recreational equipment and facilities are provided, including boats and canoes on the river, bicycles, saddle horses, tennis, squash, ping-pong and swimming."[106] The Court concluded that, "In fact, Peace Haven presents the aspects of any ordinary country club, except that the members of the former are said to profess a common interest in metaphysics."[107] The Court held that the organization was not entitled to an exemption as fulfilling either moral or mental improvement of men and women, religious, bible, charitable, benevolent, educational or scientific purposes. In the course of its opinion it noted that Peace Haven had "no tenets, ritual, dogma or other characteristics of a religious organization except, possibly, the solicitation and receipt of funds."[108]

In *Religious Society of Families v. Assessor of Carroll,*[109] the organization claiming to serve religious purposes had tenets but the trial court in passing on its exemption found some of them

105. 175 Misc. 753, 25 N.Y.S.2d 974 (Sup. Ct. 1941).
106. Id. at 755, 25 N.Y.S.2d at 976.
107. Id.
108. Id. at 755, 25 N.Y.S.2d at 977.
109. 73 Misc.2d 923, 343 N.Y.S.2d 159 (Sup. Ct. 1973).

to be illegal (the apparent espousal of suicide and murder of the very aged), some scientific (fostering decommercialization, homesteading, solar power, decentralization of production, population control and more generally scientific humanism) and none of them to be religious as religion is traditionally defined. The court looked to the dictionary, some very old opinions and Augustus Hand[110] for traditional definitions. For itself the court noted: "Petitioner totally denies the existence of God and totally relies upon human reason. This requires that it be excluded from the company of religious institutions."[111]

An earlier case[112] involved some land in Riverdale in the Bronx used as a retreat for the religious training of members of a Christian religious order. The facts of the case suggest that the deep spiritual and educational purposes of this organization were carried out with great seriousness. The court found that the organization was devoted exclusively to religious and educational purposes. The facts that the organization was not a recognized sect or denominational church, that it was incorporated under the Membership Corporation Law and not the Religious Corporation Law, that it was not open to the public, and that it had few members were not decisive. The court accepted a public benefit theory[113] and noted: "The public

110. Id. at 926, 343 N.Y.S.2d at 162 citing the oft-quoted passage from United States v. Kauten, 133 F.2d 703, 708 (2d Cir. 1943):

> It is unnecessary to attempt a definition of religion; the content of the term is found in the history of the human race and is incapable of compression into a few words. Religious belief arises from a sense of the inadequacy of reason as a means of relating the individual to his fellow-men and to his universe—a sense common to men in the most primitive and in the most highly civilized societies. It accepts the aid of logic but refuses to be limited by it.

111. Id. at 926, 343 N.Y.S.2d at 162–163.

112. Outer Court, Inc. of the Order of the Living Christ v. Miller, 161 Misc. 603, 292 N.Y.S. 674 (Sup. Ct. 1936), aff'd mem., 256 A.D. 814, 10 N.Y.S.2d 208 (1st Dept. 1939), aff'd mem., 280 N.Y. 825, 21 N.E.2d 881, 11 N.Y.S.2d 252 (1939).

113. "However, exemption from taxes originated in an effort on the part of governmental authorities to compensate landowners for services supposedly rendered to the government; in other words, it is intended as a reward or

benefit received in return for tax exemption is found in the religious nature of the work carried on by relator. The propagation of the Christian religion, the training of teachers and the preparing of others to carry on the work of the Order is an asset to the community and to the State."[114]

In *Gospel Volunteers, Inc. v. Village of Speculator,*[115] the tax status of two camps used by a nonsectarian evangelical organization for the promotion of Christianity was at issue. The camps contained lodge houses, cabins, picnic areas, a large sand beach, an island and facilities for basketball, tennis, shuffleboard, miniature golf and water-skiing. The program included religious services each weekday morning, several weekday evenings and two major services on Sunday. Daily prayers and seminars were held and numerous religiously oriented films were shown each week. Evangelists, bible teachers, preachers and missionaries regularly visited the camp. The court found the organization's purposes to be the promotion of the spiritual, moral, social and physical well-being of its members and found these purposes coincident with the moral or mental improvement of men and women, religious, bible, tract, charitable, benevolent, missionary or educational purposes (or two or more such purposes) of the statute. The court noted:

> Moreover, considering the general character of present-day organizations devoted to the promotion of religious purposes, it is virtually impossible to draw fine distinctions between the spiritual, moral, social, mental and physical improvement of an individual. Thus, all of respondent's purposes appear necessarily incidental to its primary purpose of promoting the Christian religion, and upon a reasonable interpretation of the statute, are within the intendment thereof.[116]

---

compensation for services rendered in the performance of some function deemed socially desirable." Id. at 610, 292 N.Y.S. at 681.

114. Id. at 609, 292 N.Y.S. at 681.

115. 33 A.D.2d 407, 308 N.Y.S.2d 785 (3d Dept. 1970), aff'd mem., 29 N.Y.2d 622, 273 N.E.2d 139, 324 N.Y.S.2d 412 (1971).

116. Id. at 410–411, 308 N.Y.S.2d at 789 (citation omitted).

The fact that the organization was not a part of a recognized sect or denominational church and therefore incorporated under the Membership Corporation Law rather than the Religious Corporation Law was not found to be controlling by the court.

In *Watchtower Bible and Tract Society of New York, Inc. v. Lewisohn,*[117] the Court of Appeals held that the Jehovah's Witnesses were organized and conducted exclusively for religious purposes within the meaning of paragraph (a) of section 421 rather than for missionary, bible or tract purposes within the meaning of paragraph (b) and thus New York City property used by the society to carry out its purposes was exempt from taxation under Local Law No. 46 of 1971. The Court found that the society was the "ecclesiastical governing body of a recognized religious denomination with its own beliefs and form of organization,"[118] and fielded over one and a half million ministers and missionary evangelists in more than 200 lands. It also noted that "the great weight of judicial authority has uniformly held that the preaching activity of Jehovah's Witnesses from house to house is done as ministers of the gospel and it is held that it is religious preaching."[119]

The last point mentioned focused on the activity of an organization in deciding whether the organization served a "religious" purpose. In *America Press, Inc. v. Lewisohn,*[120] at issue was New York City's restoration under Local Law No. 46 of 1971 to the tax roll of property owned by a nonprofit corporation de facto controlled by the Jesuit order and used both as a Jesuit residence and as offices for the publication of two magazines (*America* and *Catholic Mind.*) In addition, the property

117. 35 N.Y.2d 92, 315 N.E.2d 801, 358 N.Y.S.2d 757 (1974).

118. Id. at 97, 315 N.E.2d at 803, 358 N.Y.S.2d at 760 (citations omitted).

119. Id. at 98, 315 N.E.2d at 804, 358 N.Y.S.2d at 760 (citations omitted).

120. America Press, Inc. v. Lewisohn, 74 Misc.2d 562, 345 N.Y.S.2d 396 (Sup. Ct. 1973), aff'd mem., 48 A.D.2d 798, 372 N.Y.S.2d 194 (1st Dept. 1975), appeal denied, 38 N.Y.2d 708, 382 N.Y.S.2d 1027 (1976).

was used for the holding of Masses and by the John La Farge Institute, an organization devoted to ecumenical and interracial concerns. The City Tax Commission restored the entire property to the tax rolls on the ground that *America* and *Catholic Mind* were essentially secular journals, mere counterparts of *Time* and *Newsweek*. The court characterized the publication of magazines interpreting current events from a Christian-Catholic viewpoint an extension of the church's work and found that the property was used primarily for religious purposes. The activity at issue in *American Bible Society v. Lewisohn,*[121] was the publication and distribution without comment of the Bible. The court held that a corporation organized for such purposes "when neither the corporation nor its corporate activity is directly associated with an organized religious denomination or with an organization having as its avowed purpose the furthering of a recognized religion"[122] is not devoted to religious purposes under paragraph (a) but is rather an organization developed primarily for bible purposes under paragraph (b) of section 421. Thus property owned by such an organization in a jurisdiction such as New York City, where the property was located, which has taken action to remove the exemption from bible organizations, is not entitled to exemption.

In attempting to restate the law of New York as to what a religious purpose is, the characteristic of a religious purpose being carried out by an organized religious denomination (traditional or new) would seem to be of considerable importance. It constitutes a decisive difference between the *America Press*[123] and *American Bible*[124] cases and was of clear significance in

121. American Bible Society v. Lewisohn, 40 N.Y.2d 78, 351 N.E.2d 697, 386 N.Y.S.2d 49 (1976).

122. Id. at 81, 351 N.E.2d at 698, 386 N.Y.S.2d at 50.

123. 74 Misc.2d 562, 345 N.Y.S.2d 396 (Sup. Ct. 1973), aff'd mem., 48 A.D.2d 798, 372 N.Y.S.2d 194 (1st Dept. 1975), appeal denied, 38 N.Y.2d 708, 382 N.Y.S.2d 1027 (1976).

124. 40 N.Y.2d 78, 351 N.E.2d 697, 386 N.Y.S.2d 49 (1976).

the *Watchtower Bible*[125] case. However, two earlier cases—*Outer Court*[126] and *Gospel Volunteers*[127]—suggest it is not necessary to be part of a traditionally recognized sect or denomination but both cases appear to have involved organized and stable groups that did not belong to any other church. An early trial court decision—*Peace Haven*[128]—suggests that for an organization to be characterized as religious it must have tenets, ritual or dogma, and another early trial court decision—*Religious Society*[129]—suggests that such tenets must espouse a belief in the existence of God and the fallibility of human reason.

No New York case in which a religious purpose has been found or assumed has involved an organization other than Christian or Jewish (although as *American Bible*[130] shows attachment to Judeo-Christian beliefs alone is not sufficient). It would seem therefore that the difficult question of the exemptability under the religious category of an organization meeting other criteria of religious purposes but espousing non-Judeo-Christian beliefs is still very open in New York.[131] Similar doubt exists as to how the courts would rule on an organization whose tenets did not include belief in a supreme being, although *Religious Society*[132] would appear to require a belief in God. The emphasis the courts have placed on being a recognized religious denomination might, however, protect from taxation, for example, an ancient eastern "religion" that did not espouse a

125. 35 N.Y.2d 92, 315 N.E.2d 801, 358 N.Y.S.2d 757 (1974).

126. 161 Misc. 603, 292 N.Y.S. 674 (Sup. Ct. 1936), aff'd mem., 256 A.D. 814, 10 N.Y.S.2d 208 (1st Dept. 1939), aff'd mem., 280 N.Y.825, 21 N.E.2d 881, 11 N.Y.S.2d 252 (1939).

127. 33 A.D.2d 407, 308 N.Y.S.2d 785 (3d Dept. 1970), aff'd mem., 29 N.Y.2d 622, 273 N.E.2d 139, 324 N.Y.S.2d 412 (1971).

128. 175 Misc. 753, 25 N.Y.S.2d 974 (Sup. Ct. 1941).

129. 73 Misc.2d 923, 343 N.Y.S.2d 159 (Sup. Ct. 1973).

130. 40 N.Y.2d 78, 351 N.E.2d 697, 386 N.Y.S.2d 49 (1976).

131. See Note, New York's Real Property Tax Exemptions For Religious, Educational, And Charitable Institutions: A Critical Examination, 44 Albany L. Rev. 488, 490–91 (1980).

132. 73 Misc.2d 923, 343 N.Y.S.2d 159 (Sup. Ct. 1973).

belief in God. It is far from clear, however, as to how a new and largely unknown order without a tenet requiring belief in a supreme being would fare in New York.

As suggested above the nonestablishment clause of the First Amendment[133] looms over these questions. In 1969 the Supreme Court, by a seven-to-one vote in *Walz v. Tax Commission,*[134] upheld the constitutionality of the granting of property tax exemptions to religious organizations for religious purposes under Article XVI section 1 of the New York State Constitution (as implemented by section 421 of the Real Property Tax Law). The claim had been made that the grant of an exemption constituted an indirect contribution by the government to religious organizations and so violated the nonestablishment clause. The decision rests upon a number of grounds—not the least important of which is the fact that such tax exemptions have been granted by local jurisdictions for many years and exist today in all states and the District of Columbia. An important theme running throughout the various majority opinions is the neutrality requirement of the nonestablishment clause holding that government may not legislate to benefit religion over nonreligion, or one particular religion over another.[135] Justice Harlan in his concurring opinion phrased the issue with considerable clarity by noting that courts must carefully review, "the circumstances of governmental categories to eliminate, as it were, religious gerrymanders. In any particular case the critical question is whether the circumference of legislation encircles a class

133. The First Amendment provides in part that "Congress shall make no law respecting an establishment of religion or prohibiting the free exercise thereof..." It has been made binding on the states under the Fourteenth Amendment.

134. Walz v. Tax Commission of New York, 397 U.S. 664, 90A S. Ct. 1409 (1969).

135. This principle was brought to prominence by Justice Black in Everson v. Board of Education, where he said: "The 'establishment of religion' clause of the First Amendment means at least this: Neither a state nor the Federal Government can set up a church. Neither can pass laws which aid one religion, aid all religions, or prefer one religion over another." 330 U.S. 1, 15, 67 S. Ct. 504, 511 (1947).

so broad that it can be fairly concluded that religious institutions could be thought to fall within the natural perimeter."[136] In finding that the New York arrangement met the neutrality test, he said:

> The statute that implements New York's constitutional provision for tax exemptions to religious organizations has defined a class of nontaxable entities whose common denominator is their nonprofit pursuit of activities devoted to cultural and moral improvement and the doing of "good works" by performing certain social services in the community that might otherwise have to be assumed by government. Included are such broad and divergent groups as historical and literary societies and more generally associations 'for the moral or mental improvement of men.' The statute by its terms grants this exemption in furtherance of moral and intellectual diversity and would appear not to omit any organization that could be reasonably thought to contribute to that goal.
>
> To the extent that religious institutions sponsor the secular activities that this legislation is designed to promote, it is consistent with neutrality to grant them an exemption just as other organizations devoting resources to these projects receive exemptions. I think, moreover, in the context of a statute so broad as the one before us, churches may properly receive an exemption even though they do not themselves sponsor the secular-type activities mentioned in the statute but exist merely for the convenience of their interested members. As long as the breadth of exemption includes groups that pursue cultural, moral, or spiritual improvement in multifarious secular ways, including, I would suppose, groups whose avowed tenets may be antitheological, atheistic or agnostic, I can see no lack of neutrality in extending the benefit of the exemption to organized religious groups.[137]

Justice Brennan also appears to have found support in the neutrality doctrine for his concurring opinion. He begins his analysis by observing that granting property tax exemptions to

136. Walz v. Tax Commission of New York, 397 U.S. 664, 696, 90A S. Ct. 1409, 1425 (1969).

137. Id. at 696–697, 90A S. Ct. at 1425–1426.

religious organizations serves two basic secular purposes of government:

First, these organizations are exempted because they, among a range of other private, nonprofit organizations contribute to the well-being of the community in a variety of nonreligious ways, and thereby bear burdens that would otherwise either have to be met by general taxation, or be left undone, to the detriment of the community.[138]

He rejected an attempt to avoid the neutrality issue by limiting the question to real property used exclusively for religious purposes on the grounds that it is simplistic to assume that a religious organization's public welfare and sectarian activities can be separated.[139] The second secular purpose is stated as follows:

Second, government grants exemptions to religious organizations because they uniquely contribute to the pluralism of American society by their religious activities. Government may properly include religious institutions among the variety of private, non-profit groups that receive tax exemptions, for each group contributes to the diversity of association, viewpoint, and enterprise essential to a vigorous, pluralistic society.[140]

He lists the many purposes enumerated in the New York exemption statute as showing a general scheme that encompasses both of these purposes, the suggestion being that religious purposes are only one of many means of achieving these ends. Justice Burger echoes these observations in his majority opinion[141] while at the same time limiting to some extent

138. Id. at 687, 90A S. Ct. at 1421 (citation omitted).

139. He notes that "the same people who gather in church facilities for religious worship and study may return to these facilities to participate in Boy Scout activities, to promote antipoverty causes, to discuss public issues, or to listen to chamber music. Accordingly, the funds used to maintain the facilities as a place for religious worship and study also maintain them as a place for secular activities beneficial to the community as a whole." Id. at 688, 90 S. Ct. at 1421.

140. Id. at 689, 90A S. Ct. at 1421–1422 (citation omitted).

141. "The legislative purpose of a property tax exemption is neither the advancement nor the inhibition of religion; it is neither sponsorship nor hostil-

the importance of the neutrality principle.[142]

The establishment clause of the First Amendment prohibits legislation that would prefer one religion over another. Thus the application of an exemption provision, such as section 421, so that one kind of religion, e.g., traditional religions based on Judeo-Christian beliefs, received exemptions and another kind, e.g., a new sect without theistic beliefs or standard ritual, did not would probably be impermissible. In *Washington Ethical Society v. District of Columbia*[143] the Court of Appeals reversed a district court decision denying a property tax exemption granted to property regularly used for religious worship to the Washington Ethical Society, an ethical culture group. Dur-

ity. New York, in common with the other States, has determined that certain entities that exist in a harmonious relationship to the community at large, and that foster its "moral or mental improvement," should not be inhibited in their activities by property taxation or the hazard of loss of those properties for nonpayment of taxes. It has not singled out one particular church or religious group or even churches as such; rather, it has granted exemption to all houses of religious worship within a broad class of property owned by nonprofit, quasi-public corporations which include hospitals, libraries, playgrounds, scientific, professional, historical, and patriotic groups. The State has an affirmative policy that considers these groups as beneficial and stabilizing influences in community life and finds this classification useful, desirable, and in the public interest. Qualification for tax exemption is not perpetual or immutable; some tax-exempt groups lose that status when their activities take them outside the classification and new entities can come into being and qualify for exemption." Id. at 672–673, 90A S. Ct. at 1413.

142. "We find it unnecessary to justify the tax exemption on the social welfare services or "good works" that some churches perform for parishioners and others—family counselling, aid to the elderly and the infirm, and to children. Churches vary substantially in the scope of such services; programs expand or contract according to resources and need. As public-sponsored programs enlarge, private aid from the church sector may diminish. The extent of social services may vary, depending on whether the church serves an urban or rural, a rich or poor constituency. To give emphasis to so variable an aspect of the work of religious bodies would introduce an element of governmental evaluation and standards as to the worth of particular social welfare programs, thus producing a kind of continuing day-to-day relationship which the policy of neutrality seeks to minimize. Hence, the use of a social welfare yardstick as a significant element to qualify for tax exemption could conceivably give rise to confrontations that could escalate to constitutional dimensions." Id. at 674, 90A S. Ct. at 1414.

143. 249 F.2d 127 (D.C. Cir. 1957).

ing the course of his opinion, Warren Burger, then a circuit judge, stated: "To construe exemptions so strictly that unorthodox or minority forms of worship would be denied the exemption benefits granted to those conforming to the majority beliefs might well raise constitutional issues." At issue in cases of this sort is whether the activity claiming exemption should be characterized as a religion for First Amendment purposes. In this regard the term "religion" as used in the First Amendment has been interpreted quite broadly by federal courts. In *Torcaso v. Watkins,*[144] a case involving the denial of a commission to the office of Notary Public to an appointee who would not declare his belief in God, the Supreme Court stated that a state could not constitutionally pass a law that aided "those religions based on a belief in the existence of God as against those religions founded on different beliefs."[145] In *Malnak v. Yogi,*[146] an action brought to enjoin the teaching of transcendental meditation in public schools as violative of the establishment clause, the court found the doctrine, that there exists a field of life present everywhere as the ultimate reality, is of a religious nature. *Walz* suggests a broad interpretation of the term "religion" emphasizing its functions in fostering moral and spiritual improvement, in acting as a stabilizing influence in society and in promoting moral and intellectual diversity.[147] For a statute to be held constitutional under the establishment clause as not promoting religion, e.g., by conferring a tax exemption, it must be found that the reason religions are supported (exempted) under the statute is that they primarily promote some secular pur-

144. 367 U.S. 488, 81 S. Ct. 1680 (1961).

145. Id. at 495, 81 S. Ct. at 1683–1684.

146. 440 F.Supp. 1284 (D. N.J. 1977), aff'd, 592 F.2d 197 (3d Cir. 1979).

147. Indeed it might be argued that Walz requires that when a statute establishes a class that has as its unifying rationale the promotion of moral, spiritual and cultural development, which class plainly encompasses traditional religions, its application so as to extrude from its coverage organizations whose purposes are to further these values would be impermissible as favoring religions over other organizations established to carry out the essential purposes contemplated by the legislation.

pose, e.g., moral, spiritual and cultural improvement. It would follow then that an organization primarily devoted to these purposes could not be denied statutory support (exemption) on the ground it was not a religion. Thus when New York courts are confronted with some of the difficult questions arising with respect to the nature of religion, it would seem they will have to consider whether the property in question is devoted to these broader purposes as well as its status under a narrower conception of religion.

### *Moral or Mental Improvement*

As noted above the moral or mental improvement of men and women has long been an exempt purpose.[148] In the 1971 legislation bifurcating the statutory provision this purpose was listed in paragraph (b) of subdivision 1 of section 421.[149] The following year it was moved to paragraph (a).[150] The legislative history suggests that this purpose was designed to cover only such organizations as the YMCA, YWCA, Boy Scouts and Girl Scouts. A 1972 memorandum of the Senate Rules Committee commenting on chapter 529 states:

> Real Property Tax Law, §421. The purpose of this bill is to provide that real property owned by certain nonprofit organizations organized for the moral or mental improvement of men, women and children (Boy Scouts, Girls Scouts, Y.M.C.A., Y.W.C.A., etc.) may not become subject to taxation by local action pursuant to the provisions of Chapter 414 of the Laws of 1971.
>
> The subject bill amends paragraphs (a) and (b) of subdivision 1 of section 421 of the Real Property Tax Law to provide that such organizations may not be made subject to taxation by local action. The effective date of such act has been set to apply to assessment rolls with taxable status dates occurring on or after January 1, 1972. This conforms to

148. See note 59 and accompanying text, Chapter 2 supra.
149. 1971 N.Y. Laws, ch. 414.
150. 1972 N.Y. Laws, ch. 529.

the January 1, 1972 effective date of Chapter 414 of the Laws of 1971.

Scouting organization and Y's provide a public benefit to the people of our State, render substantial services to the communities in which they operate and provide tremendous help in combating juvenile delinquency. They assist in the education, training and development of our youth and their preparation for a useful adulthood.

The imposition of real property taxes upon such organizations would impose severe financial hardship on them and undoubtedly cause substantial curtailment of their programs.[151]

This reading of the legislative history was adopted by the Appellate Division in the *Presbyterian Residence Center Corp. v. Wagner*[152] case discussed above.[153] It has also been so construed by Counsel to the State Board of Equalization and Assessment.[154]

## *Conclusion*

The above analysis describes a conflict in the interpretation of the three terms, "charitable," "educational" and "religious," which designate the exempt purposes the New York Constitution provides cannot be altered or repealed by the legislature. One line of interpretation has given these terms a fairly narrow construction. Public benefit was removed as a criterion of charitable purposes, although under the traditional law of charities this factor lies at the very heart of the concept charitable. "Education" has been construed in a manner that appears to limit its extension to instruction conducted in a school-like setting, although it is usually given a much broader meaning centered on the idea of developing an individual's capacities whether in the context of formal schooling or otherwise. Finally there is some suggestion that "religion" may be narrowed to requiring an

151. New York State Legislative Annual 266 (1972).
152. 66 A.D. 2d 998, 999 411 N.Y.S. 2d 765, 767 (4th Dept. 1978).
153. See text accompanying note 58 supra.
154. 5 Op. Counsel SBEA No. 17 (1975).

acceptance of Judeo-Christian beliefs or some traditionally theistic set of beliefs. Any such narrowing, however, would probably give rise to serious First Amendment problems if it worked to deny the exemption of an organization that did not hold such traditional views but was devoted generally to fostering moral, spiritual or cultural improvement. A ruling of this nature would very likely involve the preference of one religion (traditional religions enjoying the exemption) over another, as "religion" is meant for First Amendment purposes, and thus be constitutionally impermissible.

The narrow interpretation of these terms appears to have been prompted in large measure by concern over the erosion of the tax base caused by the granting of exemptions to groups that would be covered by giving these terms a broad rendering. Chapter 4 suggests that this concern is largely unwarranted and has no basis whatsoever with respect to the exemptions provided to charitable, educational and religious purposes. Indeed such concern may be impermissable under the Constitution of the State of New York as suggested by the Court of Appeals in *Diocese of Rochester v. Planning Board of Brighton.*[155] There, in refusing to uphold a land planning board's rejection of an application to build a church and school because of the potential adverse effect upon property values and loss of potential tax revenues such construction might cause, the Court stated:

> Section 1 of article XVI of the Constitution of this State provides that "real or personal property used exclusively for religious, educational or charitable purposes" shall always be exempt from taxation, and such institutions have been granted tax exemption, (Tax Law, §4, subd. 6). Thus the paramount authority of this State has declared a policy that churches and schools are more important than local taxes, and that it is in furtherance of the general welfare to exclude such institutions from taxation. This being the case, it cannot be seriously argued that

155. 1 N.Y 2d 508, 136 N.E.2d 827, 154 N.Y.S.2d 849 (1956).

the decision of respondents denying this permit because of a loss of tax revenue is in furtherance of the general welfare.[156]

The narrow interpretations find a plausible basis in the form of the statute. First, no definitions are given of these three terms. Second, its lengthy enumeration of purposes, many of which would normally be included within the meaning of the constitutional purpose, may suggest a restricted compass for these three terms. It is, however, highly unlikely that this was the intention of the legislature when it drafted the statute. It is also extremely unlikely that when these three purposes were lifted into the Constitution that they were intended to have narrow meanings. Moreover, the narrow interpretations, capricious and confusing in their development, appear to have no considered policy underpinnings and to rest in large part on a prediction made in the early 1970s regarding New York State tax base erosion that was based upon erroneously made findings predicated on questionable data and which in any event have very little to do with charitable exemptions. Finally, one can discern a more recent trend in the interpretation of those terms that gives them the broader and more flexible meaning they have always had in the law of charities.

156. Id. at 524–525, 136 N.E.2d at 836, 154 N.Y.S.2d at 861.

# 6

# The Theory of Charitable Real Property Tax Exemptions

This chapter examines the two principal justifications for exempting nonprofit charitable organizations from real property taxation. First, the exemption can be viewed as a form of government subsidy to the provision of services by property-owning exempt organizations—a subsidy effected by eliminating what would otherwise be a fiscal liability of these organizations, thus leaving them more funds to carry out their activities. This is sometimes referred to as the tax expenditure approach since the tax exemption is viewed as functionally equivalent to taxing the organization's property and making a direct grant to it in an amount equal to the tax.[1] Tax exemptions, it is said, have the same impact on the government's budget as direct expenditures because they represent revenues foregone by the government.

1. Professor Stanley S. Surrey, an important voice in the development of the tax expenditure approach, in explaining this approach with regard to income taxes (and for these purposes there are no salient differences between income and property taxes), has said: "The tax expenditure concept in essence considers these special provisions as composed of two elements: the imputed tax payment that would have been made in the absence of the special provision (all else remaining the same) and the simultaneous expenditure of that payment as a direct grant to the person benefited by the special provision." S. Surrey, W. Warren, P. McDaniel & H. Ault, Federal Income Taxation 241 (1972).

The second way of viewing the charitable real property tax exemption is as a necessary means for rationally defining the tax base. Under this view, it would be argued that since the property in question should not as a matter of the normative structure of the tax be included in the tax base, it is exempted. This way of characterizing the exemption will be referred to as the tax base approach. Justification of the tax exemption will vary depending on which view is taken. At this point it might be noted that nowhere in the law of New York—relevant statutes, their legislative history or in judicial interpretations—are either of these concepts explicitly brought forward as underlying the exemption.

## The Tax Expenditure Approach

The view of the tax exemption as a tax expenditure or government subsidy is widely held today.[2] Subsidies are justified because recipients are deemed to be furnishing important public benefits that warrant the encouragement provided by the exemption (or subsidy). The property in question would normally be included in the tax base, but is excluded in order to achieve a social objective unrelated to the raising of revenue and the normative structure of the tax.[3]

Generally there are two kinds of activities said to provide benefits of a public nature justifying the exemption. First are

2. For a brief review of the tax expenditure concept and an indication of some of the most important writing that has been done on the topic, see Feldstein, A Contribution to the Theory of Tax Expenditure: The Case of Charitable Giving, *in* The Economics of Taxation (H. Aaron and M. Boskin, eds. 1980).

3. "The public finance standard for evaluating a tax instrument is a broad base capable of providing large amounts of revenue at relatively low rates. This standard, then, implies that the tax instrument contains few, if any, exemptions to the general rate of tax and, in this sense, possesses a high degree of tax neutrality." Gabler and Shannon, The Exemption of Religious, Educational and Charitable Institutions From Property Taxation, *in* IV Research Papers Sponsored by the Commission on Private Philanthropy and Public Needs 2542 (1977) [hereinafter cited as IV Filer Commission Research Papers].

those the government would otherwise have to provide as, for example, private primary schooling and those the government would normally provide if there were no private organizations furnishing the benefits as, for example, the services of private hospitals. Second are those activities the government might not ordinarily undertake to provide but which offer benefits available to many members of the community. Private museums open to the public at large would be an example. A private organization devoted to reviewing and criticizing the work of the local legislature would be another example. Presumably everyone in the community would benefit from its activities. In the aggregate, churches and religious organizations are thought to engage in activities falling under the second kind of public benefit since for constitutional reasons they cannot be supported by the government. With the exception of this last group and perhaps those organizations functioning to provide an outside evaluation of government activities, no fine line can be drawn between the first and second kinds of public benefits as governments in modern times have come to undertake an increasingly wide variety of services to the public.[4]

Even though an organization may be providing a public benefit, it is questionable whether the exemption mechanism is the most suitable means for providing support to organizations or whether other means, e.g., direct grants, are as well or better suited to serve those goals. A major argument in favor of the exemption as a means of confering a subsidy is that the decision as to the nature of the public benefit and the manner and extent of its provision ought to be a matter of private choice rather than collectively arrived at through the legislative process—"that independent centers of power with a large measure of private control should be encouraged."[5] It has also been noted

4. See Ginsburg, The Real Property Tax Exemption of Nonprofit Organizations: A Perspective, 53 Temple L. Q. 291, 306–313 (1980).

5. Bittker, Charitable Contributions: Tax Deductions or Matching Grants? 28 Tax L. Rev. 37, 39 (1972) [hereinafter cited as Charitable Contributions].

"that the tax exemption promotes a pluralistic approach to the provision of various services that would otherwise drift into the public domain."[6] These services are likely to be conducted "by private groups with more imagination, diversity, flexibility and perhaps even economy than by government agencies."[7]

In general, it is this study's conclusion that a system accommodating dispersed initiatives in providing services of a public benefit will more satisfactorily achieve the common good than one concentrating initiative in one centralized organization. It is entirely up to private individuals whether they want to establish a nonprofit organization eligible for the exemption. No authorization from a government agency is required. It is private individuals who decide that there is a need to be met. As long as the organization fits within the general eligibility requirements of the exempting statute, the most important of which is that it must be devoted to certain specified purposes, it must be given an exemption. The exemption having been given, the leaders of the organization are largely free to decide the various characteristics that will ultimately define the organization, such as its size, where it locates, its legal structure, the manner in which its exempt purposes are to be carried out and how and by whom it should be governed. Of equal importance, in many statutes the nature of exempt purposes are fairly broad. For example, "charitable" purposes have been construed to include any purposes beneficial to the community.[8] Thus, considerable freedom is given to the initiators of nonprofit charitable organizations to discover new public needs to be met, previously unrecognized, and to establish solutions to these new needs.

6. IV Filer Commission Research Papers, supra note 3, at 2542.
7. Charitable Contributions, supra note 5, at 39.
8. See Restatement (Second) of Trusts § 368 (1959). Under section 501(c)(3) of the Internal Revenue Code, the term is to be used in its generally accepted legal sense as an express reference to the law of trusts. See Treas. Reg. § 1.501(c)(3)-1(d)(2)(1959). See text accompanying note 45, Chapter 5 supra.

Government agencies cannot be expected to discover all of society's developing needs. There may even be something in the nature of government that inhibits its discovery of society's needs. Indeed, the history of charity has shown instance after instance of private individuals becoming sensitive to emerging public needs and founding charitable organizations to meet these needs, which are in time taken over by the government as the problem finally comes to be seen by a larger number of people.[9] It is also the case that government agencies by their nature are not, in general, as flexible and creative in experimenting with solutions to new problems.[10] A pluralistic society with two separate systems for implementation of man's social conscience through the discovery and satisfaction of public needs—the governmental system and the system of private charities—is more likely to evolve to a higher level polity than a society with only one such system.[11] Support to the charitable sector through the exemption mechanism works so well pre-

9. See e.g. Charitable Contributions, supra note 5, at 39.

10. On a related point Professor John G. Simon has eloquently noted that, "The goal of experimentation and innovation clearly depends on congeries of initiatives, some or many of them unorthodox, idiosyncratic, irreverent, absurd. The hard fact is that this process is usually irreconcilable with ongoing constituent control." Simon, Foundations and Public Controversy: An Affirmative View, *in* The Future of Foundations 58, 82 (F. Heinmann ed. 1973).

11. Professor Lawrence Stone has noted of the role played by nonprofit charitable organizations that "It is often a unique pathfinder in social welfare and the sciences to be followed only at a later date by governmental or profit-oriented resources." Stone, Federal Tax Support of Charities and Other Exempt Organizations: The Need for a National Policy, 28 U.S. Cal. Tax Inst. 27, 39 (1968). In listing the functions of nonprofit activity the Filer Commission in its summary report began with "initiating new ideas and processes" and quoted former Secretary of Health, Education and Welfare Wilbur J. Cohen as follows: "There are critical reasons for maintaining a vital balance of public and private support for human services not the least of which is the continuous task of innovating areas where public agencies lack knowledge or are afraid to venture. . . . The private sector is adept at innovation, and at providing the models government needs." Report of the Commission on Private Philanthropy and Public Needs, Giving In America 42 (1977). It closes this section by noting that "Once successfully pioneered by nonprofit groups, and having established their legitimacy and worthiness, new ideas and processes can be, and often have been, supported and expanded by government." Id. at 43.

cisely because of the freedom with which charitable organizations can operate in discovering and satisfying public needs. These advantages are well suggested by John V. Gardner:

> One of the most interesting examples of the government's relations with the private world involves those activities that are tax-exempt for educational, scientific, religious or charitable purposes. The implications of this tax exemption have not been well understood. The state is saying, in effect, that these activities are in the public interest, and, more important, that it is in the public interest to encourage the conduct of these activities by nongovernmental groups and individuals.
>
> It would be difficult to exaggerate the importance of this policy in preserving and fostering the pluralism so characteristic of our society. The fact that our system encourages such diversity of initiative in the vitally important areas of education, science, religion and philanthropy has contributed to the richness and variety of our national life.[12]

Subsidies to private organizations providing public benefits through the mechanism of direct grants would involve these organizations in politics in the purest sense. Regular appearances before legislative committees would be required, and their work would be vulnerable to political influence and pressure. Freedom from this kind of outside control is critically important for organizations whose essential nature is to experiment and innovate.[13] Subsidy by direct government expenditures, uncertain from one year to the next, makes long-term planning very difficult and generally does not promote stability.[14] In contrast, the benefits of tax exemptions are certain and provide a greater degree of financial certainty than a system of government grants.[15]

12. J. Gardner, No Easy Victories 140 (1968).
13. See Charitable Contributions, supra note 5, at 39.
14. See IV Filer Commission Research Papers, supra note 3, at 2543.
15. This view assumes that the purposes of exempt organizations are in some sense more fundamental and rest on values that are more enduring than many of those regular government concerns and so should not "be subjected to the vagaries of periodic legislative review." Property Tax Exemptions, supra note 13, at 296.

A major objection to the exemption system as a means of aiding activities providing public benefits centers on that part of the system many of its proponents find most desirable, viz., its low visibility and essentially unpublic nature. Opponents argue that it is far more difficult to ascertain the cost of the subsidy when provided by an exemption than by direct grants. Principles of good government, it is said, require that programs supported by the government be regularly reviewed and weighed against the competing needs of other government programs.[16] Aid to exempt organizations is administered by revenue committees and tax authorities rather than the substantive committees and agencies that might normally have jurisdiction over these agencies.[17] Circumstances and policies change, and a system of direct expenditures is more responsive to changing needs.[18]

Another major objection to the exemption scheme is that the amount of the subsidy, based as it is on the assessed value of the exempt property, may bear very little relationship to what would be considered an appropriate amount if the decision were based on the actual needs of the organizations or of society's needs for the services provided by the organization.[19] A

16. See IV Filer Commission Research Papers, supra note 3, at 2544.

17. See Warren, Krattenmaker & Snyder, Property Tax Exemptions for Charitable, Educational, and Governmental Institutions in Connecticut, 4 Conn. L. Rev. 181, 302 (1971) [hereinafter cited as Property Tax Exemptions].

18. "Indeed, it is, the permanence of the exemption that limits the options available to government policy makers since it reduces their flexibility in adjusting to current circumstances. An organization or activity deemed worthy of an exemption at any one point of time may not necessarily be so evaluated in 5 or 10 years. Yet, many exemptions last far longer than that since nothing is harder to retrieve than a preferred tax status." IV Filer Commission Research Papers, supra note 3, at 2544.

19. "It would be sheer coincidence if the value of the tax exemption were to match the value of an appropriation based on actual needs for the service in question. Under a direct grant, there is at least the potential for approximating these needs on a year-to-year basis. Measures of public needs are admittedly imprecise, but they would seem to be more accurate than a value that results from a determination of land and improvements valuation and the prevailing

further point is sometimes made that as only wealthy organizations enjoy the advantages of the exemption and renting organizations do not, the system works an inequity.[20] Critics of the exemption scheme become most alarmist when they describe the "snowball" effect of granting exemptions. They assume that each exemption granted causes a reduction in the tax base, which in turn increases the tax burden on the remaining taxable property. In response to this increased burden, more organizations will file for exemption and the process will "snowball."[21]

It is also said that the exemption is inefficient because it encourages exempt organizations to invest more of their funds in land and buildings than they would in a world without taxes.[22]

A final set of objections raised against the exemption scheme responds to a perceived intergovernmental unfairness that in many instances the exemption is mandated by the state legisla-

---

local property tax rate." IV Filer Commission Research Papers, supra note 3, at 2544. It may be also that the exemption causes these organizations to overinvest in property and consequently to use their funds inefficiently in their efforts to achieve their primary goals.

20. Property Tax Exemptions, supra note 17, at 300.

21. See IV Filer Commission Research Papers, supra note 3, at 2545. This somewhat troubling possibility assumes that property becoming exempt erodes the tax base by removing a taxpayer from the community and consequently increasing the taxes on those who remain. Below the validity of this assumption is examined.

22. In this connection Dean Netzer has pointed out that:

> Subsidy in the form of tax exemption has two other real, although less obvious, costs. First, like any subsidy other than a straight cash payment, tax exemption is a relatively inefficient form of subsidizing worthy purposes. The value of the subsidy is a function of the extent to which the tax-exempt organization uses costly land and buildings in its operations. Property tax exemption encourages such organizations to use more, and more valuable, real property than they would use if they had to pay property taxes, but were given a no-strings cash subsidy. Real estate is made cheaper relative to labor and other inputs, and organizations are induced to be less labor-intensive and more real-property-intensive. This bias in the choice of inputs is not one that has redeeming social values.
>
> Related to this, the tax exemption leads to some inefficiency in urban land use, by encouraging taxexempt organizations to use more land than they would under other forms of subsidy. Where there are alternative uses for the sites, the inefficiency is real, not theoretical.

Netzer, Property Exemptions and Their Effects: A Dissenting View, Proc. 65th Am. Conf. Tax., Nat'l Tax. A. 268, 283 (1973).

ture but paid for by local governments, whose tax bases are reduced by these exemptions.[23] Frequently it is nonresidents of the municipality who benefit from the exempt organizations, e.g., the students of a "national" university in an Upstate township, although the residents bear the burden of the tax.

In sum, if the tax exemption were repealed and a system of direct government grants substituted for it, the antiexemptionists would list some of the following advantages. The amount of the subsidy would be rationally related to the needs of the community and the organization. Organizations would not be induced to overinvest in property. Local governments and their taxpayers would not be called upon to support organizations benefiting a community far wider than that comprised by their municipality. And government could exercise some control over the level and direction of public support given to these organizations.

There is one important assumption that the tax expenditure argument makes that should be recognized in assessing its validity, viz., that if the tax exemption were removed, the real property now exempt would produce a tax (equal to the tax rate times the property's assessed value). It is assumed that either exempt organizations would pay the tax or, if they were unable to and ceased operations, that their property would be transferred to new owners in whose hands the property would be assessed at the same value as before the transfer and who would be able to pay the tax. If, however, neither of these eventualities occurred—if, for example, as a result of the removal of the exemption an exempt organization abandoned its property and no one else picked it up—no new and additional tax revenues would be collected from the property, and the tax burden of the taxpayers who existed before the exemption was removed

23. See IV Filer Commission Research Papers, supra note 3, at 2545. "The state legislature may feel unduly benevolent when it can make generous contributions to some worthy causes without any obvious cost to the state." Property Tax Exemptions, supra note 17, at 299.

would remain the same. Under these circumstances the tax expenditure approach would not appear to be an apt way of characterizing the exemption since it is premised on the assumption that tax revenues are foregone by reason of the exemption.

## The Tax Base Approach

The tax expenditure approach assumes that all real property in the taxing jurisdiction is in the tax base. This assumption, however, must be examined. It may be that only a part, albeit a large part, of all real property should be included in the real property tax base just as only a part, albeit a large part, of all income is included in the income tax base.[24] If such is the case, it could be that providing exemptions to specified property is merely a way of defining the tax base by removing from the tax base certain property that, as a matter of the tax system's logic, ought not be within it and not a means of providing an "indirect" government subsidy. This line of analysis, referred to here as the tax base approach, forces a consideration of what kinds of property ought to be in and what kinds ought to be out of the tax base. So far as is known, there is no legislative history or judicial opinion in New York expressly discussing the question of the proper boundaries of the real property tax base.

The tax base could be either arbitrarily determined or it could be related to questions of tax and social policy grounded in principles of equity. If arbitrarily determined, all one need do to determine the tax base is to read the statutes that impose it. It might be assumed that an exemption from taxes to prop-

24. As Boris Bittker has said: "There is no way to tax *everything;* a legislative body, no matter how avid for revenues, can do no more than pick out from the universe of people, entities, and events over which it has jurisdiction those that, in its view, are appropriate objects of taxation. In specifying the ambit of any tax, the legislature cannot avoid 'exempting' those persons, events, activities, or entities that are outside the territory of the proposed tax." Bittker, Churches, Taxes and the Constitution, 78 Yale L.J. 1285 (1968).

erty used in a certain manner is provided merely to carve the property so used out of the tax base.[25] If, on the other hand, resort is made to principle, then in order to determine whether an exemption is provided to furnish an indirect subsidy or rather to define the tax base, one would have to consider the underlying principles upon which the tax system is built.

From one point of view, it may be thought that the real property tax is merely an historical anachronism that, because of the exigent demands of local finance, has not given way to the more progressive tendencies of modern taxation. This approach, which would assume that at society's present state of development there are no longer any principles underlying the property tax, is strongly suggested by the history of the tax, as will be seen below.[26] It has been asserted by a scholar of the property tax that the customary definition of the property tax base—one that includes all real property within a jurisdiction—is in fact nonprincipled and related to historical custom or administrative convenience.[27] Professor Thomas Heller argues:

> If a base can be known only by the statute which establishes it, then it is reasonable to argue that it is the entire statute which defines the tax and not some part of it. This would mean that the property tax base does not include charitable properties because state laws have specifically excluded them from coverage. They are not exceptions to an established base but initially defined as non-taxable.[28]

25. If the tax base were arbitrarily determined, there would be no way to tell whether an exemption was made to define the tax base or to provide an indirect subsidy.

26. Indeed, as also noted below, ability to pay has become the accepted principle for achieving equity in taxation, and in this regard one of the strongest arguments against the property tax is that it does not take account of ability to pay. See text at note 31 infra.

27. See Heller, Is the Charitable Exemption From Property Taxation an Easy Case? General Concerns About Legal Economics and Jurisprudence, *in* Essays on the Law and Economics of Local Governments 183, 223 (D. Rubinfeld ed. 1980).

28. Id.

If, however, a principled approach is to be taken, a recognition of the essential purposes of the tax would appear to be the first step in determining the proper tax base. It could be, for example, that the property tax is levied solely to defray expenses that government incurs in connection with providing services directly benefiting property. If this were so, the tax could be grounded on what is called the benefit principle, according to which the amount of the tax is proportionate to the government services a taxpayer receives.[29] In Chapter 1, however, it is shown that the proceeds of the real property tax in New York are used to finance *all* government services, most of which benefit individuals in their personal capacity and not property.[30] It would seem, therefore, that the actual goal of the real property tax is to raise money to support the wide range of services that government furnishes society. In this sense the property tax is no different than the income or sales tax. Consequently, the property tax could not equitably be based on the benefit principle because there is little relation between the amount of property taxes (determined, as these are, on the assessed valuation of property) people pay because of their connection with property, e.g., a homeowner, and the amount of government services they receive. The Gerber Commission's 1979 report suggests that the property tax may once have been related to benefit principle but is no longer:

Despite frequent and often widespread criticism, the real property tax has long been the major source of tax revenues for local governments. At one time, ownership of real estate was generally considered to be a good indication of wealth. Property tax collections, which were locally determined and levied, were used chiefly to finance local services to property (e.g., police, fire, roads, and sanitation). Property owners, therefore, benefited directly and tangibly from the services provided,

29. R & P Musgrave, Public Finance in Theory and Practice 193 (1973) [hereinafter cited as Musgrave].

30. See Note on the Governmental Services and Functions Financed With Funds Raised by the Real Property Tax, Chapter 1.

and those services normally resulted in increased property values. Levying real property taxes allowed local governments to finance local services by recapturing to a degree the increases in property values their services had created. For decades, therefore, the real property tax enjoyed general acceptance as a "good" tax in that there was a close and visible relationship between taxes and benefits received.

In recent years, however, few could agree with the proposition that real estate ownership constitutes a good measure of wealth or a reasonable basis for judging a taxpayer's ability to pay for local government services.[31]

To determine the base of a general revenue-raising tax, principled public finance theories aimed at achieving equity would ideally begin by recognizing that justice in taxation is best achieved by distributing the burden in accordance with ability to pay. Musgrave points out that "actual tax policy is largely determined independently of the expenditure side, and an equity rule is needed to provide guidelines. The ability-to-pay principle is widely accepted as this guide."[32] Seligman's history of taxation suggests that the ability-to-pay principle has predominated since the earliest days of taxation, although its implementation has changed through various stages of economic development.[33] He points out that in a primitive society the poll tax was used with roughly equitable results, since personal status in those times reflected personal ability. As civilization advanced, the poll tax gave way to a property tax based on the produce worked from communally held land, and with the development of individual ownership of land the tax on real property per se emerged. Finally, as society became increas-

31. Report of the Temporary State Commission on the Real Property Tax 7 (1979).

32. Musgrave, supra note 6, at 194. Professor Goode states that, "Fairness is generally recognized as comprising equal treatment of equals and reasonable differences in the treatment of unequals. In regard to taxation, capacity or ability to pay is the relevant aspect of equality and unequality. Income and competing tax bases derive their appeal from their relation to capacity or ability to pay." R. Goode, The Individual Income Tax 17 (rev. ed. 1976).

33. E. Seligman, Essays in Taxation, ch. I (1928).

ingly complicated and the forms of wealth and ownership and the means of production became increasingly differentiated, the income tax resulted as the fairest measure of capacity. Seligman summarizes this evolution as follows:

The history of finance, in other words, shows from one point of view, at least, the evolution of the principle of faculty or ability in taxation —the principle that each individual should be held to help the state in proportion to his ability to help himself. In the earliest indirect payments there was no idea of equity, but only of force. But with the advance of civilization and social ethics, we reach the first stage of rude equality in the poll tax. Step by step the revenue system advanced to successively higher planes. Expenditure, property, product—each of these in turn was considered the test of individual capacity and obligation toward the state; until finally in modern times revenue or income has come to be regarded as the most equitable and the most practical measure of individual and social faculty. To arrange a system of taxation a large part of which at least shall, on the whole, correspond as closely as possible to the net revenues of individuals, and which shall take into account the variations in tax-paying ability, has thus become a demand of modern civilization.[34]

The next step to specify the tax base is to decide what property ought in fairness to be called upon to help finance the broad array of government services. But first a preliminary point must be made. It is axiomatic that real property taxes are in fact paid by people, not by real estate itself.[35] Property taxes

34. Id. at 18.

35. Professor C. Lowell Harris has pointed out as first principle of property taxation that: "The property tax, like every tax, is really a tax on *people*. 'Things,' such as real property, do not in a meaningful sense, bear tax. The property tax must be thought of as a device to tax people according to their (a) ownership, (b) use, or (c) other tie to property." C. Lowell Harris, Constitutional Restrictions on Property Taxing and Borrowing Powers in New York II-1 (1967). In this connection, Harvey E. Breyer has said:

If federal budgetary receipts must be substantially increased, either to finance new programs or to permit reduction in state and local taxes, the income tax stands tall as a prospective source of additional funds. It does so partly because, irrespective of their form and no matter where their initial impact may fall, taxes can be borne only by individuals or families. The collection of tax receipts by the government

on residential property are paid for by homeowners out of their earnings or other income.[36] Property taxes on commercial or industrial property are paid for by increases in the prices charged for the products these enterprises sell or out of the net income they generate, which would otherwise, at least ultimately, be returned to the owners of these organizations as profits on their investments.[37] Who ultimately bears the tax is a question of incidence theory about which experts differ.[38] In any event, however, it is clear that it is people whom the tax finally reaches. Upon analysis, then, it turns out that the real tax base question is what people or what class of people with respect to their relation to property ought in fairness to be expected to pay the property tax. Money must be taken from someone to finance government expenditures. The principled question is whose income should go down. The answer is determined by deciding what constitutes a just distribution of after-tax income.

Who are the people connected to nonprofit charitable[39] or-

---

brings about a reduction in private consumption or saving, or both, although in some instances, this result may come about only indirectly, and those actually affected may not even understand that it is happening. In the complex case of the corporate income tax, for example, people bear that tax in their capacities as owners or, possibly, as employees if wages respond to profit levels and if the tax reduces after-tax profits; alternatively, the corporate income tax may be distributed, at least in part, among people according to their consumption of corporate products if the tax is shifted forward through higher prices. Taxes on property and on other things, including transactions of various kinds, are similarly borne by people, through diminution of sources of income or reduction in the opportunity to consume and/or to save. Meaningful debate on tax policy, therefore, should focus mainly on the distribution of tax liabilities among people, rather than on the distribution of taxes between people and things or legal entities.

Breyer, The Income Tax in the Federal Revenue System, *in* Broad Based Taxes 3 at 3 (R. Musgrave ed. 1973).

36. In the case of rental property, the tax ultimately reaches either the tenants or the owners of real property, depending on market conditions.

37. In addition, the tax may be shifted to the enterprise's employees or suppliers, i.e., ultimately people.

38. See Musgrave, supra note 29, at ch. 15.

39. "Charitable" is used broadly to include all activities providing public

ganizations who might fairly be expected to pay the property tax if those organizations were subject to the tax? There are two general classes of such people: the recipients of their services and those who contribute to their financing.[40] Thus, under the analysis so far advanced, the property tax base question for nonprofit charitable organizations owning property is whether their beneficiaries or those who make contributions to an organization for which they receive no tangible return (referred to as "contributors") should in fairness be liable for the tax or not.

If a property tax were imposed upon nonprofit charitable organizations and shifted to their beneficiaries, this would mean that part of whatever funds they contributed to these organizations in return for their services would be used to defray the tax. In assaying the appropriateness of subjecting the beneficiaries of charitable organizations to this tax, there are two general categories of charitable organizations to be considered: first, those organizations providing relief to the poor, the distressed or the underprivileged. The beneficiaries of these organizations are hardly in a position to pay a tax to support the provision of government services. Indeed, they are for the most part "exempt" from income (and most other) taxes, i.e., it may be argued that whatever income they do receive is not considered

benefits: activities that might be classified under the terms "educational" and "religious" as well as "charitable."

40. For completeness' sake, there are two other classes that might be reached: employees and suppliers to these organizations. Employees could, in effect, be made subject to the tax by receiving lower wages, i.e., the incidence of the tax would be shifted down to them through a reduction of wages. Since it is likely the case that many employees of nonprofit charitable organizations already receive lower compensation than their counterparts in the "profit" sector of the economy and since it is likely that any further lowering of compensation might result in their leaving their positions with these organizations, this class would at least only marginally seem available to defray the tax. (In this connection account should be taken of the fact that many nonprofit charitable organizations make considerable use of volunteers.) Likewise, in our market system it is improbable, in general, that suppliers would offer their goods and services to nonprofit charitable organizations at a price lower than they could fetch in the open market, and so they too, as a class, would not be a potential target for the tax.

as being in the income tax base. If ability to pay is the touchstone of taxability, these beneficiaries should surely be exempt. Furthermore, in many instances they are recipients of government transfer payments, e.g., welfare, food stamps, medicare, medicaid, etc., financed in large part out of taxes collected to support general government services. It is also the case that most of the services received from this category of charitable organizations are in the nature of emergency aid and, as such, do not promote the greater material well-being of their recipients as is the case with most normal personal-consumption expenditures. It would seem, therefore, entirely appropriate not to look to the beneficiaries of this class of charitable organizations for payment of the tax, i.e., entirely appropriate to define the real property tax base in such a manner as not to subject them to tax. Furthermore, as a practical matter, this class of recipients could not pay the tax.

The second general category of nonprofit charitable organizations provides services that may be broadly characterized as promoting the moral, spiritual, cultural or educational development of recipients who may not be penurious or distressed but who are unable or unwilling to pay for their full costs. It would seem to be a perfectly legitimate social policy judgment not to include within the tax base payments made for the consumption of such intangible items as spiritual solace or educational enhancement. As will be noted below, it is of benefit to the community to have these goods made available on as wide a basis as possible. Enabling these organizations to charge a lower price for their products because they are free of the tax assures a wider provision of these goods. It must be admitted, however, that this is a more difficult "tax base" argument to defend. A more essential reason for exempting this type of charitable organization may be to encourage the provision and consumption of their services deemed beneficial to the general public welfare by enabling these organizations, through the provision of a tax exemption, to charge a lower price for their services. On this view the exemption might more appropriately be conceived as a tax expenditure.

In any event, there is only limited room to increase the charge to recipients of benefits from these kinds of organizations without seriously undermining the purposes for which these organizations were established. For example, if tuition at private universities were increased, even with attempts to raise additional scholarship income, New York universities would become institutions that only the rich could afford to attend. Furthermore, many of the most talented New York students might decide to go to school elsewhere. A similar point applies to ticket prices for theatrical performances.

In most circumstances, to keep financially viable, these organizations must receive contributions to meet their full costs. As a practical matter, if these organizations were made subject to the real property tax, most of the funds to defray it would come from these contributions.[41]

This leaves contributors to nonprofit charitable organizations as the only remaining candidates to defray the property tax, i.e., the ultimate tax base question becomes whether the contributors to nonprofit charitable organizations owning property should be called upon to pay the tax[42] in addition to contribut-

41. If additional contributions would not come forward to meet the costs of the new tax, the organizations would have to reduce their operations to the extent necessary to produce savings out of which the tax could be paid. If this occurred, the beneficiaries would feel the burden of the tax in a reduction in the level of services provided for them.

42. Contributors would in effect pay the new tax even if they did not increase their contributions since the tax would in fact be defrayed out of their contributions. (This would certainly be the case where all of the funding for the organization came from contributions.) This can be seen by assuming the exemption were repealed. Before the exemption's repeal all of their contributions would have been used to support the organization's activities. After the repeal part of their contributions would be used to support the organization's activities and part to defray the tax. Analytically, they would be in the same position as contributors who before the repeal only contributed an amount equal to that part of their after-repeal contribution which was devoted to the organization's activities and who then after the repeal increased their contributions in an amount sufficient to defray the tax.

ing to their general support. There are a number of good reasons why the contributors to nonprofit charitable organizations might not in fairness be included within the tax base, or put somewhat differently, that the act of contributing to charitable organizations should not give rise to tax liability. First, it has been shown that the property tax is a general tax used to support all government services.[43] Contributions to charitable organizations support services very similar to the public services provided by government—in some cases services the government would undertake to provide if they were not furnished by the charitable organizations; in other cases services not traditionally provided by the government but clearly of general benefit to the public.[44] Contributions to these organizations should not be subject to tax since their intended purpose and effect is to support the financing of public goods, similar to those supported by taxes, which provide wide social benefits.[45] In effect, contributions are similar to the payment of a voluntary tax. Second, contributors have already paid the property tax and received direct benefits in their capacity as homeowners, consumers or investors in profit-making organizations and should not be expected to contribute additionally to the provision of government services by reason of their support of nonprofit charitable organizations from which they receive no direct benefits.[46] Individuals investing in a profit-making

43. See text accompanying note 30 supra.

44. See text following note 63 infra.

45. A discussion of the concept of a public good is given below. See text accompanying note 56 infra.

46. Antiexemptionists will argue that contributors receive benefit or utility from making their contributions (elsewise they would not make them). It is unmistakable, however, that the satisfactions one may receive from contributions to charity are of entirely different order than the benefits received from purchasing tangible consumer goods or owning a dwelling place, and such a difference justifies their exclusion from the tax base. Those who would disagree with the tax base arguments advanced here would hold that such a difference does not justify their exclusion from the tax base. See, e.g., Kelman, Personal Deductions Revisited: Why They Fit Poorly in an "Ideal" Income Tax and Why They Fit Worse in a Far From Ideal World, 31 Stan. L.Rev. 831 (1979). In some

organization expect to receive a return on their investment and, indeed, that return may have been reduced somewhat to defray the real property tax liability of the organizations in which they invested. In other words, their investments will not only produce a return for their exclusive benefit but will also generate funds sufficient to pay the property tax related to their investment. Contributors to a nonprofit charitable organization receive no such monetary return, and thus, unlike investors, have no additional funds with which to pay the tax as a result of their contributions. These considerations are elaborated upon in a slightly different context below.[47]

However the exemption is explained or justified[48]—whether

---

instances, it may be the case that contributors receive some direct benefits from their contributions, e.g., the contributor to a nonprofit ballet company who frequently attends the performances. But even in such instances, it is usually the predominant effect of the contribution to benefit many others and the distinction holds.

47. In the analysis made so far no mention has yet been made of an important contributor to many charitable organizations: the government. Recently an increasingly large number of charitable organizations have been receiving increasingly larger amounts of support from various governmental grant-making agencies. It would generally speaking be nonsensical to look to these government agencies to defray a newly imposed property tax on charitable organizations since they raise funds to make these grants by taxation. That is, it would be absurd to impose a tax financed by increasing taxes. This approach, of course, would not be absurd if the taxes collected to pay the newly imposed property tax were levied on a different tax base than the property tax base, e.g., a state sales or income tax might provide funds to make grants to an organization, which in part would be used to meet the organization's local real property tax liability.

48. In the following discussion similarities will be evident between the analysis of the real property tax exemption as it relates to contributors and the federal income tax charitable contribution deduction. These similarities result from the recognition that property does not pay property taxes but rather that people pay property taxes by virtue of their various relationships to property, e.g., as property owners, consumers, investors, etc., and finally that people pay property taxes out of income. If the federal income tax charitable contribution deduction were not provided, contributors would have to pay income tax in respect to their contributions. Similarly, in the analysis developed here, if the property tax exemption were removed, part of a contributor's contribution would be used to defray the charitable organization's (new) real property tax liability. The similarities having been identified, the analysis has been extensively informed by Professor William Andrews's seminal article on the charita-

as a tax expenditure or as a principled means of defining the tax base—its effect is to increase the tax burden of those who are subject to the tax, i.e., without the exemption their taxes would be lower.[49] This is made clear by considering what would happen if the exemption were repealed.[50] For these purposes taxpayers can be divided into two groups: first, those who contribute to charitable organizations ("contributors") and second, those who do not ("noncontributors"). Both groups consume and accumulate wealth.[51] Indeed, it is assumed here that nearly every use of income that an individual might make, other than applying it to the use of exempt organizations, would constitute consumption or wealth accumulation and to some degree ultimately be reached by the property tax. If the exemption were removed, one or more of three responses would result. First, contributors might increase their contributions in order to provide for payment of the tax. In this case, the level of charitable services would remain constant and because of the increased tax receipts coming from organizations now subject to the tax, noncontributors' tax burden would be lessened with a consequent increase in the amount of their consumption and wealth accumulation. On the other hand, contributors would have less income for consumption and wealth accumulation. The level of consumption and wealth accumulation and the level of charita-

---

ble contribution and medical care personal income tax deductions. Andrews, Personal Deductions in an Ideal Income Tax, 86 Harv. L.Rev. 309 (1972) [hereinafter cited as Andrews].

49. There is one unlikely possibility where this might not be true, i.e., if the exemption were not available contributors to charitable organizations would not make contributions but would spend the amount of their contributions in a manner that would not be reached by any taxes of the taxing jurisdiction. See note 53 infra.

50. The analysis made below would also apply if exemptions were merely cut back, limited or reduced in some way as distinguished from being eliminated altogether. The analysis is clearer, however, when total repeal is assumed.

51. Consumption and wealth accumulation includes all economic activity presently reached by the property tax either directly as in the case of homeowners or indirectly as in the case of consumers, investors, etc. See text accompanying notes 35–38 supra.

ble services would remain constant, but there would be a shift in consumption and wealth accumulation from contributors to noncontributors. Second, contributors might continue to contribute at the same level as before the repeal. In effect, part of their contributions would now be used to pay the tax and the level of goods and services provided by charitable organizations would be reduced.[52] On the other hand, the tax burden on noncontributors would be reduced as a result of the increased tax receipts, and consequently they would have more money for consumption and wealth accumulation. Noncontributors would benefit and the recipients of charitable services would suffer. There would be an increase in consumption and wealth accumulation and a decrease in level of charitable goods and services. Third, contributors might stop contributing to charitable organizations altogether. The level of services provided by charitable organizations wholly dependent upon support from contributors would drop to zero. Monies used before the repeal for charitable contributions would be used for consumption and wealth accumulation and thus be reached by the tax.[53] Consequently, noncontributors' tax burden would be reduced and, as a result, the level of their consumption and wealth accumulation would increase. Contributors would also increase the level of their consumption and wealth accumulation as presumably money used before the repeal for charitable contributions would now be used for consumption and wealth accumulation. There would be a sizeable decrease in the provision of charitable services and an increase of similar dimensions in consump-

52. See note 42 supra.

53. More broadly, they might be reached by other taxes supporting government services, which might also cause a reduction of the tax burden of noncontributors. It may be, however, that such monies would be used outside of the jurisdiction for consumption and wealth accumulation and thus not be reached by any tax that would support the government of the jurisdiction in which the property of charitable organizations is located. In this case, the repeal would not result in the lowering of noncontributors' tax burden, and it could not be said categorically that the effect of the exemption is to increase the tax burden on those who are subject to the tax.

tion and wealth accumulation. Of course, in actual practice if the exemption were repealed it is likely that all three responses would occur more or less together, i.e., some contributors would continue to contribute at the same level as before the exemption, some contributors would increase their contributions and some would cease contributing altogether. In all cases there would almost certainly be a reduction in the tax liability of those who were subject to the tax before the repeal and this shows that the virtually necessary effect of the exemption is an increase in their tax burden.

In these terms, a tax base approach to justifying the exemption would turn upon a judgment that only consumption and wealth accumulation ought to bear the burden of tax, i.e., be called upon to finance general government services, and that contributions to charitable organizations do not constitute consumption or wealth accumulation. On such a view, the intended effect of the tax would be to reduce consumption and wealth accumulation to finance general government services but not contributions to charitable organizations. Focusing on the first case given above,[54] which assumes contributors would increase their contributions to pay for the tax if the exemption were repealed, a tax base approach would maintain that this would be an unjust result because contributors have already reduced the level of their consumption and wealth accumulation by making their contributions in the first place, and it would be

54. As suggested above, the second case is similar, if not identical to the first case, since in the situation covered by the second case of contributors not increasing their contributions in the face of repeal, their contributions can be analyzed as consisting of two parts: first, that part which is used to support charitable organizations' general operations (not including the new property tax liability) and second, that part which is used to pay the new tax. See note 42 supra. Thus, in the second case contributors are also reached by the tax, and if there are reasons why contributors should not increase their contributions as they would in the first case that justify a tax base approach to the exemption they would apply to the second case as well. Since the point to be made is more easily developed by examining the first case, it is used, but, if the point holds, it applies as well to the second case.

inequitable to have them further reduce their consumption and wealth accumulation by increasing their contributions to pay for the tax. This inequity becomes especially apparent when it is recognized that the decrease in the level of contributors' consumption and wealth accumulation because of their increased contributions would result in an increase in the level of consumption and wealth accumulation by noncontributors. While it is true that the effect of the exemption lays a heavier burden on the consumption and wealth accumulation of noncontributors than would be the case without the exemption, this is entirely appropriate since only consumption and wealth accumulation are targets of the tax. Furthermore, contributors are reached by the tax insofar as they engage in consumption and accumulate wealth.[55] In fact, contributors would also bear a heavier tax burden on their consumption and wealth accumulation as a result of the exemption. Consumption and wealth accumulation are reduced to finance government services and the measure of consumption and wealth accumulation does not include charitable contributions.

Above it was said that the principled question is whose income should go down to finance government expenditures, and that this question, in turn, is answered by deciding what constitutes a just distribution of after-tax income. One compares the amount of income left to various taxpayers for consumption and wealth accumulation after these amounts have been reduced by taxes to see whether a fair distribution has resulted. Under the tax base approach advanced here, contributions are initially eliminated from taxpayers' income because in this view they are not available for consumption and wealth accumulation, and the reductions made by taxation of the remaining incomes,

55. In much of the analysis, reference is made to the tax burden of noncontributors being increased because of the exemption. It should be recognized that contributors are noncontributors in most of their economic activities, i.e., "contributors" use most of their money and wealth in a way that would characterize them as "noncontributors."

with their resultant after-tax distributions, are tested for fairness. Ability to pay is measured after contributions have been removed from income.

At bottom, the tax base approach rests upon one's assessment of the validity of the distinction between consumption and wealth accumulation on the one hand and contributions to charitable organizations on the other. These two categories of economic activity are, for these purposes, considered to be radically different. As shown, whereas direct and tangible benefits are provided to those who consume and accumulate wealth, no direct and tangible benefits are provided to those who contribute to charitable organizations as a result of their contributions. Rather, direct and tangible benefits are provided to others, viz., the recipients of charitable goods and services.

There is another difference, also suggested above, between these two kinds of economic activities that can be construed as supporting the tax base approach. In most cases, charitable organizations provide what economists call public or collective goods[56]—goods that benefit all of society more or less equally and are of such a nature that the receipt by one person of a benefit provided by a charitable organization in no way diminishes the quality or quantity of the benefits received by any other person in the community. Everyone is benefited to some extent by the presence of a hospital in the community as everyone potentially has a need for its services at some time and all are made equally secure by its presence.[57] Similar arguments can be made for museums, churches, schools and the wide variety of other kinds of charitable organizations. Thus, contributors to charitable organizations are contributing to the support of public goods. Public goods are subject to the "free-rider"

56. See Musgrave, supra note 29, at 52–56.

57. Hospitals provide direct benefits to those who are ill and must use them and what, in contrast, might be called indirect benefits to all those who have no present need for their use but may very well in the future have such a need. Such indirect benefits are, however, very real and tangible.

phenomenon. Once such a good is produced, people cannot be excluded from enjoying its benefits. Consequently, since partaking of the good will not be dependent on payment for it, people will find it in their interest "to share in the provision made by others as a 'free rider.' "[58] There may be many who derive satisfaction from these goods being provided, for whom it is of distinct value to live in a community with such goods, but who choose not to support them because others do. In this sense, contributors not only provide direct benefits to the recipients of the goods and services of charitable services—those who take soup from the Salvation Army or those who attend a chamber music concert—but also benefit those who prefer to live in a community providing such goods. Such is not the case with most items of ordinary consumption and accumulations of wealth that largely benefit the individual consumer or wealth accumulator alone. Thus, contributors not only provide direct benefits to others, receive no direct and tangible benefits in return for their contributions, but, in addition, by their contributions provide public goods that benefit all of society.

In summary, there are principled grounds for not including within the tax base contributions where, in the senses described above, the purpose and effect of such contributions are to benefit others and not contributors. Furthermore, because of the public good aspect of most goods and services provided by charitable organizations, the increased tax burden resulting from the exemption that falls upon those who free-ride upon these contributions is fair since they in fact benefit from the provision of these goods. These differences between what has been called consumption and wealth accumulation on the one hand and contributions to charitable organizations on the other provide convincing grounds for the tax base approach.

The tax base approach advanced above has as an important element the assumption that charitable goods are public goods

58. Musgrave, supra note 29, at 53.

—goods that are of benefit to the community as such, as distinguished from private goods benefiting individuals in their individual capacity.[59] Contributions to support these public goods should not be included in the tax base precisely because they primarily benefit the public.[60] A closer examination of the public good concept is needed because of its centrality to the tax base argument.[61] Again as a preliminary matter, a distinction must be made between two categories of charitable goods: goods that tend toward relieving the suffering of the helpless and goods that tend toward promoting the cultural, spiritual, moral and educational development of all.[62]

The public nature of the first category of charitable goods—those intending to relieve the distress of the helpless—is self-evident. It is socially desirable to have available organizations to provide relief to those in distress who cannot help themselves. Everyone in the community benefits from the care that these organizations furnish to needy individuals. It is not necessary to look to humanitarian principles or notions of morality to see that society is made more stable and secure by the provision of these services.[63] In modern society most of the services provided by organizations in the first group would be undertaken by the government if they were not provided by these organi-

59. It is the case, however, that many goods considered charitable for purposes of the argument advanced here may be of direct benefit to a relatively few individuals, but, nevertheless, provide substantial and tangible benefits, although perhaps indirect benefits, to the community as a whole. Likewise, private goods providing direct benefits to individuals may provide indirect benefits to the community as a whole. See note 67 and accompanying text infra.

60. It is because the effect of the contribution is primarily to benefit the public and to return to the contributor benefits of an entirely different nature than the direct benefits enjoyed by the public that contributions are not considered consumption or wealth accumulation.

61. What is said below about public goods also relates to the tax expenditure approach.

62. Andrews draws a similar distinction and calls the first category "alms for the poor" and the second "philanthropy more broadly defined." See Andrews, supra note 48, at 347 and 356.

63. Many, in addition, believe that a just and fair society is preferable when its polity is informed by humanitarian principles.

zations. In fact, in most communities substantial government agencies exist to furnish these services, which are supplemented and complemented by private charitable organizations.

Justification as public goods for the second group of charitable activities—those devoted to promoting educational, cultural and moral development—may not be as readily apparent. An analysis of this type of public good might begin by concentrating on the nonprofit nature of these organizations and distinguishing in an economic sense between the act of investing in a for-profit venture and the act of contributing to a nonprofit charitable organization.[64] It is accepted doctrine that the primary and ultimate purpose of investing is the prospect of realizing a profit in return for placing one's money at risk. In contrast, the primary and ultimate purpose in contributing to a charitable organization is to make possible the provision of its goods or services. Investors may have as an incidental purpose the provision of a particular product to the public, but their ultimate and determining purpose is the realization of profit. Contributors, on the other hand, have as their ultimate and determining purpose solely the provision of a charitable good or service.

There is a second important element entailed in the "economic" purpose of contributing to the support of charitable organizations. A university would not be a university without students. No one would bother to organize and finance a ballet company if it were not going to give performances to the public. Inherent in the essential nature of these activities is that they be availed of and that they be availed of must be a primary purpose of one's contributing to them. Typically, a part of this latter objective is that that the goods be made available on a wide basis. Those who support universities seek a steady flow of

64. Although the discussion of the nonprofit nature of charitable organizations is focused upon the second category of charitable goods—goods promoting cultural and moral development—it applies as well, of course, to the first category of charitable goods—those relieving the distress of the helpless.

well-educated graduates to go into society to take the leadership roles they have been trained for. Those who support cultural activities seek as many performances as possible or wide access to these benefits. In contrast, an investor might decide to limit the scope of a product's output if by doing so a greater profit could be realized on the investment. In sum, it is part of the essential nature of nonprofit charitable organizations to provide goods or services and to have them availed of. Their ultimate objective is to have these goods or services used by their natural consumers, not for gain or for any other ulterior purpose.[65] As will be developed below, this characteristic coincides

65. The essential economic nature of nonprofit organizations has been very well stated by Professors Baumol and Bowen:

> Nonprofit organizations as a group share at least two characteristics: (1) they earn no pecuniary return on invested capital and (2) they claim to fulfill some social purpose. These two features are not wholly independent. Any group which sought to fulfill no social purpose and earned no financial return would presumably disappear from the landscape. Moreover, its goals themselves often help explain why no money is earned by such an organization. While an automobile producer may take pride in the quality of his cars, he is much less likely to regard product quality per se as an ultimate objective of the enterprise than is the head of a nonprofit organization. Nor is the auto producer likely to be nearly as concerned about the social composition of his clientele.
>
> The significant point is that the objectives of the typical nonprofit organization are by their very nature designed to keep it constantly on the brink of financial catastrophe, for to such a group the quality of the services which it provides becomes an end in itself. Better research, more adequate hospital facilities, more generous rehearsal time, better training for those engaged in these activities—all these are not merely incidental desiderata. They are fundamental goals in themselves, and with objectives such as these, the likelihood of surplus funds is slim indeed. These goals constitute bottomless receptacles into which limitless funds can be poured. As soon as more money becomes available to a nonprofit organization, corresponding new uses can easily be found, and still other uses for which no financing has been provided will inevitably arise to take their place. Any lively nonprofit organization always has a group of projects which it cannot afford to undertake and for whose realization it looks hopefully to the future. Once this fundamental fact is grasped, it is hardly surprising that such groups feel themselves constantly strapped. It becomes clear that they are simply built that way.
>
> Nor is it just through its quality aspirations that the social goals of the nonprofit enterprise contribute to its financial difficulties. The concern of the typical nonprofit organization for the size and composition of its clientele often causes operating revenue to be lower than would be the case if services were priced to satisfy a simple profit-maximization goal. Since such a group normally considers itself to be a supplier of virtue, it is natural that it should seek to distribute its bounty as widely and as equitably as possible. The group is usually determined to prevent income and wealth alone from deciding who is to have priority in the consumption of its services. It wishes to offer its products to the needy and the deserving—

with the "public" nature of these charitable goods.

Typically, the second category of charitable goods are of such a nature that their recipients—e.g., students or audiences—would be unwilling or unable to pay for the benefits if admission were priced at a level to recover the full costs of the goods and *a fortiori* if priced even higher so as, in addition, to provide a return to those who contribute to their support. Recipients have more urgent needs that demand satisfaction, e.g., food, shelter, clothing, than the kinds of needs met by charitable goods of the second type. Such goods will be availed of only if they are offered at a price usually far below what would recover costs. As noted, contributors recognize this, and their ultimate purpose in making their contributions is to have the goods provided so that they can be availed of rather than to realize a profit by charging a higher price for the goods. Indeed, the result of modifying such activities so as to attract a higher price of admission would be either to alter radically their nature, as for example, by popularizing a production, or to restrict greatly the number of people who would or could avail themselves of these benefits. Such a modification would signal a radical shift in the "economic" reasons for providing financing to such activities. In these circumstances, transfers of funds to make possible the provision of such modified activities would be properly characterized as investments.

What emerges from this analysis is that contributions to the second group of activities also constitute the provision of sup-

---

to students, to the impecunious, to those initially not interested in consuming them, and to a variety of others to whom high prices would serve as an effective deterrent to consumption. In short, a low price for the product of a nonprofit group is normally an inevitable consequence of its objectives, and indeed sometimes becomes an article of faith. The ancient doctrine of "just price" is imbedded in the operations of these groups and carries with it all the difficulties which inevitably accompany an attempt to put it into practice. Baumol & Bowen, On the Performing Arts: The Anatomy of Their Economic Problems, 55 Am. Econ. Rev. 495, 499–500 (1965).

port to a public good. As a result of such support, the activities can come into being and fulfill their purposes, which include the essential purpose of being availed of by their relevant public. Such a public may not be as wide as that reached by activities in the first group. It is, however, essentially indefinite, being open to any persons interested in availing themselves of the activities' benefits. The existence of a ballet company is of benefit to the community even though only a relatively small segment of that community may take advantage of its performance. It is there for those who are interested and the possibility of their taking advantage of this opportunity is of benefit to the whole community. It is a benefit to the community to have made available, through the charitable contributions system, a wide range of the second category of charitable goods for those in the community who want to avail themselves of their benefits but would not do so if they were fully priced. The provision of these charitable goods opens up to an indefinite class of society a wide range of alternative opportunities for enhancing its members' life through participation in a variety of experiences that would not otherwise be available. It is a common good for society to have in place agencies through which an indefinite number of persons can attain the maturing and liberating insights of self-discovery and self-expression. That such goods have come to be regarded as public goods is suggested by the creation of governmental grant-making agencies such as the National Endowment for the Arts, the National Endowment for the Humanities and the New York State Council for the Arts.[66] In principle, there is no difference between providing support to relieve those in distress who cannot afford to take care of themselves and providing support to promote educational and cultural development to those who could not otherwise afford to take advantage of the opportunities.

66. Many other states and municipalities have similar agencies. See D. Netzer, The Subsidized Muse 79–95 (1978).

It may be objected that the provision of almost any good or service is of benefit to some indefinite number of persons so long as some avail themselves of its benefits.[67] For instance, the enormous range of goods and services furnished in the commercial marketplace confers benefits to their consumers. Furthermore, these consumers are willing and able to pay a price for these goods and services that returns to those who invest in their production the full cost of that production and a profit. Investment in such commercial activities are, however, included within the tax base, while it has been argued here that contributions to charitable activities should not be. As shown above, it is the return on their investment that provides investors funds to pay the tax.[68] The situation is radically different for contributors who receive no return on their contributions with which to pay the tax and rather than receiving direct and exclusive benefits from their contributions provide benefits to others. Again, this difference is real and wide enough to support a decision that those who are presently reached by the tax by virtue of their participation in commercial activities ought to that extent be within the tax base, and those who contribute to charities ought not to be within the tax base to the extent that they would be if the exemption were removed.

It might also be argued that both investors and consumers on the one hand and contributors on the other receive utility from their voluntary acts of investing, consuming and contributing. Investors realize a return on their investment. Consumers enjoy their consumption. And contributors make possible the

67. Many of these goods may also be public goods in the sense of providing employment or helping the economy generally, a good benefiting the community as such.

68. At this point in the analysis the question is why the contributions of contributors should not be included within the tax base and not whether the recipients of charitable services should be reached by the tax. Above it is argued that recipients should not be taxed and if an attempt to defray the tax were made by increasing whatever charge is made to the recipients, they would probably cease availing themselves of the charitable organization's goods and services. See text accompanying note 41 supra.

production of charitable goods. But here too, for purposes of deciding who should bear the burden of government services, the differences are sufficiently substantial to justify including the first two kinds of utility in the tax base and excluding the third kind, even though an economist would hold that any voluntary decision is "utility-maximizing."[69]

There is a sense in which the tax base approach presupposes a judgment that society is sufficiently prosperous to afford charitable organizations. It could be that the level of consumption and wealth accumulation would be so low that its further reduction resulting from the presence of the charitable exemption could not be justified. One might concede the radicalness of the distinction between consumption and wealth accumulation as against charitable contributions and the implications that flow from this distinction and still maintain that the tax burden on consumption and wealth accumulation is so severe relative to the low level of such consumption and wealth accumulation that it should not be made more so by the necessary effect of exemptions. As suggested above, repeal of the exemption would ease the burden of tax upon consumption and wealth accumulation by producing tax receipts from organizations exempt before the repeal, or, if such organizations shut down, by producing tax receipts from expenditures that would not have been made if the exemption were in force. If the exemption were repealed, however, it is very likely that the level of charitable services would be reduced. Charitable services would be sacrificed to make possible a higher level of consumption by

69. For purposes of deciding who should bear the burden of financing government services, focus is placed upon the effect of the used funds. In the first two cases the users (investors and consumers) benefit almost exclusively. In the third case those other than the users (contributors) benefit to a significant degree as well as the contributors. Analytically, three classes of people derive utility from contributions to charitable organizations: the direct recipients of their goods or services, those who find value in the presence in their community of charitable organizations even though they may not be direct recipients of their goods or services and the contributors themselves. In brief, many other than the contributors derive utility from their contributions.

noncontributors. If the level of consumption and wealth accumulation by noncontributors were sufficiently low, a decision to remove the exemption might be wholly justified. This would indicate that society could not afford the provision of charitable services at the level it had theretofore enjoyed. Another way of easing the tax burden on consumption and wealth accumulation would be to reduce government expenses. This would presumably result in a lowering of the need for taxes. In this context, the question might be recast to ask whether a society providing a minimal level of government services could afford to bear the burden of increased taxes resulting from providing the exemption to charitable organizations. A society, however, which determines that it can afford charitable services could define its tax base to include consumption and wealth accumulation and exclude contributions to charitable organizations. Such a delimiting of the tax base would be rational and based on solid social policy grounds and would not be inconsistent with any inherent logic of taxation that would preclude so drawing the tax base. Tax bases are not given a priori; they must be chosen.[70] A decision that society can afford charitable organizations and their services as the predicate for defining the tax base to exclude charitable contributions might be taken as the mark of an advanced civilization. Considerations similar to these may have been behind the questions asked by Mark Graves in a letter included in the 1927 Report of the Special Joint Committee on Taxation and Retrenchment: "Instead of exemptions being the measurement of a taxation menace, may they not be a measurement of social progress? May they not be the measurement of benefits which society is able to and should afford?"[71]

70. As Werner Hirsh, in discussing the problem of establishing an equitable tax burden has pointed out, "whichever concept is chosen as a yardstick to assess ability to pay, the choice is always a value judgment." W. Hirsh, The Economics of State and Local Government 67 (1970).

71. Preliminary Report by the Special Joint Committee on Taxation and

It may be that the property tax is best considered as a partial wealth tax. It is sometimes asserted that a wealth tax should be imposed to supplement the income tax because income alone is an inadequate measure of taxable capacity between property owners or, more radically, the wealth tax should be imposed as a means of reducing or eliminating the wide differences in the distribution of wealth.[72] Above it is argued that analysis of the property tax exemption accorded to charitable organizations shows that if the property tax were levied on these organizations, it would be their contributors who would most probably pay it. Should a property tax be levied upon contributors to charitable organizations to better measure their ability to pay? If the property tax is levied to better reach taxable capacity, as noted, contributors are subject to this tax in a number of ways, many of which are apparently correlated in a rough manner to their wealth, as reflected in their relationships to property, e.g., property owned outright, investments in profit-oriented enterprises or simply the purchase of consumer goods. As above, the issue is whether contributors' contributions to charitable organizations should be included in their measure of wealth. Here also, since contributions are not considered to be a form of consumption or wealth accumulation, the principles underlying the wealth tax would not be offended by not including contributions in the measure of wealth. Finally, it would seem to make no sense at all to argue that a property tax ought to be imposed upon charitable organizations on the grounds that its payment by contributors would operate to reduce inequalities in wealth since the very act of contributing to charitable organizations in almost every case has this effect. Thus, on wealth tax principles, it is justifiable to conclude that the exemption is

---

Retrenchment, Tax Exemption in State of New York, N.Y. Leg. Doc. No. 80, 144 (1927).

72. See Cooper, Taking Wealth Taxation Seriously, 34 Rec. of the Ass'n of the Bar of the A.B. City of N.Y. (1979).

granted for tax base reasons rather than as a means of providing an indirect subsidy.

If the government incurs expenses on behalf of the property owned by charitable organizations by, for example, providing direct services to such property, the above analysis does not hold. Just as the supporters of charitable organizations provide funds to pay their employees and for utilities such as heat and light, etc., they might also be expected to pay for government services that directly benefit these organizations. It would seem appropriate to include such property within the tax base for the limited purposes of defraying the expenses the government would not have incurred if the property used by the charitable organizations were vacant. In effect, in these circumstances the rationale of the tax may be viewed as resting on benefit principles, and to the limited extent that property receives direct benefits from government services,[73] it might be argued that such property ought to be included in the tax base.

Thus, if a benefit approach is to be taken on the question of whether or not charitable organizations should be exempt from tax, the benefits considered should be limited to those direct expenses the government incurred because of the use of the property by the charitable organizations.[74] To the extent that this is the case, the exemption would have to be justified on the tax expenditure theory, i.e., an indirect subsidy is given to these organizations, viz., the provision of free property services, to encourage their development. The benefit theory of taxation is closely related to the user-charge approach discussed in some detail in Chapter 2.

73. See Note on the Governmental Services and Functions Financed With Funds Raised by the Real Property Tax, Chapter 1.

74. As noted in Chapter 1, only a small part of the proceeds of the real property tax are used to provide such services.

# Indices

# List of Tables

# Table of Cases

# Subject Index